F. K. WEYERHAEUSER

F. K. WEYERHAEUSER

A BIOGRAPHY

CHARLES E. TWINING

Chuck Twining

MINNESOTA
HISTORICAL SOCIETY PRESS
ST. PAUL

This book was made possible by a generous contribution to the Minnesota Historical Society from Walter S. Rosenberry III and by additional gifts from Vivian W. Piasecki and Lynn W. Day.

Minnesota Historical Society Press
St. Paul

Manufactured in the United States of America
10 9 8 7 6 5 4 3 2 1

International Standard Book Number 0-87351-356-8 (cloth)

∞ The paper used in this publication meets the minimum requirements of the American National Standard for Information Sciences—Permanence for Printed Library Materials, ANSI 739.48-1984.

Library of Congress Cataloging-in-Publication Data
Twining, Charles E.
F. K. Weyerhaeuser : a biography / Charles E. Twining.
    p. cm.
  Includes bibliographical references (p.).
  ISBN 0-87351-356-8 (hardcover : alk. paper)
    1. Weyerhaeuser, Frederick King. 2. Weyerhaeuser Company—History.
3. Businesspeople—United States—Biography. 4. Forest products industry—United States—History. I. Title.
    HD9760.W487T94 1997
    338.7'63498'092—dc21
    [B]   97-3142

CONTENTS

PREFACE AND ACKNOWLEDGMENTS

A BIOGRAPHY OF Frederick King Weyerhaeuser has been under consideration ever since the publication of *Phil Weyerhaeuser: Lumberman* in 1985 because brother Phil's story, significant as it is, represents an incomplete account of his generation's role in the Weyerhaeuser saga. Phil oversaw the manufacturing end—logging, sawmilling, and eventually reforestation—while F.K.'s main responsibility was sales. But F.K.'s life involved a good deal more than his leadership of the Weyerhaeuser Sales Company.

He was always ready to assist others, most importantly Phil and the Weyerhaeuser Timber Company, lending innovation and flexibility and encouraging investment in new directions, geographic as well as manufacturing. He was also willing, albeit not always happily, to undertake many thankless but necessary tasks that go with doing business, such as representing Weyerhaeuser in various regional and trade associations as well as the general arena of public relations. Phil would occasionally deride his brother for having too many balls in the air, but that was mere banter. F.K.'s ability to juggle those balls allowed Phil to concentrate on his strength, managing the Timber Company's production line.

The brothers appreciated their differences and the fact that they complemented one another. At one point F.K. and Phil referred to themselves as "the exciter" and "the debunker," respectively. There is considerable truth in that characterization. While they struck a balance in terms of inclination, their personalities were quite similar. They laughed at the same things, starting with each other, and they were both unpretentious to a fault. Moreover, they were as close as any brothers could be.

F.K. assumed a special responsibility that Phil could not have imagined: leading the extended Weyerhaeuser family. Succeeding his uncle Frederick Edward, F.K. became chief of the clan in the 1940s, and to him more than any other goes credit for the cohesiveness still existing in that family. Naturally he was utterly devoted to his daughters, Vivian and Lynn, but so too did he love his nephews, nieces, and cousins as though they were his own children. Indeed, one of those cousins, Walter S. Rosenberry III, is the moving force behind this biography. F.K. became a father figure for Walter, as he would for many others. And his interest in young people wasn't limited to Weyerhaeusers; he became a national director of the Boys Clubs of America, and in 1972 received the Distinguished Service Award from the Big Brothers of Greater St. Paul "for outstanding personal service to the fatherless boys."

TO PROVIDE A CONTEXT for the pages ahead, there are a couple of business considerations whose background may help the reader. The first involves what was originally known as the Weyerhaeuser Timber Company. While named for Frederick, the company was established in 1900 by several upper-Mississippi Valley lumber associates. From that beginning, Weyerhaeuser family ownership has never approached a majority or controlling interest. And today, within the Weyerhaeuser Company, now a large public corporation, that family fraction of ownership is quite small. Nonetheless, Weyerhaeuser family members—most notably brothers Phil and F.K., and Phil's son George—have provided essential leadership over the years. Though Frederick's remarkable success allowed his heirs the option of a leisurely lifestyle, they have done little resting on their oars.

A second consideration has to do with the industry itself. Although many still presume that the Weyerhaeuser Company is a dominant force, that was never true. Perhaps only American agriculture is more fragmented than the lumber industry. Weyerhaeuser is certainly one of the industry's largest organizations, but its portion of production has probably never exceeded 5 percent. Even though one company may often be the principal employer in towns whose very existence depends on a sawmill, lumber has never been seriously threatened by a monopolizing influence. The advantages of combining companies have occasionally been touted, but in the end the independent operators valued their independence above all else.

Competition, often of the cutthroat variety, has been the rule, even among companies with common ownership. Why? Well, as F.K. appreciated while running his beloved Sales Company, on a day-to-day basis managers didn't much care who owned what. They cared about supplies, costs, inventories, and profits. As a result, F.K. and his colleagues spent much time and energy trying to obtain some slight competitive edge for their lumber, the 4-SQUARE advertising campaign being the most notable such effort. But when the sawdust finally settled, the main difference between 2 x 4's remained as before—the price.

AS HAS PREVIOUSLY been the case, I must acknowledge the very professional and pleasant assistance of the staff in the Weyerhaeuser Reference Room at the Minnesota Historical Society, St. Paul, home to that invaluable collection of Weyerhaeuser family and business papers. The same holds true of the Weyerhaeuser Company Archives, Federal Way, Washington, and my special friends, Donnie Crespo, Pauline Larson, and Megan Moholt.

I have already mentioned Walter S. Rosenberry III, who conceived of this project some years ago and who has been a faithful supporter all along, proclaiming from the outset—with his usual formality—that there would be no compromising "authorial independence and integrity." I also want to thank F.K.'s daughters, Vivian Piasecki and Lynn Day, for their efforts to enhance my understanding of their father and also for their goodnatured patience throughout.

Editorial assistance is always essential. In this instance, Jean Brookins of the Minnesota Historical Society Press has assumed the overall responsibility, ably assisted by Leila Charbonneau. Leila, having worked in a similar capacity on two earlier books, *Phil Weyerhaeuser: Lumberman* and *George S. Long: Timber Statesman,* was already familiar with my shortcomings as a writer, but familiarity hasn't diminished her acuteness. Once again, however, none contributed as much to the polishing of the prose as my wife, Dianne Vars. While the task was formidable, she never despaired and seldom snickered.

C. E. T., March 1997

AN INTRODUCTION

FREDERICK KING WEYERHAEUSER was neither the most famous nor the most powerful member of the clan: Such accolades would forever belong to his grandfather Frederick. None who followed would equal the progenitor's record of achievement, but among the progeny, none was more widely known and respected—and, within the family, loved—than F.K.

From that paragraph alone, a problem inherent in writing about the Weyerhaeusers is already evident: trying to keep the Fredericks straight. I acknowledged this confusion in the preface to my 1993 book, *The Tie That Binds: A History of the Weyerhaeuser Family Office*: "As you know, the Weyerhaeuser family is blessed with an abundance of Fredericks. It is a fine old name, but creates something of an identification problem. Accordingly, it is hoped that the following key may be helpful. The original Frederick will always be referred to as Frederick. His younger son, Frederick Edward, will be F.E. And F.E.'s son Frederick will be Fred throughout. Frederick King, son of John Philip and grandson of Frederick, will be known as he was, F.K." This formula will, for the most part, also hold in the following pages.

The plethora of Fredericks is an indication of the respect felt for the clan's founder, a respect bordering on worship. Indeed, many years later, some, including F.K., would wonder if such devotion was entirely healthy. Had the family created an idol, a myth so imposing that the descendants could never measure up to expectations? Regardless, model or idol, the shadow of Frederick was cast over the family circle for generations to come. That this could happen was ironic, for it had never been his intention.

He was of humble stock, departing the German Rhineland as a teenager in the 1850s. His wife-to-be, Sarah Elizabeth Bloedel, was born in the same region, but her parents emigrated to the United States when she was an infant. Frederick and Sarah would have seven children—John Philip (or J.P. as he came to be known), Elise, Margaret, Apollonia, Charles, Rudolph, and Frederick Edward. All would marry, and six of them would have children of their own.

Sarah and Frederick first met in rural northwestern Pennsylvania, near Erie, where their families had settled. Although they definitely noticed each other, Frederick was as yet in no position to get romantically involved. He had little money, no real profession, and was only beginning to understand his new land and its language. It wasn't, of course, simply coincidence that both young people later found themselves in Rock Island, Illinois. Frederick had discovered his life's work—the lumber business—and the future seemed promising if not secure; the Panic of 1857 had everyone's attention. Regardless, Frederick and Sarah married on October 11, 1857, and tiny John Philip arrived on November 4 the following year. Sarah's sister, Anna Catherine, also lived in Rock Island, a circumstance that would prove important in a business sense as well as a family one. Frederick and brother-in-law Frederick Carl August Denkmann became formally associated in 1860, hence the partnership of the lumber firm Weyerhaeuser & Denkmann. Since Denkmann's skills were largely mechanical, he assumed responsibility for the sawmill, and the outside work devolved to Frederick. This division of labor worked well.

It isn't clear how the firstborn, J.P., came to meet Nellie Lincoln Anderson, but most likely it was through one of his sisters. Nellie was a local schoolteacher, and her social life primarily involved activities at the Presbyterian Church. The same was true of the Weyerhaeuser daughters. Whatever the details of their courtship, John and Nellie wed on March 26, 1890.

The 1890s were especially busy years for the Weyerhaeusers. The children were either in school or recently finished with their formal education. Lots of decisions needed to be made. Father Frederick wondered not only about his own future but also increasingly worried about what lay ahead for his offspring. As for the sons, he simply assumed that they would eventually help him in his work: They would be lumbermen. He already had Charlie's place picked out—Little Falls, Minnesota, with the fledgling Pine Tree Lumber Company. Rudolph had just graduated from Sheffield, Yale's scientific school, so he would be offered some secondary position, helping while he learned. Teenaged Fred was still studying at Andover, preparatory to entering Yale. And J.P. was expected to watch over the Rock Island interests for the time being.

Frederick wasn't thinking of retirement—after all, he was not yet sixty—but he had decided to relocate to St. Paul. Though Sarah was less than enthusiastic, in 1891 they made the move, and the daughters saw to it that their mother participated fully in the Summit Avenue social scene. It was all a little much for Fred, for he missed Rock Island and his old friends. Writing to John in July during summer vacation, while his father waited none too patiently for the desk, he allowed, "The porch is covered with St. Paul 'swells' so I don't dare go out there."

The move made good sense for several reasons. Rock Island sawmills required logs from the upper Mississippi Valley, especially from Wisconsin tributaries that dissected the northern pineries. While the general arrangements had been negotiated following the 1880 floods, resulting in the so-called timber pool, there were always specific problems to be resolved. Rock Island was far removed from the site of these activities, so in a sense Frederick could argue honestly for St. Paul over Rock Island: Being closer to work would allow more time for family. Unsaid but understood was the fact that it would allow more time for work. And, looking further ahead it was necessary to look farther afield—certainly for the region's lumbermen. In that regard Frederick was not unique, although it was becoming clear that he tended to see further into the future than most of his colleagues.

Frederick realized, along with several of his fellows, that the forest resources of Wisconsin and Minnesota were finite, and that, at least as concerned the pine, the end was fast approaching. The next move would be a major one, and the choices were limited: There were the southern pineries and the Pacific Northwest forests. Some operators had already migrated, and Frederick listened intently to their discussions of the relative advantages. Although he did tour the South, initially he was unimpressed; perhaps the social differences bothered him a bit too much. As for the Pacific Northwest, he first visited that region in 1887. Now, in the summer of 1891, he planned another trip in that direction, half pleasure—at least for others in his party of fifty-nine—and half reconnaissance.

Almost everyone in the family joined the tour, including Rudolph. Though none of them was able to attend his Yale commencement, he seemed unconcerned. He had the diploma, and that was the main thing. And now to work. Rudolph thought the plan was for him to begin at Rock Island, where he promised brother John to do "the best I can for a green hand." Rudolph assumed that he would start work in late July, after the party had left, but father Frederick surprised him, indicating that he expected Rudolph to go along on the trip. Only Charlie, J.P., and his wife, Nellie, remained behind. That had been Charlie's wish, at least until he bade the travelers farewell. "I had an idea that they were most all old people," he wrote to John and Nellie, and was "surprised to see what a jolly party they were . . . and what a large number of pretty girls there was." He had nowhere to go but home, somewhat regretfully, to his room in Little Falls.

John and Nellie, now nicely settled in the "House on the Hill," the family residence in Rock Island, had no regrets. That wonderful old house was situated on a large piece of property overlooking the town and the Mississippi, and the summer of 1891 was probably one of their most enjoyable. Business was first-rate, and J.P. must have appreciated being on his own for a change. After all, he was well into his thirties. Besides, he and Nellie were in love and had little need for family distractions. When the travelers returned in August, Rudolph wrote and got right to the point, expressing his hope that the grapes were good at the House on the Hill. Father Frederick had grown up with grapes along the Rhine and at the first opportunity had planted a sizable vineyard on the Rock Island property. If the family had any weaknesses for certain foods, grapes doubtless headed the list.

Apparently the 1891 grape crop was good, if not vintage. Elise thanked Nellie for two full baskets received in St. Paul that September and consumed within days. "I really seem to need them," she admitted. "They give me a new lease on life each year." They may have missed Rock Island grapes, but they were nevertheless immersed in St. Paul affairs. At the moment, everyone was caught up in real estate matters—specifically, where they should live and whether to continue renting or to buy. Elise reported that "Lonie [Apollonia] and I want a cosy little house on Summit Ave., but *exquisitely* furnished." She realized that their preferences served only to complicate matters: "Father laughs at us, and says we want a *little* house, but with a *great many* rooms in it." The girls feared that Frederick would take the path of least resistance and simply renovate the house they had rented at 435 Summit. (This structure is no longer standing.) A year later they were still living at 435, and young F.E. observed, "We have decided that Father does not want a new house." In the end, the women had their way; Frederick eventually purchased a big stone house at 266 Summit, next door to the James J. Hill mansion. The Weyerhaeusers were in St. Paul to stay.

Elise and Lonie were in the midst of courtships, Elise with William Bancroft Hill, a minister of the Dutch Reformed Church, and Lonie with a friend and businessman in Rock Island, Samuel Sharpe Davis. Thus when Nellie announced that she was pregnant, hers was not the only family news of interest. Reactions to the announcement were as expected. Nellie's widowed mother, Lucy Anderson—naturally one of the first to know—was thrilled. "I hope he will be a real good boy and show how he can appreciate his blessings," she wrote. "I fear that he will feel so important, Rock Island will hardly hold him." But it was not a *he,* after all, who joined the family; it was baby Elizabeth.

The September 8, 1892, birth preceded Lonie and Sam's wedding day by all of two weeks, so perhaps Elise could be forgiven the week's lapse between telegram and letter to sister-in-law Nellie: Wedding plans and preparations were anything but simple! Still, all took appropriate note of the new Miss Weyerhaeuser. Grandfather Frederick visited the baby on September 16. He was, Elise wrote Nellie, "just *too proud.*" And young Fred reported to John that the joy was widely shared: "Grandpa, Grandma and all we aunts and uncles had a general hugging match when we heard the good news."

A BOY ARRIVED nearly two and a half years later. Frederick King Weyerhaeuser was born in Rock Island on January 16, 1895. Grandfather received the news while traveling in Wisconsin, and he forwarded his congratulations from the Park Hotel in Madison: "That the good Lord will keep him so that he may be a blessing to his Father and Mother is our prayer." Grandmother Sarah's concern was for the baby's sister, so suddenly forced to share life with a brother. "Poor little girl," she wrote Nellie, "she must come to grammaw." William Bancroft Hill had discussed that very matter in his letter to the family the previous Thanksgiving. In his list of reasons for each to be thankful, he started with Elizabeth: "That she's the only grandchild, and so has the monopoly of favors. Let her make the most of her opportunity while it lasts;—such privileges are fleeting." Elise, the reverend's wife of more than two years, reacted wistfully to the news of her nephew's birth: "I'm afraid the Lord has no such blessing in store for us—we shall have to rejoice with our loved ones, and take our happiness in their children." And so it was. Of the seven second-generation families, only Bancroft and Elise would remain childless.

Uncle Fred, still the "Yalie," responded flippantly, in the manner of youth. How did the parents arrive at the name King? he inquired of his father: "At least they should have inverted the order and called him King Frederick von Weyerhaeuser."

Baby Frederick's aunts and uncles were now entering the adult stage of their lives, gradually assuming more responsibilities. The four oldest were married: John and Nellie were in Rock Island with the two children. Aunt Elise and the Reverend Bancroft Hill were settled in Poughkeepsie, and there they would stay. Aunt Margaret and Professor James Richard Jewett were preparing to move during the summer of 1895. Thanks in part to Frederick's efforts, Professor Jewett was offered the chair in Semitic Languages at the University of Minnesota, beginning with the 1895–96 academic year. Margaret was delighted at the prospect of "going home" (St. Paul), but it would be a brief stay. The professor would shortly receive another offer, this time from Harvard University, and few declined a Harvard opportunity. And Apollonia and Samuel S. Davis remained residents of Rock Island. Later, when John and Nellie left for distant parts, they would move into the old family home, the House on the Hill, and also inherit the job of providing grapes for one and all. The three youngest of the second generation, uncles Charlie, Rudolph, and Fred, were still bachelors, but that was about to change, too.

Rudolph began to familiarize himself with the Cloquet, Minnesota, operations, but it obviously hadn't been all work for him. Indeed, writing to brother John on May 27, 1896, he proudly announced his engagement to Louise Lindeke, emphatically adding, "This is *no* secret." John, by now the old married man, must have smiled. In the meantime, thirty-year-old Charlie was doing his best managing the Pine Tree Lumber Company. Life, however, didn't hold much fun for him. Little Falls was, if nothing else, little, and social opportunities seemed few and far between. As for F.E., Yale '96, he had his degree but not his health, for a time at least. In the parlance of the day, he felt "poorly," the suggested cure being lots of fresh air and outdoor exercise. Accordingly, he followed Rudolph around Cloquet and enjoyed the neighboring woods and lakes in the manner of a tourist. As hoped, nature worked her magic, and soon F.E. was deskbound in his father's St. Paul office, where he assisted as best he could.

There is no overemphasizing the importance of these relationships and responsibilities. The entire third generation, beginning with Elizabeth and Frederick King, "F.K." in later life, would be greatly influenced by their aunts, uncles, and cousins, individually and as constituents of a larger family unit. And the focus of much family activity would be the St. Paul office, first Frederick's, assisted by son F.E.; and then F.E.'s, assisted by F.K.; and finally F.K.'s. One therefore doesn't write about a single Weyerhaeuser, not then, and not now.

In the 1890s the family was growing steadily. On June 16, 1895, Apollonia gave birth to Edwin, just five months younger than F.K. The Jewetts welcomed George Frederick, or "Fritz" as he would be called, just over a year later, on August 22, 1896. And despite the isolation of Little Falls, Charlie found his bride. He and Frances Maud Moon were married in Duluth on December 14, 1898. Rudolph reported the event to an absent Nellie: "Charles did finely and [the wedding] came off in good shape." Nellie missed the ceremony for good reason: She was pregnant. John Philip, Jr., arrived on January 18, 1899. Thus was completed the first group of cousins—one might say the first "contingent." The five of them—Elizabeth, F.K., Eddie, Fritz, and Phil—would become, and remain, best friends. But the closest, always, were John and Nellie's three children, Elizabeth, F.K., and Phil. This closeness was doubtless encouraged by the way their father's business circumstances changed. Grandfather Frederick was constantly seeking new opportunities; he was driven in this regard. Quite naturally, his sons became his first lieutenants, but there were soon more opportunities than sons.

In the late 1890s, however, lumber opportunities in the upper Missis-sippi Valley were fast disappearing. Even a Frederick Weyerhaeuser had to look long and hard to find standing forests, or at least forests in which the pine had not already been logged. The few remaining tracts of pineland were by then confined to the more remote regions of northern Wiscon-sin and Minnesota. Given those circumstances and the decreasing impor-tance of Rock Island sawmilling, J.P. was available to assume a new respon-sibility; and Frederick, in partnership with his best friend, Ed Rutledge, of Chippewa Falls, Wisconsin, purchased an area bordering Lake Nebag-amon in northernmost Wisconsin, twenty miles southeast of Duluth.

John and Nellie were less than excited about moving to such an iso-lated place, but Frederick offered no alternative. Someone had to take charge. John was no longer needed in Rock Island, at least not on a full-time basis, and his brothers were all busy with their own responsibilities. So finally, after a good deal of delay—this despite Frederick's pronounced impatience—John and his family began a new life at distant and lonely Lake Nebagamon.

Other members of the family appreciated the inherent difficulties. Bancroft Hill's letter of October 31, 1898, to John summarized their sympathy.

> So you are finally and fairly at Nebagamon. I am both glad and sorry—glad because I think that on the whole it was the right thing to do, and sorry because of the hardships it involves. Finan-cially I have no doubt it is the best thing, and you will be worth more money than if you staid [sic] in Rock Island. But the most satisfactory reward in later days will be the thought that you pleased father in the matter. I know that you are old enough to claim the liberty to do what your own judgment thinks best, but his heart was set on your going there, and it will be a great satis-faction to you—should he be taken away suddenly as I fear he may sometime be—to know that you pleased him in this matter. I hope the hardships will not [be] as great as you anticipate. I think of them more for Nellie than for you or the children. So far as you are concerned I know that you will bear them patiently. And as for the children I believe that the first dozen years of their life is best spent in giving them strong physical constitutions, which can be done at Nebagamon just as well as at Rock Island.

Frederick was loving and caring, but he had also grown accustomed to having his way. John's reluctance to move his family from Rock Island to Lake Nebagamon may have had to do with Nellie's comfort or his own independence. But in this contest, he was clearly overmatched. Still, if his chief concern involved raising his children, Lake Nebagamon would do just fine.

GROWING UP A WEYERHAEUSER

LAKE NEBAGAMON was and still is beautiful and isolated, to one person a vacation resort, to another a place of exile. John endeavored to make his family as comfortable as possible, building a fine house, "The Pines," on a hill overlooking the lake, not far from the new sawmill. Bancroft Hill paid them an early visit and departed genuinely impressed with the white pines encircling the house. His wife, Elise, subsequently urged her brother John to spare them, which he did, over the objections of partner Ed Rutledge. In fact, The Pines still stands in the midst of its old grove, today serving as headquarters for a summer camp.

Despite the natural beauty, Nellie would sorely miss such familiar institutions as an established church. "You don't know," she confessed to Apollonia, "how desolate it seems when Sunday comes, not to have services." There was much to keep her busy, starting with the children. Also, her mother, Lucy Anderson, was often a guest, as both companion and helper. Nonetheless, Elise observed in a letter to John, "What a lot of time Nellie will have for reading!"

Nellie did stay in Rock Island for the birth of her third child, John Philip, Jr., in January 1899, an arrival most impressive because of the baby's size. His Aunt Margaret expressed amazement that he weighed in at ten pounds; her Fritz had barely weighed twelve pounds when he was six months old. Uncle Charlie received the news of the birth

11

while in Florence, where he and Maud were in the midst of their European honeymoon. His congratulations were enthusiastic as always, and he felt happy that the grandparents had been able to spend so much time with Nellie and the children. Then he added to Nellie, almost in passing, "What a businessman Father is, always making some large deal." Charlie must have wished that Frederick would slow down, but he tended to keep such opinions to himself.

Annoying bugs aside, northern Wisconsin summers are delightful, and winter provides its own pleasures. It was the same in 1900. On January 9, Nellie penned a post-Christmas note to Apollonia, sending along their love and wishes that Eddie could be there as a skating and sledding partner for young Fred. True, there were other youngsters in the community, but not as immediate neighbors. And most were a little rough around the edges, or so it seemed. Nellie understood that even the best of mothers is no substitute for friends. As she explained in her note, Frederick was outdoors a lot, but he "would be even more if he only had a little boy to play with." Five-year-old Frederick may not have missed what he didn't know, but he surely would have benefited from having a regular playmate. In the meantime, he did the best he could, sharing by mail with cousin Eddie a sketch he had made of a train, no doubt inspired by their own little railroad, the Hawthorne, Nebagamon & Superior, which connected the Lake Nebagamon sawmill with the world. These artistic efforts, usually in the style of a comic strip, became characteristic.

He must have been lonely at times. There he was, with an older sister whom he loved but didn't always understand and a baby brother, Flippy, who was demanding and received most of the attention. And his father was absent much of the time. John was indeed missed, mostly by Nellie. Writing to him in November 1898, on the eve of her thirty-fourth birthday, she had counted their blessings: "[M]y greatest blessing being the very dearest of dear husbands. The children have both asked God tonight to keep their dear papa safe in his loving care." Prayers were a regular part of the routine, an opportunity to express devotion to God and love for one another. The practice had certainly been a part of John and Nellie's upbringing as well.

But religious responsibility didn't end with the occasional prayer. Years later, when the boys were attending distant schools, John worried about sinful influences they were likely to encounter. "You know I am a Chris-

tian," he reminded them, and "a God fearing man and one that wishes
to do God's will." Follow my example, he seemed to be saying, and if that
wasn't reason enough, he could always remind them of the one that mattered most: "Go to Church, be with Christians all you can and be a man
like your Grandfather."

Frederick and Sarah were true believers, no doubt of that. They regularly expressed thanks for life's blessings, with little mention of Hell and
damnation. At least in the context of their times, they were liberals. Frederick read his Bible daily, in German, and he believed most of what he
read, although he chose to emphasize the positive. With the strong
encouragement of their daughters, he and Sarah readily transferred their
membership from Rock Island's conservative German Lutheran Church
to the Presbyterian. The conversion not only took, it blossomed; thereafter they were loyal Presbyterians, eventually becoming stalwarts in
St. Paul's House of Hope Church.

Frederick also subscribed to the lessons of *Poor Richard's Almanac* and
found merit in many of Aesop's *Fables*. Indeed, among the latter was one
of his favorites, "The Bundle of Sticks," whose moral, "In unity is
strength," spoke to his own worst fears—that succeeding generations
would grow apart and lose their togetherness, thereby diminishing their
power and potential. The grandfather knew it would be beneficial if the
children memorized some of these lessons. And they did. Even when
they were busy with other studies, they would be reminded by their parents: "Are you learning any of Poor Richard's sayings? It is worth while
to please grandfather in that way don't you think?"

There was only one answer to that question. Frederick was not, however, a mere purveyor of parables. His audience, captive or otherwise,
realized that above all he cared, and in turn they could do no less. His
expectations went something like this: They were to be loving and devoted to the Lord, loving and dutiful to their parents, and loving and loyal to
one another. Finally, they must never, ever, do anything that would bring
discredit to the name Weyerhaeuser. To an amazing extent, his commands
and wishes were honored. And revered. The second generation seldom
acted without giving thought to how he would react. As one might
imagine, there could be an underside to all of this. While Frederick's
principles were surely honorable, it was also true that his personality could
overwhelm and intimidate. His desires determined to a very considerable

extent the course of his descendants' lives, and though his influence diminished with the passing years, it did not disappear.

When the grandchildren were youngsters they could, of course, make their parents proud one moment and disappoint the next. John was overly sensitive, no doubt of that. In early 1899, when he was working at Lake Nebagamon, having left his family in Rock Island, he felt compelled to fret on two counts. At his departure, daughter Elizabeth apparently had misbehaved, and he was hurt: "I really felt so badly that I cried," he wrote to Nellie. And then he complained about Ed Rutledge, who loved John like the son he never had: "I tell you dear he is a hard man to please. He is about as bad as father." Nellie could only urge patience, both "with Father and Mr. R.," advising John: "[B]e guided by what they wish." She also reminded him that he was very dear to his father and inquired, to make her point, "Can you imagine the time could ever come when [little] Frederick would be anything but dear to you? He would always be our precious child."

With the turn of the century, John and his family seemed fairly settled at Lake Nebagamon, at least when comfortably inside the house. Outside was another matter. In late January, Nellie reported the temperature at "20° below and very blustery, [and] tonight there is still snow falling." But winter couldn't impede progress. At the moment, Nellie was trying to organize a Ladies Aid Society. "Imagine me doing such a thing," she asked Appolonia, "and president of it, at that." The fledgling Society had already met twice, twenty or so attending, "some quite funny ones, but all seem very much in earnest." And a meeting had been held for the purpose of establishing a church. Out of twenty-nine in attendance, the majority were Presbyterians with a good many Methodists. As for the Lutherans, Nellie saw no hope: "They will not unite with us, at all." Eventually, however, she had faith that they would succeed, in the end overcoming the "many toughs."

Nellie was right; they would win. But she had little chance to enjoy the victory. She died on March 26, 1900, her tenth wedding anniversary. The cause of death was initially attributed to a ruptured appendix. Years later, John—worried about the health of his daughters-in-law— said that the cause had been a rupture all right, but the result of a tubal pregnancy, ectopic gestation. Nellie, in fact, had bled to death. John would blame himself and the isolation of Lake Nebagamon. One thing was certain—it was a terrible loss for him and the children, the first such tragedy for the American Weyerhaeusers.

The Ladies Aid Society of the First Presbyterian Church of Lake Nebagamon memorialized their founder, naming her their "*perpetual President*" and extending "to her husband, her little ones and her mother our loving sympathy and our earnest prayer that the Comforter may come to them and that they may be comforted."

What the family needed most, of course, was a wife and mother, and John wasted little time. One of Nellie's closest friends, Anna M. Holbrook, now worked at a Chicago educational publishing house, and she initially sent her heartfelt sympathy. But sympathy soon evolved into something more, romance. John courted her, and by May 1901 she was already his "busy little girl down in hot dusty Chicago." In early June, recalling a ride through Jackson Park, Anna facetiously wondered whether they should have closed the front of the hansom on such a sunny day. The two of them next arranged to visit the Pan American Exposition in Buffalo, chaperoned by Rudolph and Louise, the same exposition where President William McKinley was assassinated in September. And in July, John proposed to Anna, or Dora as he then called her. She accepted with enthusiasm.

It all may have seemed too soon and too convenient to some. Nellie's mother wrote John that she had kept the engagement a secret from those "who would make unpleasant comments, and I don't want to hear them." But the rumormongers couldn't change the facts: In 1901, John and Anna were very much in love. As for the family, they were supportive throughout. Naturally Anna had worried about their acceptance. "Oh how I shall try to have your people love me too," she wrote to John. She needn't have worried.

Sam Davis had known her as "Brooky" when she taught school in Rock Island, and his reaction was that of a close friend. After offering John congratulations, he expressed false surprise that she had accepted his proposal, "particularly as she had visited at your house & knew what a 'crank' you are." But Anna was most thankful for a note from Frederick that closed with "our best wishes and a father's love." If father Frederick approved, none who mattered could do otherwise.

But what of the children? Wasn't choosing a new mother so quickly, without their approval, inconsiderate at best? Perhaps, at least in the case of nine-year-old Elizabeth. Frederick seemed accepting, and baby Philip had other things on his mind. In truth, Elizabeth and her step-mother tried as best they could, but both had strong personalities, and, as the years ahead would demonstrate, compromise wouldn't come easi-ly to either of them. (In fairness, it should be noted that Elizabeth and Nellie had occasionally had differences as well. Many years later, F.K. recalled one specifically, when Elizabeth suggested that her grandmoth-er Anderson should go home, whereupon Nellie applied a handy hair-brush. Elizabeth may not have learned much from the experience, but her brother was surely impressed.)

While Anna and Nellie may have been close friends, their differences of temperament were striking. If Nellie was a military chaplain, Anna was the drill instructor. In the throes of love, however, she was filled with hope and optimism, recalling her class motto at Holyoke, "Eager to Be and to Do," promising "I *will be* a good wife and mother and *do* what my heart and hands find to do." They married on November 7, 1901.

Anna made the transition to Lake Nebagamon with relative ease. She arrived loaded down with books, mostly classics, and lots of ideas on how children ought to behave. All in all, they were allowed to be children, but the pressure was considerable for them to grow up quickly and to be responsible. F.K. observed (in his written "Recollections") that Anna "became a wonderful mother to us," and there seems little reason to doubt that assessment. She was, however, as she appeared—formidable. "She believed in the old Spartan virtues that were part of her New Eng-land background—hard work, and thoroughness, plus all the other basic principles of thrift and honesty." Anna's approach was consistent, and she reminded the children frequently of what was expected of them. In Janu-ary 1906, while recovering from surgery, she addressed a note to "My dear Boys," expressing disappointment at having missed their birthdays: "Now boys, here is a chance to show how much more manly you can grow before another birthday. Remember to be honest, courteous, brave and kind, the traits of character you want to foster always."

Certainly one of the best decisions Anna made was to hire her friend Aimee E. Lyford as a tutor for the children. Miss Aimee came to be far more than that. She was family, friend, and companion to the children, and surrogate mother when Anna was elsewhere, a not infrequent situa-tion, what with John's recurring bouts of depression. Life quickly became a challenge, but Anna maintained a generally cheery disposition. For the children, Aimee's foremost responsibility was education, and they attended school daily, in the Lake Nebagamon boathouse during the summers and wherever they might be during the winters. In 1904–5, it was in Pasadena; in 1905–6, at the San Ysidro Ranch near Santa Barbara; and in 1906–7, in Daytona Beach, Florida.

The fall and winter of 1904–5 was an extended period of separation, caused by John's confinement—doctor's orders—to his room in the Hotel Aberdeen in St. Paul. Anna visited when she could and occasionally brought the children along. She knew, however, that they fared better at The Pines. In mid-November, Anna told John of her plans to come to St. Paul. She wasn't sure about the children, "so happy here and get so much out of door exercise and I know *home* is the easiest place for them, but we will do what is the greatest comfort to you."

Grandfather Frederick was unintentionally hard on John, expecting more of him than he could manage, at least as concerned difficult business decisions. Frederick apparently did not realize that he was a major contributor to his son's health problems. But his grandchildren were quite another matter. They brought him great pleasure, and even when he was "instructing," both teacher and pupils enjoyed the exercise thoroughly. In 1904 he penned a note to young Frederick, thanking him for his "good birthday wishes and the seventy kisses." He then pretended to be puzzling "a good deal" over a riddle they had previously shared: How many trips across the river the man in the boat would have to make to keep the fox from eating the goose or the goose from eating the corn. (This is one of those classic folktale riddles. The characters vary in the telling from wolves and goats and cabbages to foxes and geese and corn. But the solutions are the same, one of which is as follows: The man could take the goose over and come back alone; then he could take the fox over and bring the goose back; then he could take the corn over, leaving the goose behind; and finally he could return and pick up the goose and then all would be moved to the other side safely.) Grandfather was also "thinking about the Tin Man, Dorothy, and the Scarecrow," promising to tell what he figured out when he next visited Nebagamon. The Pines may have been isolated physically, but it was hardly so otherwise. L. Frank Baum's classic *The Marvelous Land of Oz* had just been published, yet Dorothy and friends were already familiar to the Weyerhaeuser children.

At first glance, grandfather's frequent letters appear to be in German script, but when they are examined closely, one can read the English. His notes to the grandchildren were informative but usually playful and light, and more often than not they included a puzzle. Typical was one written February 17, 1906, following a trip through the Wisconsin pineries. Frederick described a wintry scene in a cutover, "full of stumps and every stump big or little had a snow white Hat on." Then he asked, "Who do you think it is who will go to the trouble and expense to put Hats on all those big and little stumps?" At the time, the children were in Daytona Beach, and grandfather feigned sadness for their circumstance. Better they should be with him where they could have fun, "in old Wisconsin, rich [with] snow and healthy Boys."

He knew, of course, that the boys had fun wherever they were. They even had fun when assigned the task of corresponding, and that was especially true of F.K., who was full of stories, many of which he illustrated in comic fashion. In June 1906, he sat down to write to his father, using his impeccable penmanship. After describing the tasty strawberries they were enjoying, he repeated an "automobile story" he had recently heard about a family who were touring in North Dakota when their car broke down. They hiked to a nearby farm and asked for a monkey wrench. The farmer allowed as how one of his "bruders" had a cattle ranch and another a sheep ranch, "but I think it is too cold for monkey ranches so far north."

Distant events would greatly influence young Frederick and his siblings. In 1900 his grandfather and associates purchased nine hundred thousand acres in western Washington from the Northern Pacific Railroad. The resulting Weyerhaeuser Timber Company was destined to be the central family business involvement and would be the major career responsibility for Philip and, to a slightly lesser extent, his brother Fred.

In December 1903, Orville and Wilbur Wright's plane made its wobbly way some 120 feet over North Carolina sand dunes, introducing heavier-than-air flight. Youngsters are surprisingly quick to learn about such innovations, and so it was with Fred and Phil. They may have been earthbound, but their imaginations were not, and though they were born during the age of steam, they would experience the age of the internal-combustion engine in all its manifestations.

And in 1905 Uncle F.E. attended the American Forest Congress in Washington, D.C. Ostensibly he was substituting for his father, but he was also a friend of Chief Forester Gifford Pinchot and had accepted the invitation with high hopes for improving cooperation between the public and private sectors in forest management. Those hopes were dashed, at least in F.E.'s eyes, when President Theodore Roosevelt departed from the prepared script and, for obvious political reasons, castigated lumbermen in general for "skinning the land." F.E. never forgot, much less forgave, and it would fall to another generation of Weyerhaeusers, specifically to F.K. and Phil, to view positively any level of cooperation with government.

But of course this had no meaning to the children in 1905. If they were concerned about anything or anyone, it was their father. John had continued to suffer occasional bouts of depression, and Elizabeth, Fred, and Phil were primarily the responsibility of Anna and Miss Aimee. They attended "classes" conducted with some formality by their tutor, and they learned their basics well. Nonetheless, everyone knew that a one-room schoolhouse with only three students, ages thirteen, ten, and six, would hardly suffice for long. Uncle Charlie was something of a meddler, but his meddling was always well intentioned. In the fall of 1905, he told John the real reason behind Frederick's recent purchase of a Minneapolis sawmill: "I arranged it so that when you get well you can have the management of that plant," adding, "On account of educating your children do you think you would care to move to Mnpls. next spring?"

A city environment certainly would have benefits, but so too did life at Lake Nebagamon. Outdoor activities naturally constituted some of the family's greatest pleasures—canoe trips on the Brule River and the opportunity to build almost anything, from tree houses to workshops. Inside their workshop they fashioned kites and model airplanes, F.K.'s special hobby, "and anything else that came to mind." Among the boys' greatest pleasures was fishing with their father. Lake Nebagamon was not an especially large lake, but in those days it was well stocked with fish, and F.K. and Phil apparently caught their share. One rule was enforced by Anna: They had to clean their own catches, and as a result, recalled F.K., "We became familiar with the 'innards' of fish and the cleaning of fish was no chore."

Such pleasures aside, life was not limited to Nebagamon. At Christmas, for example, the entire family descended on the grandparents in St. Paul—lots of adults and the five children, Ed Davis, Fritz Jewett, Eliza-

beth, Phil, and F.K. In appearance, grandfather Frederick could have been a stand-in for St. Nicholas, and he played the part well. When they sat down for dinner, grandmother occupied the head of the long table, with grandfather to her right. It was a storybook family setting, overflowing with food, fun, and love. F.K. would later remember the German songs and games, "toy trains, miniature steam engines, lead soldiers, etc.," but he also recalled thinly disguised lessons. One of the foremost was imparted by a Sarah Doudney Clarke poem, "The Water Mill." Its moral had to do with wasting time, each stanza concluding, "The mill will never grind/With the water that has passed." The poem and its message endure as a family tradition to this day.

In the end, the supposed advantages of the city would prevail. Frederick Weyerhaeuser and Ed Rutledge determined to sell the Nebagamon property to the Edward Hines Lumber Company. The decision may have been arbitrary, or they may have simply decided that John's recurring illness left them without a dependable manager and therefore with little choice. This was not a happy decision as far as John was concerned, but it eliminated the major reason for living at Nebagamon. As F.K. later described the relocation, "Father and Mother moved us to St. Paul in 1907 mainly, I suppose, to get us better schooling." After much discussion and not a little disagreement, they settled at 825 Goodrich Avenue. Anna argued on behalf of a Summit Avenue address, but John seemed to think that would be pretentious. Schooling itself proved another cause for concern.

Although he briefly attended the Irving Public School on Grand Avenue and the Mechanic Arts High School, F.K. soon enrolled in the St. Paul Academy. Its instructors were, if we can believe F.K., characters in the extreme, beginning with headmaster "Pa Fiske," who "wore no socks but he did know a lot of Latin." F. Scott Fitzgerald was a classmate, and while he and F.K. weren't buddies, they were fellow contributors to *Now and Then,* the school paper. Looking back, F.K. remembered that these were "difficult years for all of us children because we had to make the adjustment of getting along with youngsters of our own age." They would manage, of course, but their earlier upbringing of strict dependence on the family circle continued to be felt.

In the fall of 1910, Uncle Sam Davis escorted his son Eddie and F.K. to the Hill School in far-off Pottstown, Pennsylvania. On the way, in

Philadelphia, Sam, having heard that there was a gun club at Hill, bought each boy "a beautiful, double-barrel Fox shotgun." The gun remained a prized possession of F.K.'s, a heavy thing with both barrels "full choke which was only one of the reasons that I had the biggest handicap in the gun club."

AN EASTERN EDUCATION

THE SUMMER OF 1910 marked the end of innocence and relative isolation for the third-generation cousins. F.K. experienced the greatest shock, spending a month in Cloquet, Minnesota, working for Uncle Rudolph's Northern Lumber Company. The purpose was to introduce him to the business, and that was done by starting at the bottom. He was assigned to the dry shed under the watchful eye of an old Swedish lumber grader, Gus Johnson. Gus looked the boards over, one by one, marking with a crayon where to cut them off to advantage, thereby raising the grade. F.K. sawed along the marks, working ten to eleven hours a day for seventeen cents an hour. The work was not demanding, but neither was it very interesting. He must have been happy when that tour of duty ended and he could resume his vacation.

This alternated between the House on the Hill in Rock Island and The Pines at Lake Nebagamon. Wherever they were, Eddie Davis, Fritz Jewett, Elizabeth, F.K., and Phil were partners—collaborators—in all manner of activities, including the creation of a secret society, FAWN. The apparent acronym meant nothing, at least initially, although they—and the adults—later agreed that "Fierce and Warlike Nuisances" would suffice. Elizabeth seems to have become the ultimate devotee. In the fall of 1910, she addressed Phil as "Dear Fraternal Brother," promising to "strictly adhere to the straight and narrow path and never forget FAWN."

Elizabeth was writing from her room at the Walnut Hill School in Natick, Massachusetts. Anna had accompanied her east at the same time that Sam Davis was delivering son Eddie and nephew F.K. and their brand-new shotguns to the Hill School. The boys were both fifteen, and although Elizabeth had just turned eighteen, Anna realized that she was immature for her age, not ready to begin college. Life was also very different for young Philip, left behind in St. Paul, once again attending classes at the Irving Public School.

F.K. entered the fourth form (equivalent to sophomore year), and he marveled at Hill life from the beginning. His first roommate could drink a pitcher of water by pouring it directly down his throat without swallowing. Amazing. On the other hand, he reported to Anna that he had seen an airship that one of his classmates had fashioned and asked her to "tell Phlippie" that it didn't fly nearly as well as the first one the two of them had made in their Nebagamon workshop. The classes, however, proved challenging. F.K.'s later assessment was matter-of-fact: "It was a strict school and much was expected." And it wasn't just book learning that was emphasized. John Meigs, the venerable headmaster, died while F.K. was at Hill, but his widow retained her responsibilities, meeting with each boy privately in order to discuss moral questions, "personal purity," and "relations with girls, etc." When F.K. had his conference, Mrs. Meigs urged him to become something of a missionary, saving the poor loggers. Years later, when she had the opportunity to visit some western logging camps, she must have been surprised to find so many of the men living at home with their families.

Although French pronunciation was problematic, especially the nasal part, F.K. initially had the most difficulty in his German class. Writing to Anna, he accused the teacher of unfair grading and also of possessing "fishy" eyes, while allowing "the poor soul cannot help that." He did receive special tutoring in conversational German, this from one Herr Külnick, who, F.K. claimed, was a personal representative of the Kaiser. Originally there had been five in the class, but F.K. soon found himself the sole object of Külnick's attention. It was often hard to concentrate, for Herr Külnick was a character of the first order, "very German, and his shoes end in long points like a clown's, looking something like this." (The "like this" was an inevitable cartoon sketch.)

School, of course, was not all work. F.K. made friends easily, but he didn't take readily to team sports. Eyeglasses made football difficult, and by his own admission he never learned how to throw a baseball. One of the coaches suggested, no doubt because of his size, that he try the hammer throw. Although he may have tried, he didn't persevere, so he got his exercise mostly by just being active. And he became an enthusiastic fan. Writing to brother Phil, he noted that the big game with Haverford was at hand. "Rah, Rah, Rah. We will probably be hoarse for a week after."

He heard regularly from his parents, occasionally from Elizabeth, and rarely from Phil, whom he clearly missed. Grandfather was more than a little interested in developments. He addressed a cheerful note on October 12, 1910, the day after his fifty-third wedding anniversary. "Your Grandmother and I should be very thankful to the good Lord for the many years He has given us on this Earth." As for news from Hill, he was pleased: "I feel you and Edwin will do your duty and be a credit to your Fathers & Mothers and all your Friends including Grandfather and Grandmother."

While grandfather's letters struck a balance between caring and encouraging, father John held to serious topics. If it wasn't grades—and it usually was—it was health. F.K. soon could recite many of the messages by heart. "I hope you are studying hard and taking care of your eyes and health and will do yourself credit."

Having cousin Eddie as a schoolmate at Hill was helpful to F.K. in several ways. Besides being a friend, Eddie served as a buffer, diluting or dividing the family's attention. He tended to be sick more than F.K., and his grades were no better. So when F.K. reported on himself, he could always include a passing comparative reference to his cousin. Typical was a February 20, 1911, note to John: "Eddie had hard luck last week and got his first D list. I came nearer getting a B list than ever before." In the same letter, he mentioned having received a telegram from Uncle Sam inquiring about Eddie's health. They must worry "awfully easily," F.K. concluded, more even than "our family." As for himself, he had better things to do than worry; when he heard that his father was feeling discouraged, he advised Anna, "Tell him to cheer up, the worst is yet to come."

Clearly his basic education had not suffered under Anna and Miss Aimee. He managed easily enough, which is to say without working unduly hard. As the first year at Hill neared its end, he proudly report-ed another B list, including A's in French and English, "the first time I have ever had two A's at once." The end was less than a month away, with Yale entrance examinations scheduled for June 22 and 23. Eddie didn't have to worry about those exams, being a third-former (equivalent to a freshman). F.K. admitted that it had been "terrible to see Eddie go home." The cousin must have been in something of a hurry because he left behind "many of his belongings, including his Bible (think of it), day-book, brush, etc." One suspects that it wasn't so much missing Eddie that bothered him but the fact that he had to stay behind.

Summers were still spent at Lake Nebagamon but with one notable difference: Now the children were encouraged to invite friends to join them, along with cousins Fritz and Eddie. Craziness prevailed at times, but John and Anna seemed mostly immune. And the outdoors was big enough to allow periods of relief, recesses of a sort. The summer of 1913 was probably typical, John reporting to brother Rudolph that everyone had had a wonderful time, "Edwin Davis said the best in his life." Appar-ently the housekeeper had been frightened by the ferocity of it all, and for that John was sorry. As for himself, he had been through these wars often enough to realize that there was little cause for concern: "The boys make a good deal of noise but are harmless."

When the 1911–12 school year began, F.K. and Edwin were happy to return to Hill as veterans, welcoming newcomers to the campus. Grand-father Frederick was among those who noted that the boys were feel-ing more confident, more at home than previously. He also expressed pleasure that his "old friend Tom Sawyer is young enough yet to go with one of my Grandchildren to school." But there was also sad news to share with F.K. Grandmother was very sick, and Frederick asked that the boys "pray to God our Lord that He would bless her with health and strength again so she might stay with us for some time yet." F.K. and Edwin sure-ly did as requested, but Grandmother Sarah would not recover. She died exactly a month later, on November 29.

By now, F.K. was clearly enjoying himself and the opportunities that Hill afforded. In the fall of 1911, he tried out for the Dramatic Club, although, as he explained to brother Phil, "I haven't the slightest doubt but what I'll get kicked off directly, but it's fun trying." Phil joined his brother and Eddie at Hill in 1912, so the three cousins were once again reunited. Their age difference should have been significant—F.K. and Eddie were both seventeen and Phil only thirteen—but it never seemed to be. Their differences stemmed from other sources. For one thing, Phil strongly disliked writing letters. "Where is your brother Phil going to school?" Frederick facetiously inquired of F.K.

Grandfather, however, had other things on his mind in the fall of 1912, not the least of which was the contentious presidential election. The grandchildren already understood that there were distinctions between Republicans and Democrats, not to mention former President Roosevelt's Bull Moose faction. Parents and aunts and uncles were forever ready to instruct, but the elder Frederick also believed firmly in the American dream. "One of you 4 Boys may be President yet, you are all young enough," he wrote prior to Woodrow Wilson's victory. After the votes were counted, he expressed passing disappointment, reminding himself and others that "the Democrats never stayed in Power more than 4 years, long enough to make hard times and then being turned out."

The big event of the 1913 spring vacation was a trip to Bermuda for Phil and F.K., with Anna in charge. But, as F.K. remembered, once aboard ship she came down with a case of the "hives" apparently brought on by strawberries, so the boys "were on the loose, so to speak, and [we] attended our first prize fight." In a sense, this typified their ongoing challenge as teenagers—how to escape Anna's grip—and the differences increasingly involved their fascination with automobiles. In the meantime, F.K. had developed a new interest, writing. He was now on the staff of *The Record,* Hill's literary monthly, contributing short stories to the February, April, and May 1913 issues. Each was well written and imaginative, evincing a good ear, humor, and some fairly sophisticated insights.

In "The Traitor" he used as background the deteriorating world situation, particularly in reference to a presumed German threat. The scene he set in the first paragraph demonstrates a familiarity with American classics but also has an almost eerie prescience about it.

The streets of this New England city . . . wherein our story is mostly laid, were thronged with eager, excited people. The newsboys at the corners had been waving "Extras" all day with undiminished success, for the headlines were no ordinary scare-heads. An atmosphere portentious of evil seemed to pervade everything, a certain terrible expectancy, which made people talk in whispers, and start at unexpected noises. Men talked with awe of a great war which was impending, casting its shadow over the whole civilized world and threatening, if once started, to engulf all peoples in an unutterable awful chaos.

In "The Wreck in Devil's Gulch," F.K. featured two men-of-the-world discussing finances in some detail as their doomed train hurtles toward its icy grave. And finally, in "The Escape of Bill Hogan," the reader learns that F.K. already knew quite a bit about airplanes, considerably more than his lead character.

In a wicked spirit of bravado, Bill piloted his craft over the courthouse. Unlucky deed for Bill! for he did not know very much about an aeroplane anyway. Consequently, when, in endeavoring to find the "cut-out" with his foot, he smashed the set-screw on the carburetor, likewise breaking the steering gear when he tried to repair the damage, the unsteady craft took a sudden lunge downward and smashed to kindling wood on the square before the courthouse (which was tough luck for Bill). Needless to say, the Judge laughed, which showed he bore no hard feeling toward Bill, and the Sheriff . . . well, the Sheriff treated the boys all around at the inn across the street.

Grandfather continued to be an interested, supportive observer, but he couldn't help thinking ahead, doing a bit of dreaming in the process. As F.K.'s tenure at Hill drew to a close, the old gentleman expressed pleasure that everyone was doing well in school. And then he added, on the eve of his departure from Pasadena for St. Paul—trusting the winter was over—"I hope you Boys will be good and useful Men, a help to your Parents and a credit to Family and Name. We have lots of timber and you all can have Saw Mills."

It was natural that F.K. would enroll at Yale. Two of his uncles were graduates, Rudolph from the Sheffield Scientific School in 1891 and F.E. in the class of 1896. Father John had no college experience. That was unfortunate, because of all the siblings, except possibly Elise, he would likely have benefited the most from a college education. But the pressures of the moment had dictated otherwise, and after a brief enrollment in business school, John returned home to assist his father. Now, he was quick to admit his lack of knowledge, and when F.K. sought curriculum advice, his father declined. "You understand I am not a college man," he wrote, "and therefore my opinion is not worth much but I will consult with your Uncle Fred this morning and will ask his opinion." Fred's viewpoint could hardly have surprised F.K.; after all, he was an Eli through and through. The times, however, had changed considerably since F.E. roamed the halls. The curriculum may have been familiar, and there was still the fall excitement of football and the year-round fascination with girls. But now automobiles and flying machines roared about. Indeed, it was a new world.

Coincident with F.K.'s matriculation at Yale in the fall of 1913, John and Anna determined to move west. While it isn't clear what prompted this decision, very likely John assumed that he could make a greater contribution in the Idaho operations. No doubt he was correct: In Minnesota, for good reason, he felt like the odd man out. As for the Weyerhaeuser Timber Company in western Washington, its general manager, George S. Long, needed little help. John therefore initially selected Spokane as a home base.

F.K.'s introduction to college proved a bit rough, at least according to his reports. "The work isn't easy," he wrote to brother Phil, noting that he seldom got to bed until after midnight. And trying to keep everyone in the family up-to-date was "an awful job." Somehow it seemed appropriate to offer Phil a little brotherly advice: "Go out for everything you can this year." He added, "I don't think it would do any harm to do a little more extra-curricular, and a little less curriculum." He must have realized that he was preaching to the converted: Phil needed little encouragement along those lines.

Weeks passed and John and Anna were still packing in St. Paul, preparing for their western move. Anna seemed agreeable to the change and clearly enjoyed being the center of attention, accepting "goodbyes" from friends and relations. Even John promised to participate at these social occasions, provided his dress suit fit, and it did, much to his surprise. Still, he continued to worry about the boys and Elizabeth, particularly their choice of friends. "I am so glad that you are doing good work and that you are going with good boys," he wrote to Phil, "and I hope you go to Church." Much the same message came from Anna, her advice being "to make a host of warm friends among the fine boys you find at Hill—have a broad acquaintance with people through life, it means so much happiness, 'tis what your father misses most." There was truth in that; John clearly depended too much on his sons for happiness. He was already planning for the summer of 1914: "We will have a fine instructive as well as an interesting time in studying the Lbr. and land situation in this western country."

The boys must occasionally have wondered what the hurry was. They were in school, a long way in time and distance from their life's work, assuming that to be the lumber business. But parents have a different perspective, and so it was with John and Anna. The latter advised that they learn all they could "about lots of things to keep up with this business when you are through college. It will take clever hardheaded men to cope with business deals in the future and you boys will need to be alert or other men will get ahead of you in your own affairs."

For the moment, F.K.'s mind focused on other things, such as football. Once again he epitomized the diehard fan, although Yale celebrations were clearly more serious and raucous than those at Hill. In the wake of the Princeton game, a surprising victory, he reassured Phil that despite rumors to the contrary, school spirit in New Haven flourished. "They say there has been more real spirit up here than ever before," F.K. wrote, "and I believe it; not merely because the whole university marches down to the station to cheer the team off for Harvard as they did today, but because you sort of feel it in the air." Then there were girls, about whom he promised Phil the details at Christmas. In the meantime, off to Harvard for the big game. Naturally, games at Harvard were complicated by family obligations, beginning with the Jewetts, now living in Cambridge. As for the game, it proved a big disappointment.

Football games soon faded from memory. Cars were another matter, and F.K. and Phil would spend endless hours thinking up ways to convince Anna that they were mature enough to take the wheel. In the winter of 1913–14, however, nothing equaled motorcycles for excitement. Although Anna refused to believe that her boys could be so recklessly bold, so heedless, she promised to consider the matter, confident that they would "give up the idea of having one when you know how nervous and unhappy I should be about it." That was surely wishful thinking. By 1913 both had acquired minimal driving skills; and Philip was not yet fourteen!

F.K. joined the Freshman Mandolin Club in the spring of 1914, but playing second mandolin for a middling ensemble didn't prevent him from daydreaming about automobiles. Phil was going all the way to California for spring vacation, and F.K. envied his brother's opportunity to pilot the family car. "I'll bet you run the devil out of the Peerless," he predicted, and then added "an elder's advice . . . don't go over 65, with any ladies in the car."

Just when life seemed so carefree, studies aside, reality intervened. Phil took his vacation as planned, but no sooner had he returned to Pottstown than he received the disturbing news that grandfather Frederick was seriously ill. "All of Father's children are here," John reported from Pasadena on April 3, "and the next three days will tell the story if Father will get well or not." He died the next day. But Frederick's condition had not diminished John's concern about Elizabeth, now in her senior year at Vassar. He had heard nothing from her recently, leaving him with no ready explanation: "I fear she is sick or thoughtless."

The passing of Frederick Weyerhaeuser was headline news the country over. He had indeed become a legend in his own time, but within the family he was simply Grandfather. The entire clan gathered in Rock Island for the funeral. Their lives would never be the same, and in some ways the old gentleman grew larger than life after death, an unintended burden for his heirs. Emulating his success wasn't possible. They were destined, above all else, to be conservators. Still, some decisions needed to be made. For the Weyerhaeuser Timber Company, that wasn't a problem, thanks to the presence of general manager George S. Long. But the Idaho properties were another matter, and the brothers, especially Rudolph, Charlie, and John, agonized over personnel and plans for the future in the Inland Empire.

F.K. injured a knee that spring and the Reverend Hill came down to take a look, after which he advised against surgery. Surgeons, he reasoned, had probably read about the death of the wealthy Frederick, and might be more interested in fees than in the Hippocratic oath. F.K. followed his uncle's advice and recovered quickly enough to participate in the summer program planned by John. Cousin Ed Davis, friend Bob Marshall, Phil, and F.K. toured the Idaho operations. F.K. spent a week at Potlatch tying bundles of lath, a job as tiring as it was boring. Indeed, after work the first day, he lay down to take a nap and slept until the next morning. In the course of this western junket, news of the German attack on Belgium arrived.

The 1914–15 school year began in familiar fashion, with more Yale football disappointments. But there was always next year. Meanwhile, F.K. and Eddie paid the Jewetts a visit in November and attended a lecture by Uncle Richard. As F.K. described it, the audience was the Now and Then Club, "a lot of Harvard Highbrows." Following the lecture, he and Eddie served the refreshments "and afterwards ate the remnants." But the high point was a drive to a nearby school where they visited their collective heartthrob, "her majesty Doris," F.K. observing that she "had grown quite a bit and I think she is mighty attractive"—all this for the benefit of Phil.

John suffered another bout with illness that fall, and Anna urged the boys to help by writing. "He never tires of talking of you children and the kind of noble men you are to be." Christmas plans were for everyone to gather at Rock Island. And so they did, except for John, confined to his room in St. Luke's Hospital in St. Paul. And for the balance of the school year, F.K. and Phil looked forward to another summer together. In the meantime, they made plans for a cross-country auto trip, no small feat in 1915. The boys, however, were typically oblivious to possible problems, and by mid-May Anna had, surprisingly, become an ally in their plans. "Your father is getting accustomed to the idea of your coming West by auto this summer," she wrote before adding, "He still seems to feel it a questionable undertaking to cross the mountains."

F.K. appeared bent on preparing for the excursion while also doing much to encourage a parental veto. He confessed all, or nearly all, to brother Phil. "I think the paternal and maternal wrath is directed against me because I've been having the wildest time lately going to Poughkeepsie, N.Y. and around." In addition, he was two months behind in his accounts—detailed reports of allowance and expenses—a delinquency sure to upset Anna. In fact, he couldn't account for his expenses. How to explain irresponsibility, that was his problem. "I'm busted flat," he admitted, "stripped as the saying goes." And then he told of his latest adventure. He and a new friend, Lou Bennett, had gone to Poughkeepsie in Bennett's eight-cylinder Cadillac, which, according to F.K., was "the best car I ever rode in, better than any Pierce, Packard, Chalmers, Peerless or anything else." On the way home ("and don't tell the family all about this") they were arrested for speeding as they approached New York City. The explanation was simple enough: "I never saw a car that was so hard to make go slow." After spending the night at the Montclair, New Jersey, apartment of Lou's mother, they departed for New Haven before six o'clock the next morning. "That is we would have left then if we had not been arrested again for going too fast." After leaving all of their cash with the chief of police "as bond for reappearance," they raced on. "I never went so fast in my life," F.K. allowed, over seventy miles per hour. He was probably a bit scared, but apparently it was worth the fright: "We had some time."

Phil planned to join the family that week in Poughkeepsie while F.K. was stuck in New Haven taking exams. "Now when you see the family argue for me," he urged Phil, realizing that it was not likely to do much good. Duty called. He would go directly west with John "and get to work on some job or other." And that is what he did, spending a few weeks during that summer of 1915 at the Bonners Ferry Lumber Company in northernmost Idaho. He kept the employee time records and did some of the bookkeeping, admitting upon his departure that he probably left behind his share of mistakes.

When he and Phil returned to school in the fall, football was again briefly on their minds. Phil now played for Hill, and F.K. seemed more interested in his brother's success than that of his own school. The same was surely true of their parents, although each saw things quite differently. While Anna wrote Phil that she pictured her "manly boy" winning at football and later winning at "other things in years to come for yourself and the W. family," John wrote to him fretting over possible injuries. When it came to finances, he proffered the same advice for both boys: "Buy nothing you do not need, and make a dollar go as far as you can." And he closed, ever the concerned parent: "Take the deep breaths, good fresh air and good food, do not eat between meals, drink lots of good water with much love."

F.K. rebelled increasingly as the years passed, although the expressions of that rebellion were for the most part healthy ones. Christmas 1915 provides an early example. John and Anna had settled in Tacoma, making travel to and from home difficult for the boys during school breaks. And F.K. had received and immediately accepted an invitation from Lou Bennett to spend the holidays at his Wheeling, West Virginia, home. In sharing plans with Phil, F.K. wrote that he and Ed Davis would "probably play around in N.Y. till I go with Lou." He invited Phil to join the party, assuring him, "The prospects are fine in New York." After a few days, Phil and Ed could go on to Cambridge "to save our family from being queered generally." He already felt a bit guilty, although not quite enough to alter his plans. He expected, he told Phil, "to get in hellish wrong at Cambridge for not showing up. Don't you think so?"

As things turned out, Phil went to Tacoma for Christmas while F.K. and Lou partied, from New York City to Wheeling and points between. It was just as well. Phil helped to take parental attention off sister Elizabeth, which she much appreciated, and F.K. and Lou enjoyed their expected good times. Almost at the last moment, they decided to go to the prom, scurrying about for dates. When Anna heard of the details, she expressed disappointment, F.K. having invited what she termed a "chance acquaintance." He responded in kind, not to Anna, but to Phil. "Of course the family did not approve," he wrote. "They never do for that matter." It was much ado about nothing, for his intentions weren't serious: "I simply wanted to go to the Prom and did not care who it was so long as she can dance." In the same spirit, he and Lou had ventured forth for another New York weekend, returning to the campus with eighty cents between them. Even F.K. admitted that that might have been playing it a bit close.

He was now editor-in-chief of the *Yale Courant,* another literary periodical, but beyond that he was bored. Perhaps the war had something to do with it. "This college life is getting dull," he wrote Phil on January 22, 1916. "I was not born for a student and I get in a sort of rut here and don't seem to get out of it." Indeed, the boys spent more and more time thinking and talking about the war, mostly in mechanical terms, such as the effect motor vehicles had on tactics and, of course, the role of airplanes. Their parents naturally had other concerns. "I wish the War were over and nations at Peace, instead the confusion seems to grow more tense," Anna had written in a pre-Christmas note. But those were distant hopes, and in the meantime tension and confusion increased. The boys were of an age for soldiering, or at least F.K. was. John sent him a telegram on January 16, F.K.'s twenty-first birthday: "May you always be a useful and happy man." And Phil would get exactly the same message two days later, on his seventeenth.

Of far greater importance, from the boys' perspective, was a car. First they had to persuade their parents to finance the purchase and then, if successful, what to buy? On the first count, the plan was to divide and conquer, John being clearly viewed as the weaker link. The problem was compounded because the boys already jointly owned a Chalmers, garaged in Tacoma. John saw no logic in purchasing another car on another coast. But F.K. was not deterred, already imagining how they would set forth "carrying dress suits with us, visit our friends in the various metropolises and receive their hospitality." As for the kind of car, "I vote we get something *fast* and powerful. Also it must look well." Then he added, "One thing we want is individuality. We want it painted bright red or something so that there won't be anything like it on earth." But that would be their secret, for now.

In the end John gave in, agreeing to send a total of $3,000 as graduation presents. How F.K. and Phil must have celebrated! But Anna hadn't surrendered, and foolishly, by his own admission, F.K. had furnished the necessary ammunition, revealing that his spring vacation didn't coincide with Phil's. Since Anna didn't want them to be distracted by a car during classes, she telegraphed back telling them to forget the whole thing. F.K. tried again, twice, but received no answer. "Silence gives consent," he pretended, and with $125 borrowed from Eddie plus $150 of his own, he made a deposit on a Marmon. "The die is cast! The Rubicon is crossed!" Thus he announced the deal to Phil, suggesting that their father's decision was, after all, final. Nonetheless, he had written "two long wise letters containing all possible arguments" to Anna, one of which was "a masterpiece," and if that "doesn't make her reasonable, nothing will."

Their eventual victory was hardly a rout. Anna insisted that "one stipulation must hold, the car to go into storage the last day of [F.K.'s] vacation," where it would remain until she and John came east for Phil's graduation from Hill. And she held firm, despite being bombarded by telegrams. Phil wanted the vehicle badly for the sixth-form dance, his senior prom. Not a chance. F.K. sent him the final discouraging word on May 3: "Mother positively refuses. No use kicking. Car is stored."

John and Anna had other, more important, distractions. Elizabeth, or often Betsey to them and Liz to her brothers, was in love. The object of her affection was Rodman Titcomb, a 1912 Harvard graduate employed by the Smelter Company in Tacoma. John tried to persuade Phil and F.K.

to offer some disapproving "brotherly advice," but wisely, neither did so. Anna had concluded, as she wrote to Phil, that Mr. Titcomb wasn't the right man: "Mr. T. may be a fine fellow but he lacks initiative, seems to me, and I question how long Betsey would be happy on a $2500 salary per year." John was downright jealous, expressing worry over "the infatuation Elizabeth has for Titcomb; She makes a confidant of him in place of her Mother and Father."

As it turned out, it was Elizabeth who accompanied her mother east to attend Phil's graduation. F.K. was allowed to take the Marmon out of storage on June 1, and he wasted no time testing the machine. Its performance was a bit disappointing. "She'll never go 70," he informed Phil. He also warned his brother to get his accounts in order for Anna's perusal. With difficulty and imagination, he had caught up on his own, and he didn't want his brother's carelessness to offer an excuse for any parental discipline. Despite their bookkeeping efforts, things got complicated. Anna's brother died, and as a result they stayed in the East longer than planned. But as Aunt Margaret reported from Woods Hole, the four of them—Anna, Elizabeth, and the boys—finally got away in the Marmon on July 2. It was the start of a memorable summer.

No sooner had they reached Tacoma than F.K. and Phil, working together for the first time, were sent to Yacolt as assistants to John Markham, a cruiser for the Weyerhaeuser Timber Company. The area had suffered a terrible fire, the 1902 Yacolt burn, and now, fourteen years later, the salvage logging was still going on. This was dirty work, but the boys wouldn't complain. From Yacolt they followed Markham over to the Olympic Peninsula, along the extreme northeastern fork of the Satsop River in isolated and rough country. They agreed to hike in without tents and carry a minimum of rations, sacrificing comfort for speed. But the fishing wasn't good and hard work made for big appetites, which went largely unsatisfied. Still, the cruising got done, and the boys came away with an appreciation of life in the woods.

Their reward came soon, F.K. and Phil driving the Marmon to Klamath Falls, Oregon, with three special passengers: Their father, George S. Long, manager of the Weyerhaeuser Timber Company, and his son, George, Jr. "The drive down the east side of the Cascades was glorious," F.K. recalled. And as a bonus, the senior Long was "a wonderful teacher, had a great sense of humor, and was a fine traveling companion." Along the way, F.K. and Phil, now supposedly experienced woodsmen, argued over the number of board feet in various trees, George Long being the final arbiter. It was good to end the summer on such a note. Nothing would be the same again.

Phil joined brother F.K. at Yale in the fall of 1916, and both were missed back in Tacoma. Sister Liz had her appendix removed and dramatically wrote her brothers just prior to the surgery. She expressed confidence. "*But* if anything does go wrong," she added, "I want you also to know that you two boys have been mighty dear to me and I can't begin to tell you what you meant to me this summer and how greatly I appreciate your interest and loving help." She promised that upon her recovery "a new regime will enter at home and you'll all be startled at the domestic serenity prevailing." She did recover quickly, but domestic serenity proved elusive. As John later described the scene, there were endless "clashes" over Rod Titcomb: "Mother is so anxious for the best for Elizabeth that at times she is a little exacting and Elizabeth is quick tempered and there we are."

John had fallen back into what Anna described as "one of those introspective spells," feeling left out of the business activities and worrying that his sons would be similarly treated. Anna argued otherwise but to no avail. "You boys will be his salvation," she contended. "He counts on you both a heap just lots and lots, and half his trouble now is really home sickness for you I believe." This was a burden from which there was no escape.

As the oldest male of his generation, F.K. bore the initial brunt. "Equip yourself the very best you can," his mother urged, "to show your father and uncles what the brain and brawn of the next generation can do to supplement the good work they have done, and above all keep your optimism in humanity and a clear vision of high honor in all business dealings, a broad outlook on humanity and your relation as well as responsibility to the World, in big capitals."

John wrote after the 1916 presidential election, lamenting the results. Wilson's victory was, in his words, a "bitter pill to swallow but we must support the government." There would be difficult days ahead, he predicted, worse than anything since the Civil War. Equally certain, Anna would not send any more money until the boys submitted "an itemized bill of money spent," adding, "Hard World but I can't help it." They dutifully sent in their accounts, but those at home were unimpressed. Phil's "banter" troubled Anna, and she inquired how long it had taken him "to evolve that set of items." John admonished F.K., noting that the figures would not meet the standards of the lumber company accountants.

But such disputes paled before other concerns. The war raged on, and they all heard the distant echoes. Anna reminded them toward the end of January 1917 of the importance of praying: "It seems the burden of all our prayers these days should be for the sad and suffering of Europe, then that such an affliction may never come to ours and our country."

It wasn't just the war in Europe that troubled them. John was depressed over International Workers of the World (iww) labor-organizing activities in Idaho and for a time feared that a civil war was more likely than hostilities with Germany. As the international situation worsened, Anna increased her commitment to the American Red Cross, little realizing just what a job this would become.

The realities of American involvement in a world at war could no longer be ignored. The boys naturally wondered about their own participation, and with a degree of anticipation. Things, of course, looked very different from the Tacoma perspective. Pierce County had recently voted $2 million to donate seventy-five thousand acres for use as a military post, eventually to become Camp (then Fort) Lewis. Already John envisioned the boys training there "where we can see you often." Anna, for once, offered no advice. She understood the desire "to join in the war activities" but allowed as how "frankly, tis hard, mighty hard." Elizabeth had also been wrestling with fears that her brothers might become casualties in the war. "Ever since the severing of relations with Germany I have tried to argue myself into the justice of this, and I will admit, in case of actual conflict, I would want my brothers among the heroes, but the reality does seem so hard."

The brothers already knew what they wanted to do. They wanted to fly, a preference they shared enthusiastically. Others expressed doubt. John, claiming to have discussed the matter with someone knowledgeable, warned that "aviation is the most dangerous thing," followed in order by the Navy and the Army. He didn't wish to advise but added, "If I was a young man I would take the army." Anna agreed: "Like most new ventures" aviation was the most dangerous. Still, she understood why the boys were excited. "How history has been made this past week," she wrote on March 25, doubtless referring to the revolution in Russia and to the sinking by submarines of five American ships in the North Atlantic. "No wonder you boys are fired to join something." The parents could not logically argue against military preparation: "We can only be true to our beliefs when it comes to your training."

President Wilson read his war message to Congress on April 2, declaring "it is a fearful thing to lead this great peaceful people into war, into the most terrible and disastrous of all wars." Congress passed the war resolution four days later. The wait was over.

Few were prepared, but F.K. and friend Lou Bennett had done little else of late but discuss what they should do. In retrospect, their schemes seem ill conceived and impractical. Still, at the time Teddy Roosevelt and others were making plans every bit as curious. Lou hoped to organize a West Virginia flying corps, serving as the chief financier himself. And F.K. thought it was a terrific idea. In mid-April, he and Lou set off for Wheeling to get under way. John still hoped that the boys wouldn't fly. Phil wasn't mechanical enough, and F.K.'s eyesight was not good enough. The crucial factor, however, was age. Phil was a freshman, and most of his class would remain in school. F.K. was a senior, and his class immediately scattered. More than a year later, in a foreword to the *History of the Class of 1917, Yale College,* Yale President Arthur Twining Hadley observed:

> The Class of 1917 was just finishing its college course when America entered the war. On that Class more than any other fell the burden of showing what college men could do. They stood in the front rank. Their record shows how fully they accepted the burden, and how bravely they conducted themselves in the post of honor. Never has it fallen to the lot of a Yale class to write so much history in a single year.

F.K. and Lou Bennett were but two of many, and only one of them would return from that war.

THE GREAT WAR

How PREPARED was the United States for war? Most Americans had agreed with their president that they should be "neutral in fact as well as in name." But neutrality became more difficult as the months passed, particularly after the May 1915 sinking of the *Lusitania*. Indeed, military training programs were being initiated, and Yale was among the earliest to be involved. President Hadley had taken the initiative, seeking General Leonard Wood's advice on how his school might be most helpful. Wood replied that artillery officers were in short supply, and so it was that Yale organized four batteries, eventually making up the major part of the Tenth Field Artillery.

Although Phil, along with many Yalies, would serve in the artillery, prior to 1917 neither he nor F.K. had been available for summer military training. Their father had seen to that. But now everything was changed, and there was great enthusiasm for participation. When he compiled his World War I recollections in the summer of 1941, F.K. reflected, "Judged by present day standards, the Class of 1917 Yale was a very warlike crowd."

In Wheeling, in early May 1917, F.K.'s friend Lou Bennett was attempting to organize the West Virginia Flying Corps. F.K. had joined the effort and reported to Phil that the hangars in Wheeling were under construction and that they had one airplane. But all in all, things were "moving slowly," far too slowly. He thus advised his brother to finish his freshman year: "It's bad dope to leave there now." Looking ahead, perhaps Phil could get some flying experience in the summer in Wheeling, "so you can be sure of getting into the flying corps eventually."

Little went as planned. They did locate a field at a place along the Ohio River called Beech Bottom and enlisted the services of an instructor, Captain E. A. Kelly, and his plane, a Vickers Scout. Kelly, who had served with the British Royal Flying Corps before injuries grounded him, was in the United States to demonstrate the Vickers to American officials. The captain was, according to F.K., "more or less crippled, but there was nothing the matter with his imagination, his ability to tell stories, or to absorb liquor." As for the skills they had sought, that apparently was another matter, for Kelly cracked up his Vickers on the way to Wheeling. The West Virginia Flying Corps was off to a disappointing start.

Although Louis Bennett obtained the support of West Virginia politicians for his corps, in the end that didn't matter. Federal officials held firm in their opposition. Still, Bennett refused to give up. In mid-June he sent a wire to George S. Long of the Weyerhaeuser Timber Company, ordering "four million feet air dried spruce clear four sides and suitable for aeroplane construction." But the company wasn't in the spruce business; and as Long replied, "My understanding is that both the Government and European Governments have been buying green spruce direct from the mills. I doubt very much whether you would be able to buy any dry stock in our Western country." When George Long doubted "very much," the answer was a definite no. There would be no Lafayette Escadrille in West Virginia. Bennett finally gave up late in the summer of 1917, enlisting as a cadet in the British Royal Flying Corps for training at Camp Borden in Canada.

F.K. had previously decided to take another tack, helped along unintentionally by his father, who had arrived in Wheeling on May 19 and urged his son to follow an established flight-training program. With the assistance of Henry Oldenburg, attorney for the Cloquet companies, F.K. procured letters of recommendation from several prominent politicians and on May 21 applied for acceptance as a student aviator in the Aviation Section of the Signal Corps. He took his physical at the Letterman Hospital two days later, and, surprisingly, he passed. In the words of the examining physician, his eyes were "*just* good enough." When F.K. reported the results to his father and lawyer Oldenburg, both were amazed; John must also have been disappointed at the outcome.

F.K. and his father headed west together, arriving in Tacoma on June 1. There he received his orders, also dated June 1, naming him one of twenty-five in what was to be the fifth class of "aviation aspirants between 21 and 30 years of age, having three years College education," or some appropriate practical experience. Training would commence June 11 at the University of California, Berkeley, with new classes starting every week. Upon reaching "the Happy Home" in Tacoma, F.K. wrote immediately to Phil requesting that his brother tag his pictures and take care of other details: "In other words, put my remains in order." When the moment of departure came, however, F.K. wasn't feeling quite so flippant.

He wrote Phil again on June 7 aboard the Shasta Limited, bound for Berkeley. By then he was in the dumps, feeling lonely, committed to the unknown, without connections, friends, or even acquaintances. And there was no turning back. "Guess I'm a little gloomy from the gloomy start off this morning," since everyone "was pretty broken up when I left & it made me feel like Hell. Father was almost sobbing." Phil's responsibility was clear, as F.K. viewed matters. With Elizabeth's wedding to Rod Titcomb little more than a month away, it was up to Phil to keep the parents happy. "Phlip, please be home all you can this summer. . . . Father & Mother are getting old and they need you around." And he couldn't resist offering a final bit of brotherly advice: "Don't go in for that picking-up-girls stuff! I've done very little since I've been in college & while it doesn't damn a person, etc., still the highest type fellow doesn't & shouldn't. We've got an awful lot to live up to from now on. And the hardest part of it, Phlip, is that everybody is watching us." F.K. was surely right about the watching part.

Within a week at the School of Military Aeronautics, or Government Aviation School, F.K. was feeling much better, no longer an outsider. Although not overly confident, thanks to his upbringing, he had learned his manners, one of which required that he introduce himself to strangers: "Hi, I'm Fred Weyerhaeuser," he would announce, extending a hand. And the recipient had to respond in kind, a stranger no more. "There are lots of 1st class fellows here & we shall have a slick time," he soon informed Phil.

The work was challenging, but it was exactly what F.K. had envisioned and he was "enjoying it ever so much." His rank was private in the Aviation Section of the Signal Enlisted Reserve Corps, or ASSERC as it was known. This was basic training at its most basic, with no flying instruction, although some of the courses dealt with aspects of aviation such as aerodynamics, gasoline engines, weather, navigation, telegraphy (Morse code), and artillery observation. Reveille was at 6:00 A.M., followed by calisthenics and breakfast. They drilled from 8:00 to 10:00 A.M. and then had classes until noon, with two more hours of drill in the afternoons.

Though F.K. was still a little gawky, his girth at first caused embarrassment when he found his uniform blouse too tight to button. He would soon visit a San Francisco tailor, where he purchased uniforms suited to his frame. The tailor apparently got the cut right, but not the cloth. He used a winter-weight wool, and F.K. spent most of his days perspiring. "I will never forget how silly my first uniform looked nor how uncomfortable I felt in my second," he later recalled. But these problems soon passed, and by the end of July he was the happiest of students. "I never felt better in my life," he informed his father. "Am inclined to believe a little war is a good thing." And to Phil he wrote, "It's great dope," referring to the subject matter. Drills, initially all important, were now limited to an hour a day, and those in F.K.'s class already looked forward to the next assignment. He was thankful for the early start, "instead of after the US has 10 or 15,000 aviators."

His class graduated August 11, and F.K. was among the nine selected for European flight training. (This was but one more example of lack of preparedness on the part of Americans. General John J. Pershing, while wishing to keep American units intact, realized how far behind the country lagged in aviation training. Thus he arranged for Allied schools to accept upwards of a hundred American cadets per month, beginning July 1. Some of the early slots were taken by Americans already in France serving in the Ambulance Corps, but the majority of these cadets, including F.K., didn't arrive until fall.)

Phil came to see his brother off, the two of them enjoying the weekend in San Francisco. Then F.K. headed east to report to Fort Wood, which shared Bedloe's Island with the Statue of Liberty. And at Fort Wood, Private or Second Lieutenant Weyerhaeuser—he wasn't sure which—was introduced to the old army tradition of hurry up and wait.

He did enjoy the advantage of having family nearby, so he spent some free hours at Woods Hole, where the Jewetts had a vacation home. As he reported to Anna, "The relatives were very good to me and couldn't do enough." But it was almost embarrassing. "These farewells of a departing soldier are very touching but it's always an anti-climax later when you come back." He concluded with the usual request that they not worry about him. "It will be months & months before I get through training & the war will probably be over then anyway."

But it was the waiting that was over, not the war. He and his contingent sailed aboard the SS *Magnolia* in late September. "A great bunch," F.K. later described them, "with all the enthusiasm and energy in the world." Despite a difficult crossing and subsequent travel delays, that enthusiasm and mischievous energy carried them through. In many respects, college continued. And the confusion over rank continued, as was apparent when they arrived at Le Havre, although there didn't seem to be any confusion in the minds of those in charge. Here they were privates, "because the luggage of the 2nd Lieutenants had to be unloaded and we were the logical candidates for that job."

Far more sobering, however, was the sight of a hospital train filled with wounded English and Canadian soldiers. F.K. would "never forget lighting a cigarette for an Englishman who had lost both arms and was going back to 'Blighty.'" All of a sudden the war became a ghastly reality.

F.K. soon found himself in Paris, which he described as "some place!" There he and others awaited orders, and one of his roommates at the Continental Hotel was Archibald MacLeish, Yale 1915. He used his spare moments to bring Anna up-to-date: "As to our immediate future it may be Italy for our first training. Won't that be wonderful? It is [a] fine sunny climate down there on the Mediterranean and Italy has the finest aviation schools anyway. Have gotten [an] Italian dictionary and am going to start studying it soon. I don't believe it will be a very hard language to learn." When Phil received the letter, forwarded by Anna, he sent it on to Uncle Fred, knowing of his interest. (F.E. would make a practice of copying all of F.K.'s war letters in order to share them with the entire family.)

F.K. guessed right about his next assignment. A short, smiling captain arrived on the scene and rounded up the contingent, bound for the Italian Flying School at Foggia, situated almost on the heel of Italy's boot, some one hundred fifty miles southeast of Rome. The captain was Fiorello La Guardia, a U.S. Congressman and later the mayor of New York City, and he would be as popular with his troops as he was with his constituents back home.

F.K.'s unit arrived in Foggia on October 16, joining some forty Americans already in training there under the command of Major William Ord Ryan. It was a depressing scene, as his first letter home indicated: "Foggia is by common agreement the dirtiest, rottenest, and worst hole you ever saw." But that was the town itself, and surely they had to be a bit careful when publicly discussing Foggia, the birthplace of Captain La Guardia's father. The surrounding country was quite another matter, "perhaps the most beautiful I have ever seen with a fringe of mountains to [the] west (the Apenines [*sic*] I guess) and another to the east with the Adriatic just beyond." All things considered, he couldn't have been more pleased, "in wonderful company, and enjoying my work *immensely*." Two weeks of training would not change his mind. "It has really been a circus," he informed sister Elizabeth on November 2, before allowing, "Don't suppose war is all like this however."

The work had commenced immediately, "each student being given a ten-minute joy ride." At first they flew French Farman biplanes, pusher-type aircraft. The Farman seemed almost as curious then as it does now. The student occupied the first seat, over the nose; the instructor was next, immediately in front of the motor. Thus the cadet occasionally wondered if he was all alone in the world, F.K. admitting that he "would once in a while look back to see if the plane were still with him."

November 2 was a rainy day, a good day for letter writing, since "the old white flag is up today, meaning no flying." There would be many such days in the weeks ahead, for the rainy season had just begun. He reported to Phil that his instructor was letting him do almost everything now, even though "I land too *steeply* and too *fast*." On the ground, it was mostly fun and foolishness, F.K. just one of "a jolly crowd," knowing beyond a doubt that he and his comrades were without equal. Three weeks later he told of a good flight, nine minutes in all, and a fair landing, "but haven't received any gold medals as yet." Apparently he wasn't the only one experiencing problems of that sort. He described the scene along the runway when a cadet came in with a bumpy landing: "We all line up & give him the merry ha-ha. There is really a great bunch of boys here and we have a continual circus."

"Golly but it's fun to fly!" he told his mother, recognizing her as a kindred spirit. Further, he predicted, one of these days she *would* fly: "Imagine stepping into a large comfortable machine in Tacoma or Seattle . . . and waking up the next morning in St. Paul. And, believe me, it won't be long before those things will be done." But for all of the excitement and joys of flight, F.K., like all servicemen, still waited anxiously for mail call. In addition to letters, gum and candy were "always welcome," as well as books, or so he informed John and Anna. Phil was his source for other necessities. At one point, F.K. pleaded, "Phlip, for the love of Mike, go over to the smoke shop and invest about $25 in pipe tobacco, cigars and cigarettes!" and forward the packages by parcel post. "The local tobacco is terrible."

He had the "best flight I have *ever* had" on the morning of December 6. His instructor, apparently often grumpy (or perhaps frightened), announced "molto bene." F.K. was full of confidence, ready to solo. But nothing happened, and on December 7 his instructor went hunting. Any chance for an early solo abruptly ended on December 10, when one of the cadets crashed. There was only one answer—additional training.

F.K. was naturally more honest with Phil about his experiences than with others in the family.

> Flying is something like auto-driving and something like sailing. It is lots easier than driving an auto fast over a bad road; still you've always got to keep watching. It is all in getting the "feel" of the controls and in judging your speed through the air. The landing is not hard except in a side wind when you have to use your rudder just right at the right instant. We have accidents here every day and machines get busted up continually but nobody ever gets hurt. And you ought to see some of the wrecks!!

F.K. was not as blasé as he sounded. Although he didn't mention them in his letters, there were fatal accidents, and naturally he thought about such possibilities. But most of the time, the mere joy of flying sufficed. He did, however, reflect now and then. "When you get over here," he explained to Phil, "with a big war ahead of you, you certainly begin to appreciate your past blessings more. We have been mighty fortunate so far in our lives, and if the worst happens to me there isn't much for me to regret, because it will be in a good cause and there's the satisfaction of knowing that you and Liz are still at home to look out for Mother & Father." He had also insured himself for $10,000, "half payable to you and half to Liz."

His current training involved a series of maneuvers, culminating in the first brevet test, "two figure '8's at 1,500 feet and then fly for 45 minutes while maintaining a constant altitude of 3,000 feet." When all this was successfully completed, he would be an aviator. (The "brevet" was not a formal rank and so contributed to confusion about exact status.)

Now sporting a mustache, F.K. completed that first brevet in early January 1918 and immediately began work on the second. But he was less than happy over a recent change in policy denoting a second lieutenancy in aviation, presumably because there were too many first lieutenants. That hardly seemed fair. Here he had been one of the so-called honor men, sent to Europe for flight training, which had been delayed through no fault of their own, and many of those "2nd raters" left behind were already first lieutenants. John read of his son's frustration in detail: "Of course we shall go ahead and do whatever is expected of us in any case, but we are trying to have it corrected at the same time." For his part, F.K. wrote directly to Minnesota Senator Frank B. Kellogg, "calling his attention to the matter."

The basics mastered, in the next phase students performed several required maneuvers at high altitudes, after which they were to land at a "strange airdrome." Finally, they made a "raid test" involving two cross-country flights over different courses. When this had been accomplished, they became "military aviators" and received their commissions. F.K. completed his "raid" on February 7, 1918, although he wouldn't receive the rank of first lieutenant in the Air Service until March 11. Nearly five months had passed since his arrival at Foggia.

F.K. completed his second Italian military brevet in mid-February; by then he had accumulated more than twenty hours of flying time. Now he awaited his commission and the start of advanced training. At times the rank part seemed unimportant, "selfish," but he admitted that it would be "nice to wear a gold cord and sport a couple of bars." The confusion over rank had apparently been resolved, for F.K. expected to be a second lieutenant in about a month and a first shortly thereafter. Phil, still at Yale and studying military subjects primarily, hadn't improved as a correspondent. F.K. admonished him on February 18, "You *damn sphinx!*"

He was grateful, though, for the regular packages of tobacco. "Keep on sending it, old scout, whenever you feel flush." He wrote on another "rotten rainy cold day," the fourth successive day grounded. With the preliminary training completed, he expressed his regard for the French Farman, in his words "the *Ford* of aviation." While avoiding mention of fatalities, or even serious injuries, he did acknowledge that there were "smashups *all the time.*" So far, however, he had a near-perfect record, "knock on wood," explaining that it was mostly "the boneheads that smash."

The advanced flying initially involved "climbing, climbing, and then climbing." The only danger was "climbing too steep and going into a stall and then side slip and nosedive (which is bad business)." In a nosedive, there was only one course of action: "[P]ut controls in neutral, pull close into your stomach and pray to God she'll come out of it before you hit." But such excitement soon appeared a thing of the past. The March 11 celebration of F.K.'s promotion to first lieutenant was subdued. They all had long since grown tired of Foggia and of living on rumors. F.K. was eager to begin training on the new combat plane, whatever it might be. He had his preferences. "I want a big 3-engined bomber, such as was flown by Italians in U.S. They are wonderful machines, and are the machines of the future, to my mind." In this instance, F.K. would get his wish.

The boredom continued with not enough mail to ease the monotony. He acknowledged receipt of a letter from Phil, encircling the word *letter* so as to make it glow. He also claimed to have had it framed and hung over his bed "as a curiosity" and predicted that should Phil ever become famous, his letters would become exceedingly valuable "because they're so rare." For himself, he had nothing to report since "the Government seems to have decided not to use us for this war, but the war after next." He described the tedium:

> . . . go to bed about 10 p.m. (if I damned please), sleep all night and till about 10 a.m., unless the Officer of the Day makes a big row, in which case, it is necessary to get *out* of bed till he leaves room and then crawl in again. If the weather happens to be good (if I want to), I can get up at 7 and test out a Farman for the boys, but as the wind has been blowing hard for 4 days straight, it will probably blow for the next 4 too. At 11 comes 1st Mess & at 12

comes 2nd Mess. I can go to either or both if necessary. In the afternoon at 1 p.m. another fellow and I have an Italian lesson when we feel ambitious. We usually don't feel ambitious. At 2, we play bridge, or write letters, or go for a walk or do anything till 6 or 7 or anytime we like. Then we can get dinner at mess. In evening we can go to opera if there is any (it's never very good), getting home when we like, being Officers.

F.K. feared that his soul was rotting out "down here, especially when there's a big fight going on up in France, as just at present." He only hoped that the Allies could "hold the Huns till we can get an Army over here that will knock the everlasting Hell out of them." Clearly his patience was wearing thin. But things were about to change.

Phil did have one good excuse for his silence, besides his studies. He was in love; in fact, he was engaged to Helen Walker, a student at Smith College. The engagement would be on-again, off-again, ultimately ending in marriage after more than three years. F.K. sent congratulations: "Damn it, you always were a heart-killer or rather a lady-breaker!" He foresaw no romance on his own horizon—"no 'calico' I want to hitch myself up to."

In the meantime, he was learning to fly the Caproni, the trimotored Italian bomber he had hoped for. Training started on the Caproni 350— the figure denoting the combined horsepower of the three engines—to be followed by the Ca 450 or the Ca 600. He found the flying easier in some respects; with "a 3-motored rig and a friend in seat beside you who can take charge when you get tired and one or 2 mechanics in behind watching the engines, you're Jake!!" The intent was to do night bombing at fairly long distances. He expected to finish the course within the month.

But the work and excitement could not entirely obscure news from the home front. John had sent F.K. a troubling article alleging that the Weyerhaeuser Timber Company had been sabotaging the war effort. Though the charge was ridiculous, the response was subdued, the feeling being that it was best not to protest too loudly. That made F.K. mad, as he let his brother know. "If I ever get to have any power in business," he asserted, "you can bet I'm not going to let anyone talk that way about me or my Co. without calling for a showdown."

It was, of course, one thing to react from a distant place in uniform and quite another if the vantage was a desk in Tacoma. F.K. was feeling naturally full of it. Still, as he looked to the future, he thought he would settle down in some small town and run a sawmill, content with little money and less excitement.

John, assuming the worst, imagined his son at the front by April 1; F.K. happily informed him otherwise. He remained, as he wrote on April 20, "very much 'in the behind' as yet, with no immediate chance of getting killed or even of getting hurt."

But the training was not as simple as F.K. expected. Within a week he had three accidents, two of them a matter of bad luck. The first happened during takeoff when a clod of dirt hit and broke the left propeller. A piece of the prop flew through the upper-left wing and "just *missed* the aileron wire. So made a sharp turn and came in all right." The second mishap occurred while he was landing, when the wind kept blowing the plane along and F.K. could only watch as he hit a hangar door, busting part of the landing gear. "Then I knew a third was coming," he wrote Phil. And so it did, again during a landing. The wind changed and he misjudged the distance, rolled off the runway, in the end tipping over on the nose, again damaging the landing gear. "Can you beat it?" he asked Phil rhetorically. He hadn't been hurt, but he had been embarrassed. And he was a little poorer, being required to buy *vino* for the boys. His letter's closing expressed a recurrent fear. "The govt's forgotten all about us down here." It only seemed that way, for decisions were being made at the highest levels concerning how best to utilize American pilots. Finally, in late May, General Pershing approved their temporary assignment to Italian squadrons, with the understanding that should they be needed in support of American troops they would be transferred to France.

The Italian front was not terribly significant to the American high command in 1918, but the Allies knew it constituted a crucial distraction to the Germans and their Austrian allies—a distraction made all the more important when the Russians quit the war. The Italians had to be kept in the battle and, for a time, that seemed to be in doubt. The most dramatic moment had occurred the previous fall, with the disastrous defeat of the Italian army at Caporetto. Some two hundred seventy-five thousand troops surrendered, and the rest began a long retreat, south and west to the Piave River. Ernest Hemingway, then a volunteer ambulance driver for the Italians, would later describe the retreat in *A Farewell to Arms* as "orderly, wet, and sullen." King Victor Emmanuel summed up his country's extreme embarrassment: "All cowardice is treachery, all discord is treachery." F.K. and his fellow airmen were most needed where they were, supporting the Allied effort on the Southern Front.

He made his final practice bomb run on June 18. They dropped their bombs from two thousand feet, flying into a head wind that held them almost stationary. After pulling the lever, he recounted to Phil, he watched "the bombs *slowly* drop, getting *smaller* and *smaller*," and after what seemed forever, they could see "a little puff of white smoke." Now he expected to get orders within the week, "where to I don't know, but in all probability, to the big show." He looked forward both to leaving Foggia and to proving himself. And in a postscript to sister Liz, he announced that some of them were scheduled to leave Foggia on the evening of June 19. "And shall soon see action. Am so glad! Lots of Love!!" But F.K. wasn't among them.

His wait lasted until mid-July, when matters moved quickly, F.K. writing to his parents from "the front" on July 16. He assured them that his front was not at all similar to the one that had become so famous. "I am lying on a fine bed . . . in a fine little hotel. The room is as nice as you could find in the Davenport in Spokane." A month later he told of his first action in a letter to Phil. "It certainly gave me a funny sensation to see little flashes all around down below and realize that those were guns shooting at me." But beyond the "funny sensation," there was apparently no fear. "It's like a game," F.K. noted, "and the chances are all in your favor." Game or not, he was obviously beginning to wish for the end. The news from France was encouraging, what with the early American successes at places like Chateau-Thierry. It had been more than a year since F.K. had seen his parents, and he missed them. "Manys the time everyone of us wishes he were back home . . . just to see some of the old familiar things like a pullman car, or an honest-to-god American Drug store or a decent girl that can talk something besides this jabber. It's not the danger one gets to mind, it's the eternal longing for the old familiar things at home."

There was no real routine for F.K. during his assignment in Verona with the 11th Gruppo Aeroplani, 5th Squadriglia Caproni. Between bombing raids were other duties, some ceremonial, others logistical, such as trips to the Caproni plant at Taliedo, near Milan, to pick up new planes and fly them back to Verona. But the orders were seldom completed according to schedule, and so the pilots waited impatiently. Among the few benefits of these "interminable delays" were La Scala operas, another example of the incongruities of wartime. For all of the dangers involved, the airmen's experience was often abstract, if not downright surreal. F.K. commonly felt as much during his raids. "The sheer beauty of it all gave one a feeling of unreality and of being in a dream. . . . It seemed impossible that the killing of people could be the reason for flight through such a paradise!"

Military ceremonies were performed in the Italian fashion. On September 20, for example, all were ordered to Padua for a grandiose review at which the king presented decorations. Manlio Borri, F.K.'s frequent flight partner, was awarded a silver medal, but one of his fellow officers didn't receive his simply because it wasn't on hand. Neither were the Italian War Crosses, which F.K. and several of his American colleagues had been awarded. They would receive them later—much later.

On October 7, the Verona contingent learned of the first of several "false armistices." F.K. didn't need reminding that the war went on. He read a letter from his old West Virginia chum Lou Bennett, reporting that one of their classmates, Jarvis Offutt, had been shot down over France. Typically, Lou promised to "avenge Jarvis' death." And to an extent he would do so, shooting down three planes and nine observation balloons within ten days. But when attacking that ninth balloon, Bennett's plane was shot down by the covering machine guns. He received German medical attention but soon died. His death was not finally verified, however, until mid-April 1919, when Lou's mother herself came over to conduct an on-the-scene investigation.

F.K.'s final flight of the war, on November 2, proved to be the most exciting. He was flying once again with Borri, their objective a bridge at Palmanova, a distant target near the Adriatic. Visibility quickly became a problem, and they flew by compass for much of the way, F.K. feeling that passing through thick clouds in an open plane was "almost like being smothered." When they descended through the overcast, the engines cooled and "started acting up," so they dumped their bombs on what they hoped was the target and headed homeward. Then the rear motor caught fire, and they had to cut off its gas supply while the rear machine gunner got busy with his fire extinguisher. He was successful, but they now had only two engines, which meant that they were able to fly at twenty-nine-hundred feet but could not climb. Since they had to pass over enemy territory, they were subjected to antiaircraft fire and "felt like a couple of ducks on the first day of the duck season." They finally found their Verona field after a flight of more than three hours, F.K.'s longest of the war. His inspection of the bomber revealed machine gun bullet holes "right between the place my feet had been."

Devastation was not limited to Europe. F.K. learned of a terrible conflagration that had virtually destroyed the town of Cloquet, Minnesota, in mid-October. Uncle F.E. provided the details of the destruction almost apologetically. He presumed that for those who had witnessed the "ruthless destruction of the Huns, this particular loss would be only a drop in the bucket." In truth, few European towns had suffered damage comparable to that in Cloquet.

On the Italian front, the exhausted Austrian armies agreed to an armistice on November 4. There was some brief discussion about sending the Italian bomber squadrons farther north to fields from which they could strike directly at Germany, but in the meantime the war ended. F.K. and his compatriots did make one final flight of note, when Victor Emmanuel entered Trieste. Several of them crossed the Adriatic, circled Trieste for half an hour, and then flew over Venice where they buzzed St. Mark's, among other sites. It was a festive end to the long trial.

On the home front, the celebrations marking the November 11 armistice were memorable. A Rock Island friend of John reported on events in the old hometown: "The Noise is increasing and the crowds grow larger every minute. Big Parade of Heider Tractors, loaded with men from factory just went by, yelling, flags waving. Now if we could see a dog fight and a runaway . . . the noise would be complete . . . Let 'er rip Bang Bang." But some still had cause for worry. The last letter from F.K. had been dated October 8, and "we are so anxious," his father wrote to Phil.

John received the long-awaited telegram from F.K. on November 21: "[V]ery well love happy Frederick." Only then did he sit down and write his sons and son-in-law, Rod Titcomb, a letter marking the end of the war. Each received the same letter, which, in the case of Titcomb, didn't make perfect sense, at least not the part that read, "When I held you as a baby I would think with an indescribeable [sic] pleasure and pride of the day when your school life would close and when you would assume responsibility and take your place in the business world." But it didn't matter. The boys got the message loud and clear.

By November 21, when John penned his letter, F.K. was already in France, awaiting embarkation orders. He would be among the first to sail, landing in Newport News, Virginia, on Christmas Day and then proceeding directly to Rock Island, where most of the family had gathered for the holidays. By New Year's Day the four cousins were reunited, all in uniform, although Edwin had already received his discharge. Uncle Charlie reported on the gathering to John and Anna, at home in Tacoma. "How I wish you could have been down to the train with us to 'Welcome Frederick.'" he declared. "What a *splendid nice modest* boy he is . . . looking fine and appears to be in perfect health."

While enjoying the moment, Charlie was already looking ahead, his hopes identical to John's. "I have great confidence in my nephews," he wrote, "and I am selfish enough to sincerely hope that they will follow the lumber business." Reflecting on his own life, he knew he had worked hard in Little Falls, but they had sawed only about 1.25 billion board feet of timber. The Weyerhaeuser Timber Company owned some sixty billion feet, so there would be work enough for all of the nephews. As a start, he wanted John to assure F.K. that he could have a job in Little Falls if he wanted one there.

But F.K. wasn't quite a civilian yet. He had to return to Camp Mills on Long Island, where he received his discharge on January 6, 1919. While in the east, he spent time with tailors, putting together a new wardrobe. "Started wearing civilian clothes yesterday for the first time in 18 months," he informed his father on January 12. John was waiting in St. Paul, eager to get his son started in the business. But the transition from bomber pilot to businessman would not proceed easily.

F.K. wasn't alone, of course, in experiencing some difficulty moving from Caproni night raids to the everyday concerns of business. One of his comrades, Arthur "Doug" Farquhar, shared his initial anxieties. "I have to laugh when I think how many times we used to say, 'Oh, boy, if we can just live thru this war things will be jake the rest of our lives' . . . and now I never was more at sea as to what I am going to do next. My girl don't love me and this thing of really starting to *work* again is appalling." Where did the romance go? Where was the excitement?

The memories didn't fade, and the friends stayed close over the years. Doug wrote again November 12, 1920, to "Caro Fred Amico Mio." By then Doug had returned to work with the Mutual Fire Insurance Company and was married. He was happy, but the exhilaration of their service together lingered. "We are both pretty lucky boys that we had our experiences and 'fought our fight' and came back in health and happiness—only I am a lot luckier than you are because I am all safely married to a very nice girl."

Six years later, the bonds of fellowship were still intact. Fiorello La Guardia, once again a U.S. Congressman representing New York's Thirtieth District, invited his fellow "wops" to a September 8, 1926, reunion in Philadelphia, to coincide with that year's National Air Races. "Bring your best stories," the invitation read. "If about the war truth is a liability."

AND NOW TO WORK

JOHN HAD DEFINITE ideas about how young men should be introduced to the lumber business. But when it came to his own sons, some adjustments were in order. At a St. Paul meeting of salesmen and stockholders of the Weyerhaeuser Sales Company (not as yet incorporated), a proud John formally presented F.K. to friends and colleagues. Though it could not have been foreseen at the time, the Sales Company would dominate F.K.'s interest in the years ahead. Meanwhile, he was westward bound.

In late February 1919, F.K. accepted an invitation to join the Auditing Department for the retail yards of the Potlatch Lumber Company. "My idea," John informed brother Rudolph, "is to train him from the consumer of lumber back to the trees." And so the war hero headed from Tacoma to Spokane, ready to roll up his sleeves and do his civilian duty. He well understood this as the commencement of his life's work. Indeed, at age twenty-four he was the oldest of the four nephews, all of whom—everyone assumed—would learn the business. And, in F.K.'s words, "Being the oldest a lot was expected of me."

He kept Phil posted about his situation. Initially he was assigned to tag along after the retail-yard auditor to various little towns. "You really learn a heap going around this way," he observed with appropriate enthusiasm. The work was easy enough, but he had not yet figured out how to spend the weekends, with "nothing to do." His sociability, manifested earlier in school and then in the military, needed an outlet.

After about a month on the job, F.K. felt he was getting "a fair idea of the general system of managing retail yards." The accompanying problem, however, loomed large—"settling down in a dumpy little town and knowing all the neighbors." That didn't augur well for a future in the lumber industry, but as he indicated to his father on March 22, "I'll talk that all over with you when I see you."

He was soon off to eastern Washington to assist the manager of the Pullman yard. Life was still not exciting, but at least during working hours he stayed busy. As a start, he kept the books and helped unload lumber, "or wait on a customer, or fill an order, load a wagon, etc., sweep out office & in other words, to do everything possible." Although he didn't mind the work, he wondered why the manager was so inactive. Why wasn't he out seeking customers? There was an answer of sorts. The only competitor, the Standard Lumber Company, was owned by the same group. That may not have been illegal at the time, but it surely discouraged initiative. F.K. was learning, maybe more often through mistakes than otherwise.

Meanwhile, John observed from a distance, watching carefully nonetheless. He saw that the benefits of the Pullman position would soon be realized, and in late April he forwarded the March statement of the Boise Payette Yards for F.K. to study. His next assignment would be at one of Boise's seventy-odd yards. There were bound to be a few favorable situations, and John promised to inquire "as to a pleasing town to live and one that might have a comfortable hotel." But it was not so much comfort as companionship that F.K. needed. "After being with good friends so long, it sure is a change, believe me."

He did seize a rare opportunity to be with one of those friends, spending three days in Tacoma, where he hosted former comrade-in-arms Doug Farquhar. For a reunion party one evening, the two of them donned their musty uniforms and danced the night away. Anna described it all for the benefit of Phil, again at Yale. According to her, the boys "had a gala good time for there were more girls than men tho Frederick has forgotten half the people he ever met here and I fear smiled to the wrong ones and slighted the right ones." F.K. regretted nothing. "All the old gang was there and it seemed like old times," or so he informed his brother, and closed, "Am looking forward to our being together this summer." But their father had other plans.

John's personal worries continued to plague him, and topping the list were his doubts about continuing as president of the Weyerhaeuser Timber Company. Admittedly, with George Long in charge of operations, the president had little responsibility. At the same time, the position wasn't strictly honorary, and John could have involved himself more had he been so inclined. Anna did her best to encourage him to remain in place, to be patient until his sons could assume their roles. In late May, he planned a trip to the Clearwater country in Idaho, where a major development was in the offing. Take F.K. with you, she urged, "as he is full of business zeal and surely shows the right spirit and interest in all the propositions." And then she reminded John of what the future might hold. "Your next years are to be such happy ones, for soon [F.K.] will be able to discuss understandingly the perplexing business issues." F.K., about to trade Pullman and Potlatch for Blackfoot, Idaho, and the Boise Payette Lumber Company, doubted that he was ready for such discussions.

Still, there were occasions when he was not reticent about offering opinions. After studying the August figures, he wrote directly to John Mahan, manager of the family office in St. Paul, suggesting that outstanding accounts at many of the yards were too large. Mahan sent his reply to John with a postscript, "Please thank Fred for the criticism." John was, in his own words, "amused to see Frederick already making expressions as to capital, etc., amount invested, earnings as pertaining to various retail enterprises."

As things turned out, Phil, along with Fritz Jewett, spent most of the summer working on the Clearwater survey with Earnest Brigham, so F.K. once again had to content himself with the mails. And in Phil's case that was, as usual, frustrating. F.K. was still in Blackfoot in mid-August but preparing for another minor move, to Firth, "a little jerk-water outfit north of here." He allowed as how his life "hasn't been very exciting." Still, the work often challenged him—"This retail biz is surely a merry scrap all the time." And on Sundays he found considerable pleasure in the outdoors, "beating it to the tall timbers and looking for fish." He hoped that Phil would be able to join him on one of those expeditions before heading back to Yale.

Deviations from the original plan notwithstanding, it is interesting how precisely John scheduled his sons' lumber education, and how closely they adhered to his schedule. Dr. E. P. Clapp, an owner colleague, was wrestling with the same problem concerning his son James, but being a physician he had little background on which to base his recommendations. John explained his own reasoning. Son-in-law Rod Titcomb, "with several years experience in other lines of business," commenced work at the manufacturing end, specifically at the Everett plant. As for F.K., he began at the retailing end of the game, "meeting the customers, figuring the bills, auditing accounts, familiarizing himself with additional stock, like paint, coal, cement, hardware, sash and doors, and the like." John foresaw about three more months of this, after which F.K. would probably assume a position with Thompson Yards, the mammoth operation responsible for selling the products of the Weyerhaeuser Timber Company throughout Minnesota and the Dakotas. The employment arrangements are of interest, as John explained to Dr. Clapp:

> Both Frederick and Rodman receive no wages for this education which is understood by the men with whom and under whom they work. It naturally creates a friendly spirit with the fellows on the job who take great pains to show them everything worth knowing in their particular job since they understand these fellows are merely learning the business as a whole and not as a possible successor to their particular job.

Not everyone agreed with this paternalistic approach. Thomas J. Humbird, a longtime associate, complained directly when John tried personally to pay Phil's and nephew Fritz Jewett's summer wages for their work on the Clearwater survey. "It reflects on the boys," Humbird argued, "and I am firmly of the belief it is a mistake." They earned their wages honestly; let them be paid. But John constantly fretted about taking advantage. The boys, he responded, "know nothing of the return of the money to the Company by me so no harm will be done," adding, "I only want no occasion given for any criticism."

In mid-October, in accordance with John's latest plan, F.K. reported to Thompson Yards' home office in Minneapolis. Initially he was impressed, finding George Thompson to be considerate and very helpful. But F.K. had landed in the midst of big trouble, although few realized it at the time.

Thompson was a salesman *extraordinaire,* and his greatest feat was selling the Weyerhaeuser Timber Company directors on the Thompson Yards' way of doing business. Years later F.K. recalled those days and Thompson's "new type of retail selling." He seemed never to worry about competitors, and the organization was highly centralized. Prices on all items at Thompson's two hundred lumber yards were set in the main office, his theory being that if profits were not adequate, "he could make a slight adjustment in all prices and correct the trouble." Once assured of Timber Company support, Thompson grew ever more reckless, running the company "on a very liberal basis" and extending credit freely. "When the mills needed orders, he would order hundreds of cars of lumber and overstock the yards." It sounded good, especially when George Thompson was doing the talking. "The only trouble," F.K. later acknowledged, "was that it did not work." In 1919, however, few seemed to question Thompson, including F.K.

For F.K., working in the Twin Cities was akin to coming home. Moreover, during much of his time with Thompson Yards, he was a houseguest at 266 Summit Avenue, where Uncle Rudolph and Aunt Louise now resided. He appreciated their attentions, writing John that they had "tried to do everything possible to make things pleasant for me." The hosts, however, endured at least one minor irritation for a time. F.K. had bought what he described as "an old beat-up Ford," which he parked on the street in front of 266. Finally Aunt Louise allowed that "she would just as soon have me park the vehicle up the street a ways." F.K., of course, immediately complied.

Within a month, he began to experience some doubts regarding management of Thompson Yards, doubts he shared with brother Phil. "It is some system and has wonderful men in it," he noted, "although I question whether it will ever be the money maker per million feet sold that Kendall [of Potlatch] and Gamble [of Boise Payette] are." He was clearly enjoying city life and hoped that Phil would come to St. Paul for the holidays. This time Phil, again engaged to Helen Walker, didn't disappoint, joining F.K. for Christmas at 266 Summit. It was almost like old times, the cousins together. Eddie Davis wrote Phil that he "sure had a fine time in St. Paul this vacation" and added, "I think we kids are getting to like each other better every year."

Following the holidays, F.K. and John toured together, ending up in Tacoma, after which F.K. worked for a time at Everett Mill "A," the old plant. Anna enjoyed their company. "The house seems to be alive again," she happily informed Phil, allowing, facetiously, that she occasionally tired of "listening to Frederick & father discuss 2 x 4's and thick & thin dimension, flooring & ceiling." But F.K. wasn't always thinking about lumber and dimension; he took advantage of being "home," socializing whenever possible. Anna enjoyed keeping track of him, or trying to. "Frederick just came in before dinner, has been having a good time in Seattle, a dinner dance Friday night at Sunset Club, and last night at Hotel Washington," and, according to her, he was meeting "a lot of 'peachy' girls, etc."

Regarding the work experience at Everett, F.K. appeared knowledgeable, at least to Phil. "This really is the way to start in, kid. I know a little about grades, manufacturing, scaling, and other trivialities." He expected to spend another month or so at the mill "before going over to Spokane to hit Mr. [L. S.] Case [general manager of the Weyerhaeuser Sales Company] for a job." In the meantime, he had invested $2,700 in a two-and-one-half-year-old Cadillac that looked like new "but has not the speed nor the stay on the road qualities of the Mercer."

Again, John wasn't alone in his concern over F.K.'s work experience and his business future. Each of the uncles was interested and ready to help but none with more enthusiasm than Uncle Charlie. Along with a letter to F.K. marked "Personal," he forwarded the 1919 annual statement of the Edward Rutledge Timber Company, reminding him that all of the so-called affiliated companies kept their books basically the same way, so that it was possible to become acquainted with one and understand the others. Charlie didn't want his nephew to be a bookkeeper, or even to become as adept with figures as his cousin Eddie Davis. "But," he noted, "it is an awful nice and useful thing to understand accounting—assets and liabilities, double entry bookkeeping, debits and credits." Specifically, he advised F.K. to study the reports at night and then get to know a bookkeeper who could provide further instruction. And if F.K. followed his advice, his uncle promised to send "with great pleasure $100.00 to give your cashier for having helped you."

What Uncle Charlie envisioned was simple: F.K. would "come to the front as a Real Big Lumberman"; his first step would be to gain an understanding of accounting. The next rung on the ladder was the Weyerhaeuser Timber Company, and Charlie intended to ask George Long to let F.K. have a copy of his report, "and I want you to tell him that you want to study it and will return it to him." At the time the Timber Company reports were few, and those were closely guarded. "Fred," Uncle Charlie continued, "I want you to agree to 'marry' that Company. By that, I mean make it your life's work." He closed the letter by noting that "George Long is the largest man in the Timber world, and think of what a chance you have to learn under him and your father."

The interest shown by the uncles was largely a product of the Weyerhaeuser family closeness. F.K. was the oldest male of the third generation, and they were German enough to attach considerable significance to that fact, trusting that he would set the example for those who followed. Rudolph had no son, and Charlie's only son, Carl, was a teenager. Still, John would very likely have considered Charlie's direct involvement with F.K. as meddlesome—a threat to his own paternal prerogatives—had he been aware of it.

By mid-June 1920, F.K. was in Spokane as planned, being introduced to the Weyerhaeuser Sales Company and its general manager, Louis S. Case. F.K. could not yet have known that he had found his niche: At the moment he was only "anxious to get a real job," as he wrote to Phil. In a sense, he regretted leaving Everett, although he described it as "the deadest place you ever saw." But it did enjoy the major advantage of proximity to Seattle, where "time does not hang heavy." In fact, F.K. would not see Seattle again for quite a while. An immediate question concerned Phil's summer plans. He was about to take his finals, thus his brother's timely closing comment: "I hope you pass—Write me soon."

Case offered F.K. a sales responsibility in northern Iowa, and off he went, knowing little about selling and less about his territory. Several months passed before he learned that the territory included Mason City. Part of the problem was Sales Company policy. Most of its trustees were representatives of the various mills, meeting monthly to set the prices for the ensuing month. That placed those in the field at a serious disadvantage with competitors who were free to change prices on a daily basis. As a result, "If the market was strong, Weyerhaeuser Sales Company prices were apt to be too low, but if the market was weak, our prices were apt to be too high." In F.K.'s case, his prices seemed always on the high side, and he had "a very tough time selling lumber." During the six months he roamed the Iowa countryside, the price of 2 x 4's fell by half. "It was," he would recall, "an object lesson in the extreme vulnerability of lumber prices to variations in supply and demand relationship." His immediate superior, Ray Clute, tried to commiserate. "We are almost inclined to agree with you," he wrote, allowing that F.K. may have set a record, visiting thirty towns without receiving a single order.

In fact, F.K. did manage an occasional sale to lumber dealers, bragging in mid-August that he had sold three carloads! But overall, there was little activity. His father worried lest he get discouraged. "Stick to the job," he urged, advising that patience was the key: "Business is quiet and nothing much doing but it will come later." September passed with no improvement, and John could only continue giving assurances that F.K. was not alone. "Do not get discouraged even if you do not sell any lumber," he wrote early in October. "No one is."

All this experience was doubtless valuable, or would be, but F.K. wanted to get started on something with a future. He wasn't alone in this professional purgatory. Cousin Ed Davis was working away as an apprentice at the Snoqualmie Falls Lumber Company in western Washington. He wrote Phil that he had been visited by a classmate from Hill, "a good scout but somewhat like myself, in that his hardest work is trying to decide what to do." As things developed, Ed would be the first of the cousins to find his niche, managing the Wood Conversion Company in Cloquet, Minnesota.

In the meantime, the three—Ed Davis, Phil, and F.K.—toyed with the dream of purchasing their own property, complete with a sawmill, possibly on Klamath Lake in Oregon. They briefly thought that the Weyerhaeuser Timber Company might sell them a tract of timber, but George S. Long was less than enthusiastic. Oh, he would sell if they insisted, but he had plans of his own for that pine: an operating branch in Klamath Falls. The three cousins would later look the region over, deciding afterward that better opportunities lay elsewhere. Long didn't argue the point.

F.K. completed his Sales Company assignment in Iowa in the fall of 1920 and came "home" to Tacoma for a reunion of sorts. John and Anna were busy supervising the construction of a new home on the old Whitworth College property on Stevens Street. Actually, it was strictly Anna's project, with John acting as a grudging and often grumpy observer. He named the place Haddaway Hall, a slightly cryptic pun on "had her way."

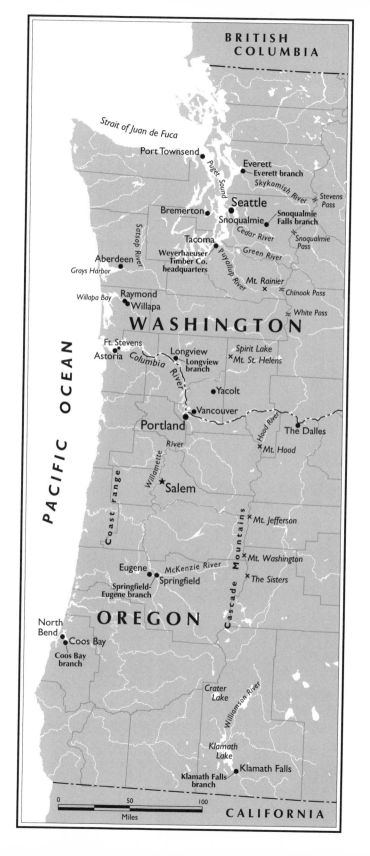

BRITISH COLUMBIA

Strait of Juan de Fuca

Port Townsend

Everett
Everett branch
Skykomish River
Stevens Pass

Puget Sound

Seattle

Bremerton

Snoqualmie
Snoqualmie Falls branch
Cedar River
Snoqualmie Pass

Tacoma
Green River
Weyerhaeuser Timber Co. headquarters
Puyallup River

Satsop River

Aberdeen
Grays Harbor

Mt. Rainier ×
Chinook Pass

Willapa Bay
Raymond
Willapa

WASHINGTON

White Pass

Ft. Stevens

Astoria
Columbia River

Longview
Longview branch

Spirit Lake
× Mt. St. Helens

PACIFIC OCEAN

Yacolt

Vancouver

Portland
River

Hood River
The Dalles

Willamette

Mt. Hood ×

★ Salem

× Mt. Jefferson

Coast range

Eugene
McKenzie River
Springfield
Springfield-Eugene branch

× Mt. Washington

Cascade Mountains

× The Sisters

OREGON

North Bend
Coos Bay
Coos Bay branch

Crater Lake

Williamson River

Klamath Lake

Klamath Falls
Klamath Falls branch

0   50   100
Miles

CALIFORNIA

John may have groused, but he didn't interfere with Anna's dream of an expansive house, magnificent gardens, and a sweeping view of Puget Sound.

Immediately after the holidays, the western Washington phase of F.K.'s education began under George S. Long himself. Long liked nothing better than to teach young men the ins and outs of the lumber business he understood so thoroughly. In this instance, the class—he liked to refer to them as his "kindergarten"—included his own son George, Jr., Edmund Hayes, Jr. (a grandson of Orrin H. Ingram, a major Timber Company shareholder), Phil, and F.K. Sometimes the work was remedial; other times it was demanding. But it was always purposeful. Long wasn't interested in anyone wasting time.

For example, the young men were assigned to the Cherry Valley Logging Company so that they might learn how logs—fir, hemlock, and cedar—were graded and scaled, Long only requesting that the Cherry Valley manager "accommodate them as you do others who drop in once in a while for a square meal." In truth, it wasn't to be quite that casual. Before leaving Tacoma, Long gave his students a handout of grading instructions that he had provided company cruisers in years past. And so they went forth with these standards in mind, soon to discover that the log rafts in the Snohomish River were not quite in accord with their mentor's instructions. The kindergarten pupils began to appreciate the difference between theory and practice.

Later, they visited mills throughout the region, following an itinerary carefully designed so that they might see the best and worst of western sawmilling. Long demanded a written report at the conclusion of the tour. Other projects included a study of the cross-arm industry, important in terms of the miles and miles of telegraph poles intersecting the country. They also worked at what was termed "chunk inspecting," the object of which was to determine the amount of breakage that occurred during logging. Long was vitally interested in the outcome, as it was an important factor in his own accounting.

By summertime, F.K. found himself serving as an assistant to Sam P. Johns, Jr., the sales manager at Snoqualmie Falls. He was busy and happy, partly because he shared a boardinghouse room with Charlie Ingram, another grandson of O.H., and partly because he could visit sister Elizabeth and her family; Rod also worked at Snoqualmie. In the meantime,

Phil was trying to help out at the Edward Rutledge Timber Company in Coeur d'Alene, Idaho, but business was so slow that there was almost nothing to do. While John sympathized on that score, he also wished his sons would focus more on their personal finances. He had recently, reluctantly, paid $20 for garage rent in Tacoma. "I had hoped that you or Frederick would have stepped up and paid the bill," he admonished Phil. But then he reminded himself of the old saying, that in the year preceding and the year following a wedding one shouldn't expect much of a man, "so I will excuse you this time." Phil and Helen had set their wedding date for that fall. The family was excited. "Fritz, Edwin & Frederick will have to get a move on themselves," Uncle Charlie commented, noting that Phil was "setting the right kind of example." In the end, however, business mattered most: "And I am sure you, Rod, F.K. and Edwin will all make good."

George Long, an expert at judging talent, suggested in the fall of 1921 that F.K. might find his best opportunity in wholesale sales in the Twin Cities. Long, with many years of selling, understood why retail buyers selected one 2 x 4 over another. Price aside, the most significant factor was the salesman himself. He also realized that his own son was ill equipped for that responsibility, for George, Jr., was painfully shy. F.K., however, seemed to have the right sort of personality. While he did not enjoy the loneliness on the road, clearly he reveled in the social aspects of a salesman's life. He was by nature friendly, good at remembering names and jokes, and quick with a smile and a greeting.

Another reason prompting Long's suggestion may have been a selfish one. His Timber Company had become heavily involved with Thompson Yards, and Long was already seriously questioning George Thompson's management. A specific problem concerned the Minnesota Transfer facility in the Midway district, between St. Paul and Minneapolis. It was too big for the retail needs of the Twin Cities, and Long wondered whether a wholesale operation might be the answer. Was F.K. interested? He was, and yet he wasn't sure. Anyway, he would give it a try. But it would turn out to be the Sales Company association, and not Thompson Yards, that would endure.

During the 1921 holidays and into the start of 1922, F.K. accompanied his father around the country, first to Pasadena for a visit with Uncle F.E., who was sadly watching his only daughter, Virginia, valiantly fight a fatal illness. Then there were meetings to attend, few of which offered any encouraging news, "and many think the outlook is not good for 1922." Regardless, F.K. had little choice but to work away at his wholesaling responsibilities in the Twin Cities. Gradually others came to concur with George Long's assessment that F.K.'s future was in sales. John noted, for example, that Bill Boner, manager of Weyerhaeuser's Everett mill, had concluded that F.K. was ideally suited to head the sales office he was planning for the Baltimore port facility. John also seemed pleased with other developments, not the least of which was F.K.'s decision to quit smoking. Like so many others before and since, however, he would lose his resolve.

By late February, F.K. was hoping "to get into wholesale business pretty quick now." He had sent out price lists and instructions to his dozen or so salesmen, though not expecting any burst of orders. John offered the usual encouragement: "Do not get discouraged but do the best you can and no one can do more." But John should have heeded his own fatherly advice. Not only did he worry about the current business depression but about the future as well, particularly whether there would be appropriate opportunities for his sons. F.E., who, given his daughter's deteriorating health, had more than enough worries himself, tried to cheer up his brother. The point at issue was whether to develop the Clearwater, Idaho, properties. Eventually they would, but in 1922 nothing was certain. "Your boys are preparing themselves to run our business," F.E. reminded, "and with or without Clearwater they will have plenty to do."

Despite the difficulties of doing business, F.K. seemed enthusiastic about his work, and the uncles, especially Charlie and Rudolph, agreed that he was first-rate. F.K., however, would shortly prove to be less than perfect. The first hint of trouble came in mid-May when Aunt Margaret informed her brother John that the Jewetts—Richard, Fritz, and herself—were planning a European tour, accompanied by Louise Weyerhaeuser and daughter Peggy. She further hoped they could get Rudolph to come along.

As it turned out, Rudolph would join the party in Europe, midway through their itinerary. That part was surely agreeable, but such was not the case when Rudolph persuaded F.K. to accompany him. In early June, F.K. had reported to his father that business was picking up, "many inquiries coming in every day and we are shipping out three or four cars from here per day." And then he dropped the *bomb,* announcing that he intended to accept Uncle Rudolph's invitation. Shortly after daughter Virginia's funeral (she had died on May 24), F.E. returned to his St. Paul desk. He left no doubt that he was disappointed about F.K.'s absence: "I am very sorry that Frederick is leaving his work at the Thompson Yards at this critical time. It is making a rather bad impression upon all of us, for there was no real point in Frederick's going to Europe at this time other than to make company for Rudolph."

F.E. exaggerated. Charlie, for example, was glad that F.K. was taking some time off. As he informed Phil, "Your brother Fred does not look too strong to me." Moreover, F.E. and Rudolph had their occasional differences. Currently at issue was Louise's cleaning of F.E.'s house in St. Paul. To F.E. and his wife it seemed overly thorough, for Louise had disposed of some of Virginia's keepsakes, assuming that this would spare the grieving parents unnecessary pain. But F.E. and Harriette viewed Virginia's possessions as remembrances to be treasured.

Happily, other things occupied the family's attention. Helen gave birth to her firstborn, Ann, on November 3. F.K., by then back on the job in the new office building of Thompson Yards, sent along immediate congratulations to his brother, "although you don't deserve much credit yourself." In Phil's wire announcing the birth, he had closed with "congratulations," leaving F.K. somewhat confused. "Presume you referred to my future," he ventured, admitting that he was "sort of considering the matrimonial plunge, but things aren't at all definite yet, Phlip." And they weren't. F.K. felt like settling down, but he hadn't found the right girl. He soon would. Indeed, his controversial trip to Europe served as the catalyst.

VIVIAN O'GARA WEYERHAEUSER

"One important interruption to my efforts to establish a wholesale business at the Minnesota Transfer occurred when my uncle, R. M. Weyerhaeuser, invited me to make a short trip to Europe with him to meet his wife and daughter in Paris." So F.K. began his "Recollections" for 1922. Actually, the trip itself was much less notable than what transpired as a result.

With Uncle Rudolph, F.K. crossed the Atlantic aboard the *Berengaria,* the largest English liner of its day, and during that crossing he became acquainted with Spencer Logan, a young man from Chicago. F.K. was approaching his twenty-eighth birthday; his sister and younger brother were both married and had begun their families. Some may have wondered whether he was destined for bachelorhood, but he had merely been waiting for the right woman. Spencer's wife, anticipating a happy development, introduced him to that young lady. Her name was Vivian O'Gara, and when they met at a house party hosted by the Logans, sparks apparently flew, the proverbial love at first sight. More important, it was love forever after.

But no whirlwind courtship happened when F.K. returned from Europe. His father and the uncles had been discussing his future responsibilities, knowing that difficult choices lay ahead. The biggest decision involved the development of the Clearwater properties, to be headquartered in Lewiston, Idaho. John was expected to provide leadership on this project, but uncertainties—awaiting railroad commitments and questioning the commitment of his brothers—would make that an arduous task. Charlie reported so much satisfaction with F.K.'s work at Thompson Yards that they were prepared to recommend his promotion to assistant general manager, second only to George Thompson in terms of active management. But of course they would defer to John's wishes, and in December 1923 he informed Phil that he intended to bring F.K. west after the New Year, "show him around and . . . offer him the management of the Clearwater." But what seemed obvious to John at that point proved to be much less so with the passing months.

Indeed, the Clearwater project would bog down under the weight of John's uncertainties, and F.K. would go elsewhere—actually several elsewheres—before he found his niche. He gave his notice to George Thompson in mid-January, clearly planning to head for Idaho, but a month later John gloomily announced that the railroads "had lost interest in the Clearwater extension so that matter is dead." He was being overly pessimistic; the issue wasn't dead, only seriously postponed. And F.K. would be going to Idaho, but to Potlatch, not Lewiston.

But while there were delays in the forests of Idaho, there were none on the fields of love. Vivian O'Gara, a graduate of St. Mary's of the Woods, a "finishing school" in South Bend, Indiana, was twenty-three when she met F.K. ("In my day," Vivian would later observe, "pretty girls didn't go to college.")

She had grown up in Chicago's North Shore society. In 1917, her "coming out year," she appeared in *Chicago Tribune* articles in October and November and in a December issue of the *Chicago Examiner*. A serious equestrian, Vivian often rode along the trails of Lincoln Park. Thomas J. and Mae Vivian O'Gara were her parents, and according to F.K., his wife "inherited the beauty of her mother and the strength of character of her father."

Born in Dublin, T.J. became a leader in the United States coal industry, at one time owning several mines in the Midwest and East. Hard times hit unexpectedly when O'Gara, Ogden Armour of Armour & Company, and W. C. Brown, president of the New York Central Railroad, were indicted for giving and receiving rebates. A compromise settlement was eventually negotiated, and the indictments were dismissed in federal court. But the damage had been done; T.J. lost many of the mines and sold his remaining O'Gara Coal Company stock in the early 1920s.

F.K.'s marriage plans surprised many, not the least of whom were John and Anna and the Weyerhaeuser aunts and uncles. Rejoicing could not be easily managed, for Vivian was a Catholic. The correspondence relating to this difficult situation has been destroyed, evidence of its embarrassing vehemence. It is known, though, that F.K. finally told his parents that they had no say in the matter. Others had to infer the same: Either they accepted Vivian or they rejected her and lost him. Given that choice, John and Anna accepted, albeit grimly. Weyerhaeusers ordinarily did not deliver ultimata, but clearly F.K. and Vivian had no choice. And that experience, standing alone together, doubtless served to increase their devotion to each other.

The intensity of the moment is demonstrated by the rapid sequence of events. They announced their engagement on March 21, and it made headline news on the society pages. The March 22 account in the *Chicago Daily News* was typical: "Miss O'Gara was a debutante of a few seasons back, and is one of the most popular of Chicago's younger social set. She is tall and slender, with golden hair—quite one of the prettiest of the North Shore belles." The report also described her as "an active member and earnest worker in the exclusive Junior League," and it noted her wartime contributions as "a member of Mrs. George A. McKlintock's famous Canteen, where she worked all day every day." There were the expected exaggerations, particularly concerning F.K.'s inheritance. "The Chaperon's Comment on Society," a regular feature in the *Chicago Evening American,* was headlined, "Fiance of Vivian O'Gara Is Worth Many Millions and Heir to More." The article began, "Well, it looks as though Vivian O'Gara made no mistake in taking a good look around in the marriage market before she settled on a life partner." At his death, grandfather Frederick reputedly left an estimated $300 million, "his holdings worth more than the combined fortunes of Morgan, Westinghouse, Gould, Mackay, Vanderbilt and Duke." This was but one more instance of the public confusing dollars, acres, and board feet, as the Weyerhaeusers would often describe such flights of fancy.

One fact emerged from all of the engagement accounts: Not a single reporter knew the wedding date. Indeed, nearly everyone reacted with amazement when F.K. and Vivian repeated their vows almost coincident with the engagement announcement in the papers, on the afternoon of March 22. The same "Chaperon" reported incredulously: "Instead of the ostentatious display one might expect, when a multi-millionaire claimed his beautiful bride, there was only a small basket of Killarney roses in the drawing-room of the O'Gara home, where the wedding took place." It was noted that Vivian's parents were vacationing in French Lick Springs, and, in their absence, brothers Alfred and Lincoln "extended the family blessing and acted both as wedding hosts and wedding guests." Representing F.K.'s side of the family were cousin and best man Ed Davis and his wife, Catherine.

Why the haste? The story, as quoted in most of the newspapers, went as follows:

> "Well," smiled Mrs. Weyerhaeuser after the ceremony, "It was this way. Mother and dad said yesterday they were going to take me to Europe for six months. Imagine! A whole half year away from my brand new fiance! I just telephoned to Fred, and now I am Mrs. Fred. That's all there is—there isn't any more."

That may have been true, except for the part about being Mrs. Fred. She would always be Vivian O'Gara Weyerhaeuser.

One suspects that the senior O'Garas had planned the European tour in hopes that their daughter would get over her infatuation. On the other hand, surely they knew Vivian better than that. F.K. would recall the circumstances matter-of-factly. They proceeded without a big wedding simply "because we feared our parents would object to the fact that she would be marrying a Protestant and I would be marrying a Catholic." In short, there seemed little purpose in delaying the inevitable, with its concomitant hurt feelings. John and Anna signaled their acceptance by coming to Chicago; T.J. and Mae would soon demonstrate theirs. As it turned out, Vivian even got her European tour. She and F.K. sailed in late May on a delayed honeymoon.

Upon their return, they would make their home not in Chicago, St. Paul, or even Tacoma but in Potlatch, Idaho. How they managed that is a story in itself. Years later, F.K. erroneously thought that the decision had been made after the honeymoon. Actually, Allison Laird, manager of the Potlatch Lumber Company, had met with F.K. in St. Paul early in March and invited him to join the organization. F.K. could not immediately commit; he had other matters on his mind, matters that Laird acknowledged. "You have been going thru one of the big experiences that can happen to any human and, of course, could not bring your mind to settle anything so important as making a decided change." That observation was included in a letter written immediately after Laird had wired F.K. the following April 18: "Your Uncle Charles, Mr. Irwin, and I have had a good conference this morning on Potlatch matters. We are a unit in wanting you to join the Potlatch organization and hope you will accept the invitation and come to us whenever you can conveniently arrange your matters. A cordial welcome awaits you and Mrs. Weyerhaeuser into our Potlatch family."

Charlie Weyerhaeuser was then president of Potlatch, and he more than anyone encouraged F.K. to accept the western opportunity. F.K. had acquired considerable experience in sales. According to John's original plan, his son's lumber training was to commence with the consumer and then work "back to the trees." He hadn't gotten back to the trees, and John's reluctance to appoint his son manager of the Clearwater involved, according to Charlie, F.K.'s lack of experience with white pine. And since Clearwater development still lay ahead, it made perfect sense to Charlie for F.K. to go to Potlatch. Indeed, when recounting the meeting with Allison Laird and Jack Irwin, Charlie, a great one for underlining, put the matter directly: "What the Weyerhaeuser family wanted was for you to get the *Sawmill* experience . . . that you *would need* to *develop the Clearwater Timber Co.* holdings when the time comes to build those mills." Charlie agreed that F.K. had served well with the Thompson Yards, but the future wasn't there. If he intended "to be a *big man* in the 'W' family, or *organization, the west* is the place to *learn* and *develop.*" He closed with God's blessing and love to Vivian.

While Charlie remembered Vivian, he may not have considered how she would take to living in Potlatch. Allison Laird considered it. "We will all try to make her happy," he wrote, "and if she will like us, there is nothing more to fear on that account." The culture shock would wait. F.K. and his bride were off to Europe. When they returned, they stopped briefly in New York City and Chicago. F.K. preceded his bride west to Tacoma, where he visited his parents in Anna's magnificent newly completed home, Haddaway Hall, for the first time. Then came Potlatch. F.K. wrote brother Phil on July 1, apologizing for having missed connections while in the East. "Felt that I should get right out to Potlatch to start hitting the ball," he explained. As for the honeymoon, it had been "a Lulu," and he hoped that Vivian would soon be joining him.

In truth, Uncle Charlie did worry about F.K.'s ability to adjust to Potlatch, the community more than the company, and tried to warn him of possible pitfalls. This was worry misplaced, for F.K. was by nature considerate and never snobbish. Still, Charlie knew that Potlatch was likely to be full of surprises. "Frederick," he began, "I know that above all things young people do not like too much advice, and it is the fatherest [sic] thing from my mind to try to give any, but,

> in talking with Carl [Charlie's son], I have said to him that he must be above the environments in which he may sometimes find himself placed, and that I wanted him at all times to act and speak in the same way, in a little place like Little Falls [,Minnesota], that he would in a large city where the people he would meet would have had the same advantages that he has had. And I have said to him that I have heard my father say a thousand times that he cared more about his credit and reputation than anything else. So, Frederick, if you consider this as advice from your old uncle, please forgive me, and will try and not give any more.

For Vivian the move to Potlatch amounted to a leap into the unknown. Years later, F.K. noted that she had "followed me loyally to Potlatch, Idaho . . . then to Minneapolis in 1925; then to Spokane in 1930; and to St. Paul in 1932." The society reporters she left behind could only imagine Potlatch. In a July 7 article, the *Chicago Daily News* placed her in "the outskirts of Spokane," living in a home "modern in every respect with the usual quota of servants and every convenience, though set in a big lumber camp." The Chaperon in the *Evening American* of August 20 was a good deal more accurate. "Potlatch, a little rough and tumble lumber town, some seventy miles from Spokane, Wash., in the heart of the big woods, is on the map for many Chicagoans at the moment, and is of considerable interest, I might add." As for Vivian, initially life there amounted to "a novel and splendid education for a girl born and reared in Chicago and enmeshed in the many social activities of the Junior League." The Chaperon claimed to have heard directly from Vivian, who commented on the climate ("delightful") and also that she was "quite enthusiastic over the change—a decided change, indeed, following a honeymoon sojourn in Europe."

How long did Vivian sustain an enthusiasm for Potlatch? That isn't known, but probably not for more than a month or two. Her new home sat on what was called Nob Hill, where the Lairds and the other "elite" resided. Potlatch's Nob Hill, however, wasn't up to the standards of Chicago's North Shore, not by a long shot. The commoners lived on another hill. Elite or common, they all lived in company-owned houses, and, as F.K. observed, "No one cared particularly about keeping up their houses; keeping them painted, or developing trees or gardens because they did not own them."

As an organization, Potlatch was also lacking when F.K. and Vivian arrived on the scene. It had begun early in the 1900s with considerable promise, thanks in large measure to its legendary manager, Bill Deary. Bill was quite the character, colorful in speech and decisive in action. When the directors were trying to decide where to build a sawmill, they tentatively picked a location that Deary arbitrarily vetoed. "No," he said, "there ain't enough water there to baptize a bastard." And he pointed to another spot on the map. "We'll build it here," he said, and the "here" became Potlatch, a company town. When Deary died, Allison Laird was selected as the new manager. Laird, a banker from Winona, Minnesota—a member of the Laird-Norton family—had little lumber experience and not a great deal of interest in the business. Walter Humiston, the assistant manager, looked after the company town and Laird looked after the bank, allowing the company to run itself. The head logger, Tom Jones, did as he pleased in the woods; the mill manager, Bill Wakeman, did the same in the sawmill; and Paul Lachmund sold as best he could. There was no overall direction, and, not surprisingly, Potlatch did poorly compared with its competitors.

Charlie Weyerhaeuser hired another Charlie, McGibbon, formerly manager of the Northland Pine Company in Minneapolis. McGibbon was notorious for forcing substandard grades of wood onto the Twin Cities market. What may have worked there, however, failed miserably at Potlatch, and in the process Potlatch lost business and acquired a bad reputation. Charlie Weyerhaeuser finally relieved McGibbon in 1923, replacing him with Jack Irwin, formerly sales manager for Boise Payette Lumber Company. F.K. was to be Irwin's assistant, giving particular atten-

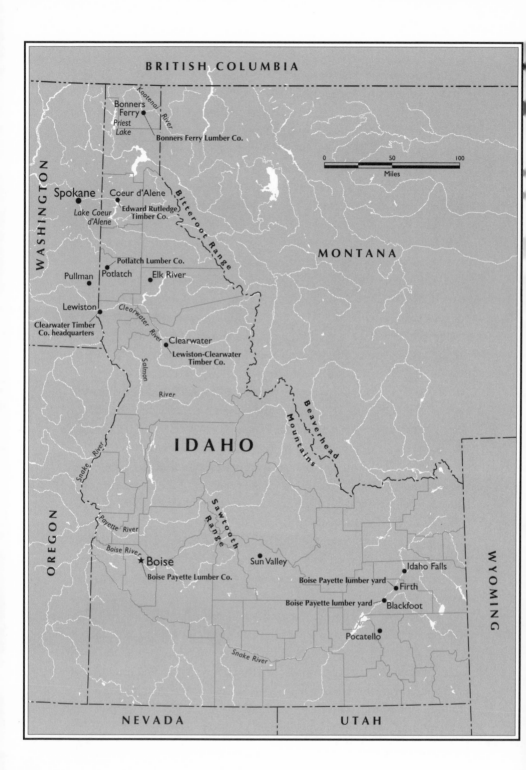

tion to improving manufacturing practices and developing sales. Slowly, things began to turn around, thanks primarily to the efforts of Irwin. He showed, according to F.K., "tremendous enthusiasm for his work" and garnered cooperation from all previously disgruntled segments of their clientele.

F.K. was serious about contributing his best, and he did for a time. It was Vivian who interrupted, though not intentionally. They had gone east for the holidays, first visiting Ed and Catherine Davis in Cloquet. While there, Vivian developed a baffling illness and became so sick that she couldn't be moved for several days. John, always eager to diagnose, concluded it was a miscarriage. F.K. later described the problem as "a ruptured fibroid tumor." Most likely, the "fibroid tumor" was an ovarian cyst. In any case, Vivian finally got well enough to travel, and they reached Chicago on New Year's morning, 1924. She still suffered, however, and was soon admitted to St. Luke's Hospital, where Dr. Arthur Curtis performed surgery, removing the benign growth. But the siege wasn't over. On January 19 the *Chicago Evening American* reported that she was "seriously ill" and that her parents were "with her constantly, as are her three brothers." And so, of course, was her husband, who slept in her hospital room.

John also came to Chicago out of concern. It was he who communicated the details to the family, although these were medically hard to follow. While the tumor had been removed, the infection raged on, and again Vivian seemed near death, unable to eat and barely able to breathe. She was returned to the operating table, where surgeons lanced her neck beneath the ear, thus allowing a buildup of pus to escape. Finally the signs were encouraging, but by now Potlatch seemed to F.K. very distant and relatively unimportant. John worried on both counts—about Vivian's health and his son's responsibility. "How would it be," he naively inquired of F.K. in mid-February, "to let Vivian stay with her parents six, seven months where she would be with her friends and have the best of attention and you stay at Potlatch." Allison Laird took a more understanding approach. "Do not worry about the situation here," he wrote in late February. "We want you to come just as soon as it is proper and no sooner."

For a time, doctors feared the possibility of another operation, this to remove gallstones; but it proved unnecessary. Still, Vivian's convalescence would be lengthy, and F.K. decided that they had best find a place to escape the remainder of Chicago's winter. For reasons that are unclear, they selected Pass Christian, Mississippi, on the coast just west of Gulfport. Once again, Allison Laird offered every encouragement, observing that it "seems to be the right thing for you to do," and he sincerely hoped that "the southern sunshine and its milder atmosphere" would hasten Vivian's full recovery. She slowly began to feel stronger, and by mid-April F.K. had returned to Potlatch, leaving Vivian in the care of her parents.

Vivian eventually joined her husband in Potlatch later that spring, but she was not happy. She found little to interest her, especially when F.K. was absent. He admitted as much to his father, and the response should not have surprised him. It was, however, an extremely insensitive response, and it hurt. To F.K.'s observation that Vivian "dreads being alone terribly," John expressed absolutely no sympathy: "If you cannot leave home now and then, I am sorry because you are in the wrong business." And then he proceeded to share the business facts of life. "Your Grandfather was away [from home] half the time. Last year I was away 186 nights. How can you take my place if you cannot go away from home?" That question was curious because, as both father and son well appreciated, John's business contributions had never been significant.

Once started, John had difficulty stopping, citing brother Fred's similar problems with Harriette who, whenever she objected to her husband attending to responsibilities, became "sick or nervous." Don't let that happen to you, he warned, all too pointedly. It was simply a matter of telling Vivian "to gather herself together," and if she could not, then "you had better get some minor position where you can be at home all the time." He went so far as to admonish, "Be a man." On the surface and considering the source, such words seem not only uncalled for but also incongruous. But fathers and mothers often maintain expectations for their children that reflect their own disappointments and failings. With effort, F.K. doubtless understood.

Apparently Anna wrote a similar letter. Once again a parental challenge had been issued, and once again F.K. had to respond, making his and Vivian's position clear. They came first; it was as simple as that. John soon retreated: "I hope and pray that this matter will not put a barrier between us." F.K. would forgive. There was no choice in that. Besides, such injuries were hardly critical, even if they left some scars. Fortunately, F.K. could always depend on his siblings to understand. Phil and Helen were then living in Coeur d'Alene, convenient enough for weekend visits, so the couples got together frequently. Thus reinforced, they could share numerous experiences that placed John and Anna's current snit in perspective. And John, whatever his momentary worries, placed the highest value on family ties. "I am so thankful to the Lord that you and your brother and sister are going to remain good friends," he wrote Phil in May 1924. Indeed, nothing could alter that friendship. Nevertheless, all three had other commitments. For F.K., home was wherever Vivian happened to be, and home ought not to be Potlatch for any longer than absolutely necessary.

John's unhappiness was most likely rooted in the uncertainties of the Clearwater development. Supposedly he was the one in charge, but he convinced himself that his brothers were not supportive. Worse, he decided that Charlie was interfering, assuming a role in the process that co-opted his own. Charlie had led a contingent into the Clearwater country, in part hoping to assist in the selection of a manager. That really annoyed John, especially since he still hoped that F.K. would fill the post. Anyway, on July 31 John informed F.K., "I am turning all Clearwater stuff over to C.A.," adding, apparently for the record, that Rudolph was "on a grouch when I saw him last in Spokane." That took care of two out of three brothers. "I have much to be thankful [for] living two thousand miles away," he reminded himself, meaning St. Paul.

John couldn't really turn over the Clearwater simply by passing along papers to brother Charlie. At that point it was not so much a matter of who was in charge, for the summer months were largely devoted to railroad surveys and debate over likely sites for a mill. The final decision involved building a very large sawmill in Lewiston, and this necessitated lengthy negotiations with city officials and private landowners. One thing was certain. The Clearwater development was bound to be expensive. And another thing: F.K. was chomping at the bit, anxious for more responsibility. The uncles understood this and appreciated that it was, for the most part, a healthy desire. But at the time there were few positions available. Rudolph assessed the situation accurately, recognizing that "the younger generation are restless and want to keep things moving, and do not stop to realize that things cannot always go as we wish." Among that restless generation, F.K. led the way. Uncle Charlie continued to talk about the Clearwater opportunity, but F.K. thought he saw more and more delays on the horizon. And then there were other questions, such as, would Lewiston be any more agreeable a place to live than Potlatch?

On October 16, he sat down and wrote to Charlie, responding to the question whether he would be willing to wait six months for a Clearwater decision. At the time, F.K.'s answer seemed final. "I have decided not to consider the Lewiston development any further for myself," he noted, explaining that he and John had discussed the matter the previous weekend. The problem of choosing a manager was larger than many in the family assumed, involving "much more than the giving of employment to the grandchildren. The first requisite, as I see it, is that he be a mature experienced lumberman who can command the confidence of all the stockholders, the Denkmanns and Humbirds as well as the Weyerhaeusers."

F.K. indicated that he would be seeing Allison Laird within the week and would then submit his resignation from Potlatch. Following that he planned to meet with George S. Long and "put in my application to build the next [Weyerhaeuser Timber Company] mill at Longview, or wherever it will be, and run it, contingent on my getting an interest in the business." Withal, F.K. wanted his Uncle Charlie to understand how much he had appreciated the Potlatch experience. "My leaving here is due to the fact that the reason for staying here (the Clearwater development) no longer exists for me, also that I am not needed here."

But Clearwater was far from dead. In fact, within two weeks the four brothers met in St. Paul to discuss aspects of that development, starting with their choice for its manager. On October 25, Charlie, Rudolph, and F.E., with John present, agreed to offer F.K. the position of general manager of the Clearwater Timber Company. Now F.K. was in a quandary, having thought the matter was behind him. Either a new decision was demanded or a reiteration of the previous one. He telegraphed Charlie on November 2: "Father suggests I discuss future plans with you, Uncle Rudolph and Uncle Fred." John and F.K. were Tacoma bound on November 4.

F.K. did meet with Rudolph and F.E.—Charlie was out of town— and the offer was repeated, although John, for reasons of his own, chose to confuse the issue by suddenly bringing into question his son's readiness. F.E. was losing patience with his older brother, but he bit his tongue: "In any event, the management has been offered to him, and I suppose he will let us know in a few days whether he elects to accept it." F.E. heard the very next day when F.K. came to the St. Paul office. Again, he respectfully declined, informing his uncle that he had decided to accept a position with the Weyerhaeuser Sales Company. "In a way I am very sorry that Frederick is not going to take the Clearwater," F.E. informed John, "but, in his own interest and his wife's, I think he is choosing wisely in going into the Sales Department."

F.E. indicated much the same to F.K., his "hunch" being that the decision to join the Sales Company was a prudent one. The uncle's only apparent disappointment was over F.K. and Vivian's decision to live in Minneapolis. F.K. later explained that John had influenced him. "Father urged me to move to Minneapolis rather than St. Paul on the theory that one's relatives like one better at a distance than nearby." It may have been good advice, although F.K. was quick to note that over the years, "my aunts, uncles, and cousins have been wonderful to us."

THE WEYERHAEUSER SALES COMPANY

WHETHER JOHN was irritated by F.K.'s rejection of the Clearwater opportunity is hard to say. Certainly he was not pleased that F.K. and Vivian had decided to leave the West. But it was better in his view that they were moving to Minneapolis than St. Paul. Was Phil next in line for Clearwater? No one seemed to know except perhaps John, and in January 1925 he wasn't talking. He did send Phil a couple of items on extraneous matters, advising that they be forwarded to Frederick, "care Weyerhaeuser Sales Co., St. Paul." One clipping concerned "A Good Reputation":

> Must be made—can not be inherited.
> Is oftentimes the best friend we have.
> Is worth too much to be risked for the sake of money.
> Will pay big dividends if we take an interest in it.
> Is the best antidote in the world for circumstantial evidence.
> Must be earned—can not be bought.
> Is soon lost among bad companies.

Good advice, but Phil didn't bother to pass it on. Neither son needed such reminders.

Nearly thirty years later, in 1954, as president of the Weyerhaeuser Sales Company, F.K. addressed his group on its history. It began with grandfather Frederick's emigration from Germany in 1852, and not much was left out. The conclusion, however, was special. F.K. observed that "one of the fundamental principles that has always existed in our organization has been a deep belief in timber as an investment." That principle had been tested many times, but it endured, F.K. noting with a smile that it seemed to prove "that you can be right about anything if you wait long enough." And he also stressed "the principle of honesty and integrity. We believe in telling the truth about our products and our transactions."

The Weyerhaeuser Sales Company was still in its infancy when F.K. joined it in the fall of 1924. Its origins dated back to the period following Frederick's death in 1914—perhaps earlier. F.E. recalled in a letter to John in June 1920: "When I first came into Father's office, with the enthusiasm of youth, I thought we ought to have a more comprehensive knowledge of our whole business and began its study." The most obvious need was for a common system of bookkeeping, and thus an Auditing Department was organized so as "to bring our accounts into such uniformity that comparisons could be made." There was an immediate reaction: "Managers were insulted, their honesty was questioned," and the plan might have been aborted had a case of fraud not been uncovered in one of the Cloquet offices. So, auditing early came to be accepted, albeit reluctantly.

But that was only a start. Were there not other ways, better ways, for the affiliated mills—separate organizations involving common ownerships—to operate? What advantages might be gained by cooperating in a variety of activities? Among many examples that illustrated past problems, the one most cited is said to have occurred when the Northern Lumber Company of Cloquet sold a carload of shingles to a Chicago wholesaler, who in turn sold the same carload to the Rock Island Lumber and Manufacturing Company. In short, two Weyerhaeuser affiliates—the original seller and the final buyer—had lost, unknowingly, the middleman's profit to an outsider. The incident may have been apocryphal, however, since there is no record of it.

In 1915 F.E. had called a meeting of representatives of the so-called Northern mills—the Minnesota mills—and reminded them that "they were working for one group of stockholders and that if they could not work in harmony we would put somebody over them that would have authority to produce better results in our sales department."

J. E. Rhodes had been employed in the St. Paul office studying sales problems of the Weyerhaeuser group, concentrating on questions of lumber trademarking (the standards for species and grade marking). When Rhodes departed to become secretary-manager of the Southern Pine Association, he was replaced by Louis S. Case, former sales manager for the Chippewa Lumber and Boom Company of Chippewa Falls, Wisconsin. At Case's invitation, representatives of the affiliated northern pine and western pine producers met in Chicago in August 1915. All who attended agreed as to the seriousness of the problem they collectively faced. F.E., already convinced of the importance of a common sales organization, was determined to push the issue.

"We tried to interest everybody in our crowd," he recalled in his letter to John. But it wasn't easy. Inertia ruled. "It is almost amusing to me *now* to remember the all day session in our office called to consider the advisability of having a Sales Company":

> I argued and pled and argued without making the slightest impression. Finally one after another had to buy tickets, call on relatives, and what not till Mr. Case, Mr. [A. W.] Clapp and I were left alone. Case turned to me almost in despair. I replied, "They did not say no—we'll go ahead with our plans." It may have been wrong to have assumed this responsibility but I still think our action was wise.

Subsequently, the Northern mills agreed but not the Idaho operators. Some were not selling lumber anyway, and others "insisted that one salesman could not sell Idaho & Northern White Pine at the same time, etc." George Long approved the selling of Weyerhaeuser Timber Company's Douglas-fir; so, overall, F.E. was encouraged. The Northern mills would cooperate as their operations gradually wound down, and at the same time the Weyerhaeuser Timber Company's business would dramatically increase. That factor justified the name Weyerhaeuser for the Sales Company, F.E. reasoning that since the company "was to become the child of the Timber Co. in a few years, I saw no objection." Shortly, the Idaho mills also opted to join the Sales Company, and by January 1917 only the Southern Lumber Company remained outside the fold.

Concurrent with the establishment of the Sales Company was the commencement of a common advertising arm headed by George Lindsay, also working out of the St. Paul office. Lindsay needed a name for his organization, and he insisted that it must be identified with the Weyerhaeuser Sales Company. Thus Weyerhaeuser Forest Products came into being. F.E. supported use of the Weyerhaeuser name, reasoning that the advertising program would likely safeguard sales policy, particularly as it pertained to the trademarking of lumber. And it was trademarking that soon split the alliance.

Idaho producers called their lumber white pine, and it was, although western white pine (*Pinus monticola*) was significantly different from the eastern species (*P. strobus*). F.E., raised where eastern white pine had been king of the forest and the marketplace, argued against the use of the term *white pine* for the western product, "putting our name [Weyerhaeuser] on Western Yellow pine lumber and selling it as White Pine." And if one manipulates the species, why not grades as well? Despite assertions that lumber dealers were basically honest, they all knew that upgrading lumber was common, and F.E. made his position clear: "I don't want my father's name there to help support the deception." This would indeed be the basis of future battles, with F.E., and later F.K., favoring trademarking the Weyerhaeuser products to protect the public and themselves. Thus the problems of sales and advertising became inextricably mixed.

F.E.'s leadership in the cooperative cause was largely unappreciated, or so it seemed to him. Ray Clute, one of the first salesmen, recalled those early years, from inception of the Sales Company in March 1916 to its incorporation on December 2, 1919. The Sales Company and F.E. were "one and the same. . . . He alone during its early years and in its most critical moments provided the courage and the will to bring his hopes for it into fruition." But "fruition" wasn't ensured simply by incorporation.

Sales was only one of several cooperative possibilities. The Auditing Department may have been created largely in response to demonstrated fraud, but as a common effort it would endure. Other cooperative ventures, however, ran the gamut, and some ran aground. By 1920, C. A. Barton of Boise Payette and Allison Laird of Potlatch announced their withdrawal from the Logging Committee, angering F.E., who expressed surprise that they considered their logging methods "good beyond need of further study collectively and of improvement." John Weyerhaeuser chaired the Manufacturing Committee, which languished. William Carson headed the By-Products Committee, whose work culminated in the establishment of the Wood Conversion Company in Cloquet. The Legal Committee obtained general support, since "effects on the pocket book are easily figured." But a cynical F.E. observed in June 1920 that the Insurance Committee had enjoyed "the happiest existence—its Chairman [William Irvine] has let it sleep from the beginning." His conclusion was simple: "I think our crowd is lacking something in courage and much in imagination and vision."

That hadn't seemed to be the case earlier in the year. On February 24, 1920, the Sales Company directors publicly announced a startling change in policy. Over recent months there had been runaway inflation in the lumber markets, creating momentary delight among many dealers but fear for the long term among others, including the Weyerhaeusers. Central to their concern was the possible intervention of, or at least serious inquiry by, the U.S. Congress. The essential element in Sales Company policy was price stability, that "at least until June first, which covers the whole period of Spring buying, [the Weyerhaeuser mills] will make no advance in prices over the scale in effect early in January." As expected, reactions were mixed.

But this action had no more than a symbolic effect, for soon, as always, the market had the final say. The depression of 1920–21 settled the matter of price, and as prices fell precipitously, so did sales. And the return of hard times renewed doubts about the need for a Weyerhaeuser Sales Company. Surprisingly it was John who assumed leadership, and at no other time in his long career did he do so with such firmness and purpose.

Undoubtedly it was brother F.E.'s circumstances that moved John to action. This was when F.E. was exiled in Pasadena, not only feeling estranged from the business but helplessly watching his daughter slowly die. John put together a lengthy summary of his views on Sales Company problems, to which he appended eleven specific criticisms, starting with, "It has not produced the desired volume of business during 1920 and 1921." Obviously, if business had been good, the crisis could have been avoided. But it was just as well that the basic problems be faced now rather than later.

There was no shortage of questions, some of which seemed eternal. For example, where should the Sales Company office be located? Three years earlier, in 1919, George Long had argued in favor of the West, convenient to the mills; but, as Charlie Weyerhaeuser reported, "Mr. Long in his usual nice way says there is no hurry about this decision." F.E. thought a western location would be a mistake, admitting that he might be "prejudiced," the Sales Company providing his only contact with the business, "and if it leaves St. Paul, I shall be stranded." Then there were the continuing doubts regarding the ability of salesmen from one region to sell the products from another. Bill Boner, the Weyerhaeuser Timber Company's manager in Everett, Washington, strongly believed that they should employ "special Fir men and that the pine manufacturers should do the same thing." Louis Case could only shake his head at that suggestion, observing that this would revive "the old system of selling where each mill marketed its own stock."

And so it went, differences between manufacturing and sales personnel and between regions. There were, of course, some undeniable facts. The practice throughout the industry was to sell lumber on the market, which meant selling at prices that moved the greatest volume of product. All mills produced substantially the same lumber, sawing generally in accordance with grades as defined by the respective trade associations. The Aladdin's Lamp of the lumber industry was volume, and it followed that large producers of lumber required a large-volume sales organization. As John would argue the case: "While it is essential that the eventual sale of the lumber be constantly borne in mind during its manufacture and that this manufacturing be carried on in close touch with and intelligent advice from the Sales Department, still the selling is in itself a separate function distinct and apart from the manufacturing."

John invited any and all who might contribute, including, of course, his sons. But they were not treated preferentially. F.K., for example, received his final invitation in a May 4, 1922, letter, John expressing disappointment "that you have not presented some suggestions or ideas" that might be beneficial to the future of the Sales Company. In effect, F.K., Phil, and others were "ordered" to be in Tacoma early on May 22, "so we can organize and get ready for good hard work on May 23rd and 24th."

Naturally, F.E. received an invitation, and Tom Humbird, officially the Sales Company president, personally asked F.E. to serve on the soon-to-be created executive committee. F.E. declined. "I have had my turn at bat," he wrote brother John. "I have been out of the game for three years," he added, continuing the baseball analogy, "and I have lost much if not all of my nerve." He wished his brother well, maintaining that "the

Sales Co. has done well, and will do better, if it is supported, but there must be an end of questioning its very existence." He admitted that he had worn himself out "with the cooperation game" and expressed the hope that one of his brothers would succeed him in that effort. A week later he wrote again, mostly about his daughter's continuing decline. But he still thought about business occasionally and wondered "whether the Sales Co. will be blown up in Tacoma."

The feared blowup did not occur. At the conclusion of deliberations on May 24 there seemed a strong commitment to continue the effort, full speed ahead. While not all of the problems were resolved, there was agreement to work cooperatively at improving the organization. In short, there would be a Weyerhaeuser Sales Company for the foreseeable future. F.E. took no immediate notice, but within the month sent his heartfelt thanks to brother John. The timing worked out well, the market improving significantly.

AND THAT, in general terms, was the situation when F.K. joined the Sales Company in the fall of 1924. Such a move had been contemplated by Louis Case for some time. As early as the spring of 1919, when F.K. was just beginning work with the Auditing Department of Potlatch, Case had observed in a letter to John, "I sincerely hope that it will not be long until [F.K.] will get into the wholesale end of the game and be with the Sales Company." Case apparently remained convinced that F.K.'s talents were in sales, inviting him to return to Minneapolis for the Sales Company. As F.K. recalled his decision, "Sales appealed to me a lot more than manufacturing largely because our problem was more to move the product of the mills than it was to manufacture the lumber." As John had reminded those attending the Tacoma showdown, sales and manufacturing were interrelated but distinct operations. Soon he would have one son in each, and who knows, he may have planned it that way.

F.K.'s wholesaling territory covered Minnesota, Wisconsin, Iowa, and northern Illinois. His sales personnel varied in ability, the mills tending to pass along their least productive salesmen. But F.K. was already exhibiting his own management style, most obviously his emphasis on dedication and loyalty. Although the methods may have been simple by later standards, as he put it, "We knew each other well and got along." Getting along would always be the key.

F.K.'s biggest initial problem was with the "Cloquet crowd," particularly Harry Hornby, manager of the Cloquet and Northern lumber companies, which operated jointly following the 1918 fire. Hornby had never been a Sales Company advocate and would push direct sales whenever business slowed. His sales manager was a disagreeable chap named Albert Taylor, who forever maintained that his product was worth more than the market price, especially in slow times. Joe Wilson managed the Johnson-Wentworth Company, which escaped destruction in 1918. According to F.K., Wilson and Taylor "hated each other and Harry Hornby did not like the selling job being done by the Sales Company." As a result, F.K. spent a good deal of time in Cloquet, trying to keep the pieces together. There would, he said, have been no peace whatsoever had not Uncle Rudolph occasionally intervened. They should have insisted that the Cloquet mills operate under a single management, but "the old fogies" were allowed to remain in place and continue their outmoded practices. One of the principal changes involved new competition from the Pacific Northwest, specifically from their own Weyerhaeuser Timber Company, and soon from the Clearwater Timber Company as well, where brother Phil would become the manager.

Phil's decision to assume that responsibility should have ended the family squabbling over Clearwater, but it did not. John continued to fret, convincing himself that his brothers, particularly Charlie, disapproved of his handling of matters. The expense that would be involved in the development only increased his anxiety. Charlie tried his best to reassure him. "John," he wrote, "the greatest tribute that we can pay father and mother's memory is for we four brothers to stick together and work in harmony in the future the same as in the past." As for himself, he would prefer to lose all the money invested in Clearwater rather than let "any hard feelings come between you and me."

Charlie meant every word of it. He took genuine pride in watching his nephews come into their own. For example, while he was visiting Dick Keizer's Chicago office, F.K. happened to drop in. Keizer worked for the Sales Company, selling all of its lumber east of Chicago through wholesalers. "It was a real source of pleasure," Charlie observed for John's benefit, "to hear your son Frederick talking lumber business." But the atmosphere in Keizer's office wouldn't stay pleasant.

When one thinks of the pre-Depression economy, it is usual to picture a scene of "roaring" activity, with demand and prices constantly on
the rise. Such, however, hardly described the economy as a whole. As
economists and historians have pointed out, serious imbalances existed,
one of the worst involving American agriculture. While farmers and rural
communities may have been relinquishing their dominance to factory
workers and cities, they remained a critical factor in the nation's economy, and to no segment were they more important than the lumber
industry. What diminishing demand didn't accomplish, overproduction
and intense competition did. As lumber prices fell, so did profit margins.

Concurrent with this decline was the worrisome, and for the Weyerhaeusers somewhat embarrassing, introduction into the marketplace
of products from new mills, not only from Phil's Clearwater company but
also a bit later from Weyerhaeuser Timber Company mills in Longview,
Washington, and Klamath Falls, Oregon. F.K. would admit that trying to
sell additional lumber under those conditions "undoubtedly depressed the
market further." But what was to be done? F.K. asked himself that question in the fall of 1925. "Business is very quiet," he reported to his father.
"We are not getting the volume of orders we should be getting but do
not exactly know what to do next." For one thing, he thought, they could
look at their own organization and see if new arrangements might
improve efficiency. His responsibility for the so-called Minneapolis District provided a pattern for change. Indeed, Louis Case was on the road,
"making certain changes in the organization which should improve things
very much." At least that was the hope. They foresaw the establishment
of other district offices operating in Chicago, Toledo, Pittsburgh,
Philadelphia, and New York City. Simultaneously, a basic policy change
was inaugurated, that of selling directly to the retailer, the assumption
being that these offices would allow for a greater degree of attention to
those retail customers. All of this activity would dramatically diminish the
role of Dick Keizer.

Such concerns suddenly became unimportant to F.K. Vivian gave
birth to a baby girl, Marianne Nell (named for mother Anna Marie and
F.K.'s natural mother, Nellie), on November 2, but the infant died the following day of a birth injury. Moreover, Vivian nearly died. Thus in less
than two years, she had endured two life-threatening traumas. Although

she was still young and basically sound, these sieges had to have taken a toll, emotionally and physically. She gave no outward indication of any long-term effects, but in fact her health had suffered. She would never quite regain her full strength and resilience.

For the moment, those around her felt helpless. Condolences were of course inadequate, but John tried his best. "Our hearts go out to you in this time of sorrow and disappointment," he wrote, reminding them and himself that he had suffered an even "harder blow once, when I lost Frederick's mother. Keep up your courage, and all will come out right in the end." It seemed inappropriate to mention business, but he nonetheless did, noting that at Potlatch they had thirty million feet more piled than a year earlier.

Two very different matters occupied F.K.'s attention during the first half of 1926. One had been simmering for some time. Certain major shareholders, apparently led by Dr. E. P. Clapp, had conducted behind-the-scenes negotiations with a New York City banking firm—Goldman, Sachs and Company—relative to a possible sale of the Weyerhaeuser Timber Company. On the one hand, there was nothing wrong with such considerations; after all, stock in the Timber Company was only an investment, and when a chance arose to sell such an investment at a profit, why not do so? But the Weyerhaeusers didn't share that cavalier view. The Timber Company constituted the most important part of Frederick's legacy, and in their mind, to sell it would have been to discredit their heritage.

This issue came to a head early in the year. On January 7, William Carson wired George Long: "Dr. Clapp anxious to have Timber Company conference St. Paul soon as possible. Thinks you and [Bill] McCormick should be present. I believe New York bank should make cash offer. My opinion sale best interest of stock holders if conditions satisfactory. At any rate believe directors should have chance to consider proposition." Long, however, better understood the position of the Weyerhaeuser brothers, and he offered little encouragement, suggesting only that the question ought to be posed at least in "a semi-official way." Indeed, that spoke to the source of the Weyerhaeusers' ire: Others had been conspiring behind their backs, making plans without consultation. It amounted to treason, as F.E. saw it. John, still serving as Weyerhaeuser Timber Company president, felt hurt, but apparently not so much because of the "conspiracy" to sell as because of neglect from within—and that included his brothers.

Writing to F.K., he left no doubt as to the depth of his depression: "I seem to hurt people unintentionally. Getting old, and useless." And then he announced his intentions. "On account of my self respect I cannot continue as a trustee, much less as President of the W. T. Co." He asked F.K. not to discuss his complaints "with Charlie, or any of my brothers," and closed instructing that he "destroy this letter." F.K. obviously didn't follow orders, but he was also upset over the situation, and particularly those plans to sell the Timber Company.

John, too, was bothered by talk of a sale, admitting a month later that things "like the Clapp matter happen to me often" and reiterating his desire to resign as Timber Company president. F.K. recommended that they take direct action, buying out those who wished to sell. John expressed doubt that any money could be made "speculating" in the Timber Company but promised to consider the matter. As was F.K.'s habit, he outlined his plan in a confidential letter to his father, listing three objectives: first, to obtain stock control in behalf of the Weyerhaeuser and Denkmann families; second, "to materially increase the [Weyerhaeuser] family's interest" in the Timber Company; and third, "to remove dissatisfied stockholders from the Co."

F.K. claimed that he had given the plan "very careful thought" and had consulted with people who felt "very positive that the thing can be done." He had even gone so far as to contact Blair & Company, a banking firm, to inquire about obtaining a substantial loan. His basic idea was to establish a holding company that would retain the stock of those wishing to stay, and buy out, with borrowed money at 6-percent interest, those who wanted to sell. F.K. got little more than a lecture for his efforts, his uncles summarily vetoing the plan. Further, they "scolded me for undertaking serious discussions with bankers without their being aware of what I was doing." F.K. later acknowledged, in view of the Great Depression, that "it was probably fortunate" his plan had been squelched. That was an understatement. At the time, of course, few foresaw an economic depression as severe as the one that began in 1929, but the brothers didn't need any such dire predictions. John advised, "The Clearwater T. Co. will take all the funds the Timber Securities Company [the family holding company] has and then some." As for the

Denkmann family, he noted that they were already committed to a multimillion-dollar investment in Florida.

F.K. didn't give in immediately, however. He was still pushing his plan a year and a half later but to no avail. John suggested he put the matter in perspective, that "when things are dragging on the bottom as they are at present few people care about making investments." Others, though, would argue that they should be buying when the market was down. As it was, in mid-1928, John agreed with F.E. that they would be ill advised to increase their indebtedness. In fact, for a time Weyerhaeuser family members may have been more interested in selling than was then apparent or later admitted.

If John and his brothers came down a bit hard on F.K., they had to applaud his interest and willingness to step forward. Their mode of action was seldom assertive; they preferred to bide their time, maybe even, in John's words, to hope and pray. The third generation was not yet making the final decisions, but it was clear that they were waiting in the wings and none too patiently.

The second major activity in 1926 involved the reorganization of the Sales Company, with F.K. assuming greater responsibility. By now John, who had earlier remonstrated with his son for being a stay-at-home, was offering quite different advice. Rest, cut down your traveling, "quit smoking and eating too much." John cited himself as an example of what happens when one tries to do too much. And he concluded with a poignant postscript: "Do not take my advice unkindly. I am your second or third best friend."

Although F.E. and F.K. had disagreed over Timber Company ownership strategy, that did not affect their relationship within the Sales Company. Here they were allies. F.K. was now officially the assistant general manager, next in line to assume leadership. F.E. had shared some of the plans for reorganization with his nephew in mid-July, and F.K. responded enthusiastically, concurring that the changes "would be of tremendous benefit to all concerned." First listed, though not of greatest importance, was the location of the Sales Company headquarters. While it remained in Spokane, F.E. still believed that it should be in St. Paul. F.K. agreed, although it isn't clear whether logic or personal preference was the decisive factor in his thinking. The likelihood that either F.E. or his nephew would seriously consider calling Spokane home was small indeed. Central to relocating the headquarters to St. Paul was convincing George Long of the importance of customer convenience. "To my mind," F.K. observed, "the location of the head office in Spokane is analogous to the establishment of the management of the Potlatch Lumber Company in New York City."

F.K. happily filled in the organizational details of the balance of F.E.'s outline. To most in the company, this seemed to involve considerable change, but it actually represented implementation of policies and programs F.E. had long envisioned. F.K. suggested that the board limit its meetings to twice a year, preferably in the Twin Cities, and that an executive committee be established, meeting monthly. This committee would be chaired by the president of the Sales Company and would report to the board. The president and the general manager would live in St. Paul, with offices in the headquarters. This plan was put into effect, even though T. L. Humbird was currently president and resided in northern Idaho.

The relocation proceeded without large controversy. The biggest hassle involved implementation of the district office system, especially as it applied to Dick Keizer's Chicago office. Formerly responsible for all wholesaling around Chicago and points east, in its new role it became just one of several retailing offices. Rudolph, among others, objected vigorously, arguing that Keizer understood Cloquet's problems. F.K. informed F.E. of the impasse: The change from wholesale to retail was agreeable, but Rudolph didn't want Keizer "relegated to a position in charge of one small district." Rather, he wanted him to continue to supervise all eastern sales. But there was to be no compromise, and in the end the uncooperative Keizer was fired. Despite considerable fallout, F.K. was correct in his late-summer prediction that it would soon "blow over." He also reported that he was sending Lincoln O'Gara, Vivian's younger brother, to Rutledge "to learn something of the lumber business," after which Lincoln would do some retailing. "[I have] a very high opinion of his ability and know he will make good." In this prediction he was also correct.

These were busy days for F.K. When he wasn't traveling, checking on the various new offices, he was in St. Paul, thinking about his own midwestern markets as well as Sales Company general policies. Following a visit to Kansas City, he determined that they should raise prices on many of the Idaho pine products, and he took the liberty of recommending just

that to Sales Company president Humbird. The response was not encouraging. Humbird reminded him of the three fundamentals by which they
operated: Run the mills to capacity; sell the lumber at the market price;
and keep the product moving. True, they hadn't succeeded in adhering
to the first, but they had done their best with the other two. Humbird
certainly approved of any effort that might result in more money from
their lumber, but he argued, "For a few of us to try to raise the level of
price would be like undertaking to bale the Atlantic Ocean dry with a
quart cup." Instead they should adjust their ideas "to things that are rather
than things as we would like to have them." In other words, they should
meet their competition head on and sell their products as effectively as
possible. He admitted that getting the Sales Company to respond to market changes was difficult by reason of the company's size, if nothing else.
How to benefit from the advantages of cooperation without suffering the
disadvantages inherent in size was another one of those puzzlements.

F.K. accepted Humbird's reasoning—he could do nothing else,
especially since F.E. agreed with the president—but he wasn't entirely satisfied. For example, Humbird presumed that any improvement in the
marketplace was unlikely, whereas F.K. was optimistic, thanks largely to
favorable farm prospects. Also, was it enough simply to meet the competition? If they were eventually going to cut prices, shouldn't they do so
more aggressively, "going the market one better"?

He believed that despite the hard times, as a sales organization they
could and should be doing a better job. Once again F.K. summarized his
views for F.E.'s consideration. He foresaw a crisis in continuing to move
the product of the old mills while confronting the need to move an additional seven hundred million board feet per year from Clearwater and
soon from the Timber Company's new operations in Longview, Washington, and Klamath Falls, Oregon. Not only were they "threatened with
a lack of profits, but with tremendous losses in the future." Accordingly, "every method for increasing the efficiency of the Sales organization
should be resorted to, and all personal preferences and considerations
should be subordinated to the success of the selling program itself." Then
he described his view of the situation:

We have at one end of the chain, the salesman soliciting orders—
at the other end, the mills shipping them. The process to be fol-

lowed between these two points can be adjusted and varied for the best results. The conveyance of stock information, also any information with regard to prospective manufacture, log supply, etc. can be readily transmitted by letter or wire from the mills to an Eastern office. The vital link in the process is the use of this information in the light of actual trade conditions in the East. It is my firm belief that our greatest weakness today is the lack of constant personal contact on the part of our management with the daily and almost hourly fluctuations in trade conditions where the lumber is being consumed.

And, of course, F.K. had detailed recommendations in hand, beginning again with relocation of the headquarters from Spokane to St. Paul.

John received a copy of F.K.'s letter and responded immediately. Regarding the location of Sales Company headquarters he cared not a bit, although he admitted he was among those who had favored a Spokane location, "near where the lumber is made." What did worry him was an inkling that F.K. was about to assume greater responsibility. In this he was entirely correct. Louis Case, general manager since the Sales Company's beginning, was not in good health and was on the verge of retiring. "Now Frederick," his father advised, "do not let them throw this load on your shoulders. It will shorten your life."

While father and the uncles did not agree in every instance with F.K.'s assessment of conditions and plans for the future, they all surely appreciated his enthusiasm. And, judging by John's admonitions about accepting additional responsibilities, they were all feeling comparatively old. Still, F.E. had not yet relinquished leadership; he retained his own opinions of tactics to increase sales. His was a different approach, as noted in an August 1, 1927, letter to John. "I am hopeful," he wrote, "that we may be able to do more in our publicity efforts in promoting the sale of our own woods by relating our advertising more directly to our own products."

Thus he introduced, almost casually, what would become the famous 4-SQUARE advertising program.

4-SQUARE

WHEN F.E. and F.K. discussed a "new" advertising program in 1927, they referred only to specifics. Advertising, and the debate over its effectiveness, had been going on for a decade. Indeed, the subject had been one of F.E.'s early concerns, the responsibility of the so-called Publicity Committee chaired by George F. Lindsay. Unlike many committee chairmen, Lindsay took his assignment seriously—too seriously in the view of George S. Long, who soon made his opposition known. In the fall of 1917, Lindsay presented his initial plan to the General Advisory Committee, which oversaw the entire cooperative effort. That committee, without benefit of Long's counsel, voted unanimously in favor of the proposal.

Lindsay left the meeting full of enthusiasm, eager to design a logo and to develop a trademarked, grade-marked, guaranteed product and then organize an advertising campaign. On May 1, 1918, Weyerhaeuser Forest Products, Inc., came into being, the advertising arm of the affiliated companies, working in cooperation with the Weyerhaeuser Sales Company. One of Lindsay's first actions was to hire Carl L. Hamilton, a recent forestry graduate from the University of Minnesota, as his assistant. Subsequently, Lindsay contracted with the George L. Dyer Company, a New York City advertising firm already famous for popularizing the Gillette razor.

In a sense, the battle lines were drawn before the war began. Long was a true believer in the need for graded lumber on an association or district basis; years earlier he had been instrumental in obtaining a widely acclaimed agreement on the grading of white pine among upper-Mississippi Valley producers. But what Lindsay envisioned went far beyond that. At the same time, he possessed little understanding of marketing realities of the western mills where there was as yet no agreement on any kind of marking. A board is a board is a board was Long's basic contention, and the only difference the customer cared about was a difference in price. Further, a man might shave every day with a Gillette, but how many times in his life did he buy lumber? In short, who were the customers that mattered? Long thought he knew the answer; they were the retailers.

It was hard to argue with George Long, but Lindsay and Hamilton—with the crucial support of F.E. and F.K.—still believed that advertising Weyerhaeuser lumber would benefit Weyerhaeuser mills. After all, it had worked wonders in other areas. But they also agreed that trade, grade, and species marking of lumber were essential in order to guarantee what was advertised. And although he wouldn't admit it to Long, Hamilton expected the Weyerhaeuser lumber to be just a little better than the lumber of competitors. The millmen were all too familiar with "sweetening the grade," and they recognized it for what it was, subsidization. And, while not saying so, that is exactly what Lindsay and associates had in mind.

But progress was slow, and though they advertised, nothing they did could be called revolutionary. All that would change, however, in 1926 when Carl Hamilton and a few of his colleagues held what would today be called a brainstorming session. The result provided the basis for the 4-SQUARE program. It isn't clear who coined the name—very likely it was Hamilton—but the name stuck. This was the answer they had been seeking, a method of making the Weyerhaeuser product distinctive, thereby improving its marketability. The term 4-SQUARE had a double meaning—always an asset in a marketing campaign. Not only did it inform buyers that the lumber would be exactly squared at the ends, but it also connoted fairness in business dealings. Those opposed to the program, such as George Long, had no trouble with the fairness suggestion, but trimming and marking was another matter.

tion, relieving F.K. of "a lot of anxiety and friction," and allowing him to devote his "whole attention in this territory to marketing western products." That part of the job was only just beginning.

F.K. couldn't ignore Cloquet, but at the moment other matters were foremost in his mind. On August 28, Vivian gave birth to Frederick King, Jr., and the family held its breath. But all went well. When the baby was little more than two months old, he weighed nearly thirteen pounds and, according to the proud papa, "seems to be prospering." Vivian was, too, and the three of them were preparing to travel to Chicago and points east. One purpose of the trip was to attend another reunion with "the crowd that I was with during the war." In addition, the Yale-Princeton game beckoned. But as always, there was business, which continued to be slow. F.K. ascribed this largely to public preoccupation with the upcoming national elections. On the way home, however, he planned to call "on different eastern accounts which we wish to sell lumber to for Cloquet shipment," he wrote his father on November 7.

The election was a landslide victory for Hoover, who buried Democratic candidate Al Smith by more than six million votes. F.K.'s reunion of wartime buddies also proved to be a success, with some seventy in attendance. As for the football game, it had "the wrong result but nevertheless we enjoyed it very much." The only real disappointment that fall was Cloquet's lumber sales. F.K. had gone east convinced that something could be done to improve them. He returned convinced otherwise. "There does not," he reported to his father, "seem to be the need for an Eastern source of supply that existed several years ago." This problem, or some variation of it, was inevitable: What benefited one district was often detrimental to another. Indeed, that spoke to the Weyerhaeuser Sales Company dilemma. In this instance, the influx of Idaho white pine, coupled with Weyerhaeuser Timber Company shipments by water to Atlantic coast terminals and railroad hauls from those ports, was flooding the marketplace. But Cloquet aside, good news abounded: "Our mills are acquiring a very fine reputation for their products in Eastern markets and apparently our sales organization is building up a loyal clientele of customers." Without question, the 4-SQUARE program attracted attention, with new retailers enlisting by the day.

Then, at least momentarily, there was cause for alarm. Baby Frederick came down with scarlet fever in January 1929, although he soon seemed to recover. In early March, the six-month-old weighed more than twenty pounds and was about to take his first steps. "He is remarkably strong and healthy," F.K. reported, "and gives us a great deal of pleasure." There were, however, other family concerns. John agonized, this time for good reason, over his financial indebtedness to the Rock Island Plow Company, brother-in-law Sam Davis's farm-machinery company. In writing to F.K., John didn't mince words: "I am worried to death."

F.K. tried to be encouraging, reporting that he had recently met with F.E. and cousin Ed Davis and had had "a fine chance to talk" about Plow Company matters. He thought they might do some reorganizing, "which will relieve you and the others of all obligation on notes or on guarantees." F.K. was being overly optimistic. There would be no easy or quick answers. John, along with Sam and Apollonia Davis, was seriously in debt.

Responding, John assessed the situation pretty accurately. While expressing relief that F.K. had agreed to attend a Plow Company directors' meeting, he noted that lawyer A. W. "Gus" Clapp was also worried over the obligations, "where no one knows the business, and all are old, over 70." That was a major part of the problem. He also wanted to pass along some advice. "Frederick *save your money,*" he warned; "I will leave you but little." John exaggerated but only to a degree. Now he turned over Plow Company details to F.K., confident that he would manage them ably. Phil was otherwise occupied with the Clearwater; more important, he wasn't much interested.

When John got the blues, for good reason or not, he could occasionally remind himself of his blessings. He tried that tack again in a spring 1929 letter to F.K. "The Lord has blessed me with good parents, good Wives, and fine Children, and I am *most thankful.* Wealth and possession of worldly goods does not make happiness, but the fear of God and a clear conscience is as near as you can get to Heaven on this earth."

But it was F.K., not John, who had reason for worry as the summer passed. He and Vivian had rented a cottage on Lake Minnetonka, where they enjoyed hosting friends and family. Baby Frederick was no longer robust. He had lost weight, although in early August the parents thought the trouble was simply related to teething. His appetite was still good, and they continued to be optimistic. A month passed, however, and F.K. had to admit that something was seriously wrong. Now one year old, Frederick had gained no weight for the past four months. In early September he was hospitalized, to receive blood transfusions and intravenous feedings. "Just how long this condition will last we do not know," F.K. fretted. Sadly, it didn't last long; Frederick King, Jr., died on September 21, not quite thirteen months old.

The cause of death was never fully understood. F.K. would recall that he "became ill from some infection . . . and died in spite of everything we could do." From a distance, John tried to console the grieving parents. "My heart goes out to you in this hour of great affliction," he began, and closed, "May the Lord bless and keep you is my earnest prayer." F.K. and Vivian were devastated and at a loss over what to do. They only knew that they had to get away. And so they took a Far Eastern cruise aboard the SS *President Pierce,* alone together once again.

F.K. and Vivian were a world away on October 29, 1929, when the New York stock market crashed. President Hoover and business leaders the nation over initially tried to downplay the crash, Hoover observing, "The fundamental business of the country, that is production and distribution of commodities, is on a sound and prosperous basis." But confident words were of no use. The Great Depression was on, and with the passing weeks it became apparent that hard times were only beginning. While the effects may not have been immediately evident, F.K. heard enough echoes to understand the gravity of the situation. "I fear many are on the ragged edge," John observed in early November, expressing hope that F.K.'s "Chicago Company is all right." He was referring to the Midwest Investment Company. F.K. recently had become a member of Midwest's board and in his enthusiasm had solicited the support of others. In this instance, John's worries were legitimate. The company's assets were decimated, and when it was finally liquidated in 1943, it paid just eight cents on the dollar. F.K. would recall that the "experience taught me the folly of urging investments by my friends."

Two other news items caught F.K.'s attention while he and Vivian toured the Far East. The first was word of John Mahan's death on November 12. Mahan had been Frederick Weyerhaeuser's personal secretary and in that capacity managed the St. Paul family office. He would be greatly missed. The second item was the announcement that F.K. had been elected president of the Weyerhaeuser Sales Company, replacing the retiring Tom Humbird. That was fine; F.K. would do his duty. But he and Vivian were not going to curtail their travels just because of the honor. F.K. knew enough about the Sales Company to see that its problems could wait.

They returned to St. Paul early in 1930. F.E. had already departed for Pasadena, leaving a letter of congratulations on his nephew's desk. He thanked F.K. for a postcard picturing a "heathen temple" in the Dutch West Indies, noting that from his vantage, "the old House of Hope Church looks better." As for the presidency of the Sales Company, F.E. wished F.K. the best, "[B]ut, at the same time, I have some misgivings about your undertaking this strenuous job, for it seems to have proven a knockout for everyone who has held it or been closely connected with the management."

When F.K. and Vivian had accepted the presidency of the Sales Company—the decision was a mutual one—they understood that the job would require their relocation to Spokane. But before they could move, there was more bad family news. Uncle Charlie died on February 15 while he and Maud were on a round-the-world cruise. Apparently the cause of death was blood poisoning, but the specifics were never made clear. He had become ill during the passage from Egypt to India, and no treatment helped. He breathed his last as the ship entered Bombay harbor. Charlie's body was transferred to the SS *City of Rayville,* destination New York City, and it was F.K. who went east to oversee the necessary details. So F.K. and Vivian postponed moving until the spring of 1930. Their home, at 123 East 12th Street, was next door to Spokane's new Episcopal Cathedral.

One of the special sadnesses of Charlie's death was that he missed his daughter's wedding by just a few months. Sarah-Maud married Walter S. Rosenberry, Jr., on June 20. Not surprisingly, F.E. took an immediate interest in the newest member of the family. He discussed Walter's business future with F.K. via the mails. "I am very confident," he wrote, "that Brother Charles would like to have Walter with us," and by that he plainly meant in a business sense. He explained his inclusion of F.K. in the deliberation: "In a very few years, you and your brothers and cousins will be running this business, and I would wish to have your full approval of taking Walter into our organization." Ever in the family spirit, F.K. was more than willing, little knowing that present acceptance meant future problems. Further, F.E.'s apparent readiness to acknowledge an early change in leadership belied his true feelings.

Although Spokane was certainly preferable to Potlatch, Vivian did not care for its social life. Besides, she was pregnant again, so staying home was both agreeable to her and consistent with her doctor's recommendation. As for F.K., he had plenty of work to do. The Depression only made the job of selling more difficult, and this problem complicated the situation at the Idaho mills. The mills' circumstances called for drastic solutions. Brother Phil in Lewiston, in concert with cousin Fritz Jewett at the Edward Rutledge Timber Company of Coeur d'Alene, recommended a merger of the properties. The merger was effected in 1931 thanks to the efforts of many, notably Laird Bell. Phil was elected president of the new entity—Potlatch Forests, Inc.—and Fritz was chosen as secretary. F.K. became a member of its board and its executive committee. Merger did not guarantee success, however—profits would be slow in coming—but it did promise greater efficiencies and smaller losses.

One of the concurrent interests in the Inland Empire involved the possibility of sustained-yield operations. F.K. and Phil agreed that with so much discouraging news, a positive goal such as this ought to be considered. Mason & Stevens, a Portland forestry-consulting firm led by Major David Mason and Carl Stevens, offered a plan and predictions. Phil became an early convert to the sustained-yield approach, soon followed by F.K. Uncle F.E. wanted to be convinced but not Rudolph. Nor did brother-in-law Rod Titcomb. Rod had succeeded George S. Long as manager of the Weyerhaeuser Timber Company (Long died on August 2, 1930), and neither Rod nor his woods superintendent, Minot Davis, saw any future in sustained yield. If Phil and F.K. were disappointed in such reactions, they continued to talk optimistically to each other. "One of the happy aspects" F.K. retained from his Spokane tenure "was my closeness to my brother Philip who was running the Clearwater Timber Company at Lewiston."

Not surprisingly, the question of Sales Company headquarters location arose again. Tom Humbird had favored Spokane, but of course he was no longer president. Thus F.E. asked the opinions of nephews Phil and Fritz. He already knew what F.K. thought. Humbird, he noted, had argued that the office ought to be close to the mills, "where it can inspect manufacture and shipments of lumber." F.E. restated his own view "that the executives of the Sales Company should not be burdened with this sort of problem."

Although F.K. agreed, his reasoning differed somewhat. After a few months in Spokane it became apparent, he later claimed, that the head office should be in St. Paul, "where the principal officers and owners of the parent companies either lived or frequently met." Spokane was simply too far from the market and the customers. Also, the Sales Company directors who established policy, even down to setting prices, were the mill managers; and they met monthly. By the time their price lists reached the salesmen, they were out of date. Moreover, these lists were often leaked to competitors. It was indeed a curious arrangement. Finally, in 1931, the board approved relocation of the headquarters to St. Paul, taking the "first step essential to creating an effective sales organization."

So, in spite of the Great Depression, or perhaps in part because of it, there was evidence of progress. The Idaho merger effort, not yet complete, seemed a possibility. Also, the Sales Company appeared to be on the verge of reshaping itself, and the 4-SQUARE marketing program was gaining national interest. But nothing the Weyerhaeuser organization did or planned to do really mattered; there simply was little market for lumber. F.K. admitted as much in the fall of 1930. The "fundamental conditions" for an improvement were in place, "with cheap money and commodity prices thoroughly deflated." And so they waited, impatiently. "Our problem," as F.K. saw it, was "to refrain from making more lumber than we can sell profitably and develop our sales organization to the highest point of efficiency possible," exactly the charge he gave himself.

In the meantime, however, more important events were taking place. On October 20, 1930, Vivian gave birth to a baby girl, and the parents proudly named her Vivian O'Gara Weyerhaeuser. Prior to the birth, F.K. and Vivian had gone east, where they stayed for more than a month, F.K. wishing to attend the annual meeting of the Weyerhaeuser Forest Products Company in St. Paul on November 25. That was more than ordinarily important because he had in mind a change involving the advertising agency. The family arrived back in Spokane on December 1, but they would not be there for long. By the time another daughter, Elizabeth Lynn O'Gara Weyerhaeuser, was born on December 5, 1931, St. Paul was once again home, and home it would remain for many years. More vital than *where* the babies were was *how* they were; they were both healthy as could be.

GENERAL TIMBER SERVICE, INC.

F.K. had long been bothered by Weyerhaeuser's practice of having one organization sell lumber while another advertised it. Coordination between the two was not easily managed, but since sales were slow anyway, it seemed a safe time to explore ways of achieving greater efficiency.

Accordingly, in the fall of 1930, F.K. encouraged Carl Hamilton and lawyer Gus Clapp to develop tactics for increasing coordination and cooperation between sales and advertising. The subsequent proposal built on F.E.'s old concept of the committee system serving the various needs of the affiliated companies. What F.K. and his colleagues now envisioned was a "service corporation" that "might just as well be organized with the power to extend its activities into any potential field." They identified likely functions: advertising, sales promotions, sales engineering and publicity; auditing and accounting; legal services; insurance; research; engineering (other than sales engineering); timber utilization and conservation; logging engineering; patents and trademarks; and construction.

They assumed that the corporation would be conventional; that is, that it should make profits rather than operate at cost. At the same time, they should not expect more than "a reasonable return upon the capital invested." Organization would be in the form of a board of directors, made up generally of owners rather than managers. In short, the directors would be the major shareholders in "the so-called Weyerhaeuser companies." At the time, a dozen or fewer shareholding interests owned "at least 80%" in those companies and more than that in some. Those interests would become stockholders in the new service corporation "roughly in proportion to their holdings of stock in the group as a whole."

The advantages foreseen closely paralleled those put forth by F.E. on behalf of the old committee system: The plan would provide for "a more integrated, and I believe efficient organization, even if it performed no services other than those now performed by Weyerhaeuser Forest Products." The plan did not limit the scope of operations. On the contrary, F.K. assumed that cousin Ed Davis's Wood Conversion Company would be included, at least its research activities.

Gus Clapp and Carl Hamilton continued to work on specifics into 1931, Clapp drafting the articles of incorporation and a contract form, "such as might establish the working relationship between such a Service Corporation and the individual corporations." F.K. offered his hearty approval. There was no reason to hesitate. "We are receiving two or three dollars less for lumber than it can be produced for," he acknowledged, "and there seems to be no immediate prospect of any improvement." True, the major cause of their difficulties lay beyond their control. But it was also true that a portion of the loss could have been prevented and might still be alleviated "by energetic and courageous action." F.K.'s response closed with the observation that "the cost of being timid is pretty big." So the salesman F.K. had a new product to peddle—the service corporation.

In this instance, he sold successfully. A meeting was held in St. Paul on September 28, 1931, at which General Timber Service, Inc., was organized, with F.K. elected its president. It was officially incorporated under the laws of Delaware on October 9, and the stockholders met for the first time exactly a month later. F.K. had made a particular point of inviting his father, but John remained in Tacoma, fighting a cold. General Timber Service (GTS) opened for business on December 1.

In the meantime, F.K. and Vivian had settled into their St. Paul home at 294 Summit Avenue, and there they would remain, with few interruptions, until they died. Like John, mother Vivian was down with a bad cold, but baby Vivian was flourishing. "She has learned to drink out of a glass," F.K. proudly informed Anna, "and is doing a lot of other things too numerous to mention."

The plan effected for GTS varied only slightly from the original blueprint designed by F.K., Hamilton, and Clapp. To a considerable degree, it merely "legislated" what F.E. had in mind in the pre–World War I days. F.E., of course, had been less than successful in his efforts to combine and coordinate. Still, some important pieces of the original program had endured, most notably the Sales Company, the Auditing Department, the advertising arm (Weyerhaeuser Forest Products, Inc.), and the research agency, Ed Davis's Wood Conversion Company. GTS now began to assume some of those responsibilities and also to extend into other activities where coordination had not been achieved.

The record of General Timber Service, Inc., in its first year was as curious as it was complex. Working capital was provided through the issuing of "Class A stock," subscribed by the "associated ownership" to the amount of $25,000. All the assets of Weyerhaeuser Forest Products, excluding cash and receivables, became the property of GTS. This was accomplished by means of issuing 10,000 shares of "Class B stock," valued at $100,000, to the former members of Weyerhaeuser Forest Products in payment of its assets—trademarks, patents, patent rights, office furniture, and supplies.

Next came the negotiation of service contracts with the various Weyerhaeuser affiliates: Weyerhaeuser Timber Company, Snoqualmie Falls Lumber Company, Potlatch Forests, Inc., Boise Payette, Inc., the Northwest Paper Company, the Wood Conversion Company, and the Weyerhaeuser Sales Company. This did not constitute a commitment but merely allowed each company to participate to whatever degree it desired. For example, GTS offered auditing and accounting services; these were negotiated not only with the above-named entities but also with eighty-two other companies formerly served by the Auditing Department.

In addition, there were several important personnel decisions. W. A. King was one of the early appointments. He had been employed by Arthur Andersen & Company, acquiring considerable experience "in the reorganization or liquidation" of firms experiencing financial difficulty. F.K. soon recognized the abilities that King brought to the new company, and, as the Great Depression worsened, King's importance increased. The second appointee would prove even more valuable. Harry T. Kendall had been sales manager for the Central Coal & Coke Company of Kansas City. F.K. first met him at a meeting of sales managers. At that time, Charles Keith, an impressive figure, was president of Central Coal & Coke. Unfortunately, Keith had expanded operations into the West at the worst possible time, just prior to the Depression. As a result, the company failed, and Kendall found himself unemployed. But not for long. F.K. invited him to St. Paul to take a detailed look at General Timber Service and, if he was interested, to suggest how he might contribute. Kendall came, looked, and subsequently accepted appointment as general manager. He held the position for nearly twenty years.

A crucial GTS department from the beginning was its Traffic Division, led by A. G. Kingsley. The division's primary responsibility was to work with the affiliated companies in all matters concerning general railroad-traffic policies, carrier relations, and the handling of the troublesome rate cases.

But not all of the early initiatives succeeded. For example, the position of pine-mills inspector for the Idaho operations, formerly within the Sales Company, was eliminated in August. This activity had always been viewed with suspicion from the mill side of the equation, and in the summer of 1932 there simply wasn't enough lumber moving to warrant close inspection. (National lumber consumption had dropped from thirty-six billion board feet in 1929 to thirteen billion board feet in 1932.) About that time, too, the duplication of the Sales Company and GTS's Merchandising Division became apparent, and GTS bowed out.

But on the whole, F.K. was pleased with the performance of his new organization during its first year. In his president's report in December he claimed that GTS had already "fully demonstrated . . . the soundness of the idea and the very large additional benefits that are bound to accrue to the Associated Mills and to their stockholders through the continuance and judicial expansion of General Timber Services engagements."

Without doubt, however, the most significant event for the Weyerhaeusers and their fellow Americans in 1932 did not take place in mills or markets but at the polls in November. Not only did Franklin Delano Roosevelt swamp President Hoover, but Democrats also won handily at nearly every level. Republicans succeeded in only six of the thirty-four U.S. Senate contests held that year, and old-guard incumbents who ran for reelection were all defeated. In 1932, the period between the election and assumption of office still stretched until early March; given the sweeping nature of the political change and the dire economic climate, the nation's wait for the start of the new administration was a particularly impatient one. F.K. would recall the beginning of the new order matter-of-factly: "[A] series of events which fundamentally changed many things in our lives and in our ways of doing business."

Sales had increased slightly in the late summer and early fall, but by December, F.K. wrote his father, demand and prices had fallen back to "the July levels and prospects are not very encouraging." He hoped for some improvement in the spring, but he had hoped before. On the positive side, "Vivian and the babies are fine—in fact, Vivian is better than she has been for two years."

Early 1933 witnessed changes the world over, including the Weyerhaeuser realm. At the annual meeting of the Weyerhaeuser Timber Company in 1929, Rod Titcomb had been elected general manager, to be assisted by Charlie Ingram. From the start there was a degree of uncertainty regarding Titcomb's ability to succeed George Long, as evidenced by the creation of an executive committee on which Long served as chairman. John shared this concern in an early November 1929 letter to F.K. "I do hope and pray that Rodman will not be a disappointment," he fretted, and summed up the problem as he saw it: "If [Rodman] would only respect the other fellow's opinion and not make him feel so little. I respect the fellow that has an opinion, but when he starts to belittle the other fellows, he looses [sic] friends and standing among men."

As John's assessment indicates, Rod had an abrasive personal style; it stemmed from a basic insecurity. After a trial period of a couple of years, F.E. and others decided that a change had to be made. It was hard on everybody, but there was no alternative. Phil had clearly demonstrated an ability to persevere in the most difficult economic circumstances, in the Inland Empire with Potlatch Forests, Inc. While he could boast of no great success, all agreed that Phil had done as well as could be expected. Thus the Timber Company directors offered him the opportunity to manage its operation. F.K. learned of the developments from his father early in January. "Some one will be an executive," he wrote confidentially and almost mysteriously, "and if Rodman sticks to the job he will be under the executive." Then he announced: "Philip is to be that one so I understand. A great big job and I hope and pray, that he can stand the gaff." Phil accepted the Timber Company challenge, and Rodman stayed on as assistant general manager for a time. But the arrangement was awkward, to say the least.

Franklin D. Roosevelt was sworn in on March 4, and nearly everyone would remember the most famous line of his inaugural address: "So, first of all, let me assert my firm belief that the only thing we have to fear is fear itself." Although words mattered, they alone were not sufficient. Actions followed immediately, the president declaring a national "bank holiday" and calling Congress into session on March 9. Some days earlier, F.K. ran into George Prince and Dick Lilly in the lobby of the bank they owned, the First National in St. Paul, and inquired whether people were still withdrawing funds. They were, but Prince and Lilly promised, "This bank will never close." Like so many others, they were wrong. All the nation's banks suspended operations, and as F.K. put it, the holiday brought everything to a "climax."

His use of the word *climax* reflected F.K.'s hope, shared by most Americans, that the country had reached the economic nadir. And it soon seemed so. By the end of March, he noted that "business is picking up and everybody is feeling much better." This optimism continued into April and beyond. By June, F.K. appeared certain that the worst was at last behind them. "There is a real, genuine business recovery," he informed his father, "and no mistake this time." But the Rock Island Plow Company was beyond help: "[T]he upturn comes too late for us to avoid a great loss in that matter." Working to limit the losses was no easy task, but F.K. didn't seem to mind and tried his best to keep his father from worrying.

Anna died of old age on April 23, and her departure left John at loose ends. As he put it, "I am like the wind. Do not know which way I will go." He hated living alone in Haddaway Hall, rattling around in its immensity. "A man that builds a house for a *home must take care not to build it too large,*" he wrote to F.K., who tried mightily to help his father through those sad and lonely days. John worried about being a burden on his children, and he occasionally threatened to live in a boardinghouse somewhere. "Vivian and I want you to live with us in St. Paul, if you will do so," F.K. ventured, assuring John that the children wouldn't pester him and that there would be "a room and bath which could be yours permanently." John wasn't interested.

On a happier note, business continued to improve into the summer, to the extent that F.K. imagined some of the mills to be operating in the "black." That was optimism run rampant.

Sales figures for the Weyerhaeuser operations since 1929 had been truly depressing, and F.K. wondered what if anything could be done within the Sales Company to ensure its continuation beyond expiration of the current contract with the mills on December 2, 1934. Under the terms of that contract, the Weyerhaeuser Sales Company was the exclusive selling agency for the affiliated operations (the Weyerhaeuser Timber Company, Snoqualmie Falls Lumber Company, Potlatch Forests, Inc., the Humbird Lumber Company, Boise Payette, Inc., and the Northwest Paper Company). Initially, some presumed that the Sales Company would market all of the lumber produced by the several companies, but that was beyond reason. The capacity of the affiliated mills was staggering; figuring only one eight-hour shift for 300 days, it totaled nearly 1.2 billion board feet, about equal to what the Sales Company marketed during 1929, the last of the good years. Just three years later, it sold barely half that: six hundred million board feet.

Auditors reviewed the GTS figures to determine just what sales volumes would be required at 1932 prices merely to cover the operating costs of the mills. The answers were hardly surprising. None of the mills sold enough to exceed all expenses including depreciation. And only the two newest, Longview and Klamath Falls, shipped enough to cover cash expenditures and stumpage charges. They were simply sacrificing their resource to no apparent benefit, while the costs of selling continually increased. What to do?

Nothing could be done. The problem wasn't with the Weyerhaeuser Sales Company but with the world economy. Relatively speaking, the Sales Company "made a commendable record considering the conditions under which it has operated," according to a December 14, 1933, GTS report. Nonetheless, recommendations were made based on several observed deficiencies. A schism remained between mill management and Sales Company personnel. There was no "clear definition of duties and responsibilities" within the Sales Company, nor was there sufficient "delegation of authority to carry out those responsibilities." Added to that was the all-too-familiar tendency "to increase the supervisory overhead of the organization" at the expense of direct sales representation in the field.

Credit policies had been overly restrictive. And in what was likely viewed as a self-serving note, the GTS report cited "insufficient accounting analysis" as a serious problem. Without facts, the company was "likened to a boat on the ocean without a rudder."

Thanks to Sales Company general manager Harry Kendall, some remedies had already been effected. The highly decentralized district-office arrangement, in operation since 1926, was replaced by three national zones, with headquarters in Newark, New Jersey, St. Paul, and Tacoma, respectively. Zone managers were, of course, responsible for their own sales personnel and customer relations, and each zone had its own traffic office along with a credit and accounting office. Thus to a degree at least, the "delegation of authority" concern had already been addressed. Under the new contract negotiated with the mills, the management of the Sales Company assumed responsibility for prices, credits, and sales policy. Perhaps the most significant result of these changes was the streamlining, which allowed customers in a given zone to deal with a single office, regardless of the subject—prices, orders, claims, credits, or traffic rates and routings.

One organizational development was curious: Bill Peabody, superintendent at the Weyerhaeuser Timber Company's Everett mill, was selected in 1934 to replace Colonel James Long—George's brother—at the Newark headquarters. While in Everett, Peabody had also been in charge of the Weyerhaeuser Steamship Company, principal shippers for the Timber Company lumber to the Atlantic Terminals of Baltimore, Newark, and Portsmouth, New Hampshire. Upon his assignment to Newark, Peabody brought the Steamship Company responsibility with him, and so he ended up directing three separate organizations. He was manager of the Eastern Zone of the Weyerhaeuser Sales Company; he supervised the Eastern Yards (the Atlantic Terminals) for the Weyerhaeuser Timber Company; and he continued to run the Weyerhaeuser Steamship Company. This three-pronged assignment never sat well with F.E., but F.K. allowed that it "worked with reasonable efficiency." For a good many years the arrangement seemed practical, at least from a distance.

A general Sales Company meeting was held at Chicago's Drake Hotel in late March 1934. More than fifty salesmen attended, along with a number of representatives from the mills. In F.K.'s words, "It was a very impressive meeting and I was deeply impressed by the calibre of the men

The Frederick Weyerhaeuser family, ca. 1888. From left to right: Rudolph, Charles, Elise, Frederick, Margaret, Sarah, Apollonia, John Philip, and Frederick Edward

Baby Frederick King with his sister, Elizabeth, in January 1896

Nellie Anderson at the time of her marriage to John Philip Weyerhaeuser in 1890

Frederick and Elizabeth at Rock Island's
House on the Hill, Christmas 1896

Frederick King at age six

The three children—Elizabeth, Philip, and Frederick—out for a ride, ca. 1904

A Lake Nebagamon swimming party with friend and tutor Miss Aimee Lyford keeping Phil afloat, along with Elizabeth, St. Paul playmate Lawrence Noyes, and Frederick K. with an early version of water wings

The brothers developed a keen interest in automobiles and airplanes, building many models themselves. Here they are testing an early go-cart on a sidewalk in St. Paul.

Anna Holbrook Weyerhaeuser with her stepsons, Phil and Fred K., ca. 1907

Phil and F.K., nearly college-bound, along with Uncle Rudolph, sister Elizabeth, and cousin Ed Davis in front of the House on the Hill, ca. 1914

The four cousins—F.K., Ed Davis, Phil, and Fritz Jewett (with camera-shutter string in his hand)—perhaps preparing for a formal dance, ca. 1915

A summer get-together of college friends and family aboard the F. Weyerhaeuser, in its working days a Mississippi River log boat. From left to right: Fred Weyerhaeuser, Ed Davis, S. S. Davis (Ed's father), J. P. Weyerhaeuser, F. K., Willie Keeler, T. B. Davis, Lou Hardin, Tom Penney, Rufus Clapp, Joe Nagel, William Marshall, and Shorty Greebe

F.K. writing a letter in "Old Room #12," for a time his home at Campo Sud in Foggia, Italy

F.K. and Nat Robertson relaxing along a street in Naples, Italy

Ossie Watkins and F.K. flank the Signorina Fatin di Fontana and Baronessa Trêves at the baronessa's estate in Milan, Italy

The famous Caproni 350 bomber with Bill Shelton (at left), Manlio Borri, Norm Sweetser, and F.K. At far right is F.K.'s close friend, Doug Farquhar.

Vivian O'Gara Weyerhaeuser in 1923, shortly after her marriage to F.K.

F.K. the young executive, soon after joining the Weyerhaeuser Sales Company in 1924

Brothers F.E. and J.P. at the controversial Clearwater sawmill site, Lewiston, Idaho, in 1925

Business associates—largely Sales Company personnel—socializing at the Lewis and Clark Hotel, Lewiston, Idaho, in 1937. At upper left is host Bill Billings, manager at Potlatch; others include Phil Weyerhaeuser in the middle, along with F.K. and Fritz Jewett at right.

we have in the organization." Others agreed, among them Uncle Rudolph. "F.K. is sitting on the job and building up a very fine and strong organization about him," he observed for the benefit of brother John, adding, "We who are near the mountain feel that things are going fine."

Despite the promising signs, F.K. knew that Weyerhaeuser was not yet out of the woods. "Business is getting a little better," he reported to his father, "but there is still considerable uncertainty in the situation." As for himself, he was off to more meetings in New York City, after which he planned to go to Washington, D.C., for a day or two. "There is so much to do and so little time to do it in," he complained.

F.K.'s inclusion of Washington, D.C., on his itinerary may well have been tied to the piece of New Deal legislation in which he was most interested, the National Housing Act of 1934. By the end of June the act had passed the House and Senate, and F.K. and his colleagues immediately undertook consideration of its implications. It established a separate agency, the Federal Housing Administration, which, under the provisions of Title I, could insure loans to those buying new homes or remodeling old ones. Under the new law, the Weyerhaeusers found their close relationship to the managers of St. Paul's First Bancredit Corporation to be helpful. By mid-August the arrangements were becoming clear. They—the Weyerhaeuser Sales Company through General Timber Service, Inc.—would send all dealers who had purchased a carload of lumber in the past year assurance that if they were unable to get direct service from the federal agency, the Weyerhaeuser Sales Company would furnish it to them. In turn, First Bancredit would provide the money and take the notes.

The provisions of the National Housing Act were complicated. For example, the federal government would guarantee 20 percent of the total of all loans purchased by the bank but insisted that the Sales Company assume a 10-percent guarantee over and above the 20 percent. As F.E. explained it, "[T]hey wish someone else to be responsible for making collections." That made sense. The Sales Company, in turn, would ask the dealers to guarantee 10 percent for much the same reason. Regardless of the details, the important fact is that the Sales Company took advantage of the law to secure credit for its customers, and the plan worked. Further, Weyerhaeuser had taken the lead. According to the 1934 General Timber Service, Inc., annual report: "So far as we know, we are the only lumber manufacturer, or wholesaler, with a finance plan for its customers. We believe it will prove to be a very potent sales help in 1934." And it was.

From today's vantage, the initial loan amounts may seem paltry. The National Housing Act placed a $2,000 limit on loans for renovation, but the first agreement negotiated with Bancredit further limited amounts to $750, with a maturity period of not more than three years. Still, for most people, it was too good an opportunity to pass up, as the 1934 report noted: "It begins to appear that we have an opportunity to acquire a liberal education in this respect with very little risk." It was also true that in 1934, $750 wasn't paltry, and within the year, loans of up to $2,000 would be accepted.

While response to the National Housing Act marked the Sales Company's entry into the finance business, it was only the first tentative, one might say desperate, step. What followed was an amazing success story. In 1935 the Weyerhaeuser Sales Company stockholders voted to organize the General Home Financing Corporation, soon to become Allied Building Credits, Inc.; it was ABC that became the buyer of installment mortgages and modernization notes insured by the federal government. What had commenced as a "simple arrangement," not much more than wishful thinking, quickly evolved into a major enterprise. In 1936 the Sales Company concluded agreements with more than fifteen hundred lumber dealers, and in the course of the following year ABC was purchasing notes and mortgages directly, eliminating the need for the Bancredit association. By the end of World War II ABC, holding more than $30 million worth of mortgages, was virtually an industry unto itself; some feared that the tail would soon wag the dog. As F.K. then put it, "We are approaching a situation where instead of operating a finance company as an adjunct to a lumber sales program, we may be running a business as an adjunct to a finance company." The decision was reached to sell, and on October 19, 1945, the Transamerica Corporation of San Francisco agreed to purchase Allied Building Credits, Inc. (ABC is treated in depth in Chapter 11.)

While the National Housing Act was to be the most significant piece of New Deal legislation as far as many lumbermen were concerned, that was not evident at the time. Indeed, those in the industry expended far more energy on matters relating to the National Industrial Recovery Act, which President Roosevelt described as "the most important and far-reaching legislation ever enacted by the American Congress." It may well have been too far-reaching; in 1936 the Supreme Court declared the act unconstitutional. In the meantime, however, industrial leaders had labored strenuously in relation to the law: first as members of the Emergency National Committee, the Lumber Code Authority, then as witnesses, and finally as disputants over the law's provisions, particularly those involving production quotas and prices. With the Court's ruling, it seemed those labors were nearly for naught. But that wasn't exactly true. For one thing, Title X of the code, the conservation section, pointed forest management in a new direction, one that would be followed enthusiastically by the Weyerhaeuser Timber Company.

Change was in the air everywhere, and the 1934 GTS annual report carried an addendum, "Weyerhaeuser Believes That," reflecting one such change. The credo spoke to several concerns about timber, offering five responses: "Timber is a Crop; American Timber Resources are Sufficient for the Present and Future Needs of the American People; Destruction of Timber is Chiefly Due to Natural Causes; Trees, Like People, Die of Old Age; Good Forestry Varies with the Timber; [and] Cut-Over Lands Should be Burned Over to Reduce Fire Hazard."

It seemed a time for looking ahead. Even John felt cautiously optimistic in a business sense. He visited the Sales Company's Western Zone office in mid-November and came away encouraged that the demand for lumber was improving, even if "not just what is wanted." On the home front John looked forward to Elizabeth taking over "the Haddaway Plant," where he was sure she would "be happy for a time." As for his own future, he remained undecided. "I will stop at a hotel or I may move to Longview and live." F.K. was left to fret helplessly in St. Paul. "I am very strongly opposed to your living alone in a hotel or going to a city where none of your children live," he wrote John, "and I have several times told you my reasons for feeling that way." At that very moment, however, a blizzard raged outside his St. Paul office. Weather was certainly no ally in trying to convince his seventy-six-year-old father to move to the Upper Midwest.

FAMILY FIRST

As F.K. CONSIDERED his responsibilities in 1935 he felt encouraged, particularly by the organization of the Weyerhaeuser Sales Company. Thanks in no small part to the efforts of general manager Harry Kendall, that agency seemed far more responsive than previously. The change from district offices to three zone offices—Newark, St. Paul, and Tacoma—appeared to be working well. On July 17, 1933, the Sales Company had also assumed management of customer accounts formerly carried on the books of the various mills. Thereafter, credits, collections, and accounting would be handled solely by the Sales Company. Each zone office comprised two departments, a sales department and a credit and accounting department. Although the zone offices were still under the general supervision of the St. Paul headquarters, they now enjoyed far more autonomy. This permitted a faster response to local circumstances, more flexibility, and, it was presumed, increased efficiency. Most important, F.K. was happy with the personnel.

Despite such improvements, however, numerous problems remained. The volume of lumber sold during 1934, for example, exceeded the break-even point only at Snoqualmie Falls, Longview, and Klamath Falls. It fell slightly below at Everett and considerably below at both Boise Payette and Potlatch Forests. Selling, of course, was only part of the game; it didn't much matter what you sold if you didn't collect. On that score, things were looking up. As of December 31, 1934, more than 60 percent of accounts were current, and fewer than 10 percent were more than four months past due. That amounted to real progress.

Concurrent with, but not necessarily the reason for this improvement in sales, there had been an intensified advertising effort in which F.K.'s brother-in-law, Lincoln O'Gara, now played a notable role. Encouraged by an increased demand, the Merchandising Division of General Timber Service, Inc., again actively promoted the 4-SQUARE program. It also developed plans for farm buildings and soon for homes as well, in the process promoting the use of 4-SQUARE lumber to reduce costs, or so they claimed.

F.K. spent the first two weeks of 1935 on the road, dealing with both business and family matters. Immediately after Christmas, he was in Coeur d'Alene, visiting cousins Fritz and Mary Jewett, finding Fritz "very much happier than he has been for some time." The situation in Cloquet, his next stop, was decidedly different—in a word, depressing. "It has become very apparent," F.K. informed Uncle F.E., "that the lumber industry up there is doomed and that a great effort should be made to liquidate the stock of lumber and logs just as quickly as it can be done." As far as lumber production was concerned, Cloquet, along with the rest of northern Minnesota and Wisconsin, was in its twilight. For this the Depression could not be blamed. The industry had simply exhausted its resource, and it would take many years for the forests to recover even partially. In the interim, the region would be known as the cutover.

When F.K. visited Cloquet in January 1935, aside from Ed Davis's Wood Conversion Company, the Northwest Paper Company was the only plant still operating—and it was tottering. Wood Conversion was doing little better. Following its annual meeting early in the year, Rudolph described matters simply: "A very bad showing." Ed surely understood the seriousness of his problems, having received a letter from Phil flatly stating that the Weyerhaeuser Timber Company "had come across for the last time."

As for the Northwest Paper Company, F.K. could only advise its manager, Bill Kenety, that the best way to prepare to face his "thoroughly discouraged and dissatisfied" stockholders was by studying other operations "and suggest anything that might be done to improve the situation in an entirely unprejudiced manner." An eastern expert was thus hired to review the subject and offer recommendations. The subsequent study of Northwest Paper's problems doubtless saved the day, but the most significant outcome was the firing of Kenety and the hiring of Stuart B. Copeland in 1936. Manager Copeland enjoyed amazing success in resurrecting Northwest; it not only survived, it eventually prospered.

That happened much later, of course. In 1935 F.K. left Cloquet heading east, first for a Chicago meeting of the Central Zone salesmen, then on to New York City and a similar gathering for the Eastern Zone. The "enthusiasm" of both groups delighted him. While in the East, he also did his family duty, visiting Professor James Richard and Aunt Margaret Jewett in Cambridge, and the Hills, Bancrofts, and Aunt Elise in Poughkeepsie.

As always, F.K. tried not to worry his father or uncles unnecessarily. In the case of his Cloquet visit and Northwest Paper discussion, F.E. concurred. "Should have been done years ago," he admitted, hoping only that Rudolph would "not be displeased." Cloquet was, of course, Rudolph's fiefdom, but in this instance, he offered no complaint. One matter, however, couldn't be sugarcoated—the Rock Island Plow Company's indebtedness. F.K. and Ed Davis, with invaluable assistance from Gus Clapp, continued to search for a "solution." Complicating the situation, the Denkmanns were also heavily involved, and as F.E. warned F.K., "sooner or later we shall have to come to [a] showdown with the other family." Over the years, the Rock Island Plow Company would be a major headache for all concerned, especially for F.K. and Ed Davis.

A less serious but equally frustrating legacy of John's involved foolish mining investments, mostly in gold, none of which "panned out." Again, F.K. was the responsible heir, trying his best to minimize losses. Soon, however, family matters of a different sort intervened. Vivian's father, Thomas J. O'Gara, died at his Lake Shore Drive home on February 15. He had been ill for some time, "was practically paralyzed," and F.K. was doubtless correct in observing that his death must have been a great relief.

In the meantime, there was good news to report concerning the financing plan fostered by the National Housing Act. F.K.'s only complaint was that his St. Paul banker friends stood to earn some $2 million, getting this bonus "from us for nothing because we do it for the sake of lumber sales." Happily, the latest report also indicated not a single delinquency "in all of the loans we have made." F.K. was preparing to leave on another tour, this one a western swing that included a meeting with Uncle F.E. in Pasadena. In St. Paul, Uncle Rudolph seemed slightly piqued at his inability to keep track of his busy nephew. He found himself reduced to making luncheon dates with F.K., "just about the only chance I get to visit with him," he wrote to F.E.

It wasn't neglect alone that bothered Rudolph. Feeling protective as always regarding the Cloquet operations, he reacted predictably to reports of some family support for a reciprocal-tariff agreement with Canada. While he didn't confront F.K. directly, he did complain loudly to others, certain that his nephew would soon learn of his opposition. He reminded C. L. Billings, now manager of Potlatch Forests, Inc., that there was "just an imaginary boundary" between the United States and Canada, and that their "friends" the Shevlins had a large mill in Fort Frances, Ontario, and would "dump their white pine and low grade stuff at our back door at Cloquet." F.K. argued otherwise, that it would serve no purpose to attack the position of the trade associations favoring reciprocity. In addition, he thought it "wise policy" not to exclude white pine from Canada "but rather to encourage its importation in order to keep White Pine in use." F.K. didn't have to remind Rudolph that Cloquet was no longer in a position to satisfy market demand for that variety of lumber.

As matters developed, however, Cloquet was not alone in declining production. After lengthy negotiations and an agreement among union leadership, the American Federation of Labor's United Brotherhood of Carpenters and Joiners, and representatives of Weyerhaeuser's Longview operations and Long-Bell officials, the general union membership rejected the contract. By May 13, the West Coast industry was entirely shut down. The strike would last until well into August.

But even that disappointment was soon to be overshadowed. John died at Haddaway Hall on the morning of May 16, the cause of death listed as pneumonia. He had, of course, simply worn out. F.E. happened to be visiting in Tacoma at the time, so he provided the newspapers with details of his brother's life. Most of the reports embellished the facts, particularly concerning John's wealth. The *Seattle Post-Intelligencer* of May 17, for example, described him as a "billionaire St. Paul lumberman," missing the mark on dollars as well as residence. Similar stories appeared in papers across the country.

To make matters worse, on May 24 Phil's nine-year-old son, George, was kidnapped in Tacoma. A story running two days later in the *Chicago Herald Examiner* was headlined "Vast Lumber Wealth Shrouded in Mystery." After noting that the Weyerhaeusers were "famous for their resolute 'sticking together' as a family," the article quoted an unnamed business associate as asserting: "Hurt one Weyerhaeuser and you hurt every Weyerhaeuser. Then—look out." F.K. was also quoted to the effect that the kidnapping might be connected to the West Coast strike. "It may be that he was taken as a hostage or as a move for vengeance. It is a terrible situation."

He was right only about the nature of the situation. A pair of ex-convicts, Harmon Metz Waley and William Dainard, along with Waley's wife, Margaret, had recently arrived in western Washington, looking for an easy way to make lots of money in a hurry. Apparently John's *Post-Intelligencer* obituary caught their attention. The trio took a week to familiarize themselves with the Weyerhaeusers' north Tacoma neighborhood and with their daily habits. Then, at noon on Friday, May 24, George was snatched on his way home from school. His disappearance immediately attracted widespread publicity. While coverage didn't equal that given to the 1932 Lindbergh baby kidnapping and the trial several years later of Bruno Richard Hauptmann—the so-called Story of the Century—it was front-page news nonetheless. Weyerhaeuser became a household name nationwide, though obviously not in a preferred way.

At the news of the kidnapping, F.K. immediately headed west, along with all the other males of the clan. Vivian remained at home, surely keeping a close eye on Vivian and Lynn. The accounts are elsewhere available, but the important details are that a $200,000 ransom was paid and that George returned home safely a week after his abduction. The kidnappers were arrested, found guilty, and sent to prison. Also, authorities recovered a good portion of the ransom money. Raising the ransom had required some doing, and Uncle Rudolph spoke for the rest when he said, "It was a family matter." Nonetheless, John's three children endeavored to assume primary responsibility. F.K. wrote the letter to the family, with Elizabeth's and Phil's approval:

> . . . we want to set up a financial understanding with you in regard to the $200,000.00 ransom money. We want this to be a loan to

Father's three children to be repaid out of his estate as soon as possible. Three individual notes each signed by one of us are enclosed herewith. Our reason for wanting this is simply that we [the J. P. Weyerhaeuser children] do not wish to be in the position of causing financial loss and deprivation of material things to the other members of the family. Please accept these notes in the spirit in which we offer them. We want to do our part and not be a drag on everybody else. We will feel better if this is done.

It had been a bleak period indeed. John's death saddened everyone. Then there was the general lumber strike in the West. Like so many other strikes, it could have been avoided, but pride and prerogatives intruded. When it finally came to an end, no winners emerged. But the kidnapping put everything else into perspective. Naturally, the worst was feared, and all held their breath until George was safely returned. Although the awful memories made genuine rejoicing difficult, the family's relief was profound.

It took Phil and F.K. a while before they could handle business seriously again, although by mid-June both had resumed their normal routines. Phil was briefly riled by recent activities of the General Timber Service's auditors, and of course he complained to his brother. Stay out of our hair, he admonished. F.K. assumed that his auditors were doing just that, and tending to business. Nonetheless, responding to Phil's handwritten letter of June 21, F.K. apologized: "I am sorry the actions of anybody that I have anything to do with [are] the cause for this unhappy situation." He closed with the assurance that it had never been his intention "to cram anything down the throats of any of the Companies." In the meantime, he hoped Phil could be patient. Phil could and would.

Years later, F.K. and fellow Weyerhaeuser director John Musser discussed "certain principles" that had been followed through the years. Heading the list was a "confidence in trees," followed by "a confidence in the principle of decentralization of responsibility and authority." Despite the latter assertion, there had been occasions when the principle of decentralization was violated, or at least tested. For example, F.E.'s plans for government by committee certainly constituted an attempt at centralization, and so of course did the formation of the Weyerhaeuser Sales Company and General Timber Service, Inc. F.K. followed his uncle in leading such efforts, with brother Phil leading the opposition. While the two were destined to be occasional opponents, it is also true that had they not been such friends and mutual supporters, cooperation as was seen in the Sales Company would have been impossible.

In the summer and fall of 1935 sales were slow to pick up, although most remained optimistic about the future. The question was, what to do in the meantime? For the most part, the brothers labored at familiar tasks, but probably only F.K. stayed awake nights wondering how to do things better. Early in 1936 he again made a full tour around the West, and upon arriving back home found a desk covered with problems old and new. For a start, there was increasing trepidation regarding the tax policies of the Roosevelt administration. Also, Title I of the Housing Act had been amended, and as a result the Weyerhaeuser Sales Company would need to negotiate a new arrangement with the bankers. All the while, management problems at the Northwest Paper Company in Cloquet awaited resolution. The price, as F.K. forewarned F.E., would be "pretty high," exceeding his uncles' estimates. Generally speaking, though, the lumber business was improving, and F.K. predicted, "We are in for a good year."

A month passed without resolution of the Northwest Paper Company management question. F.K. visited Cloquet in mid-April, acquainting himself with the paper mill's operation "until I got choked up with the sulphur fumes." In his opinion, the basic problem couldn't be understood by studying reports. What was needed was new leadership, "management by a good business man . . . a man who knows how to deal with people, properly organize them and place responsibility on their shoulders for the work they will have to do." Accordingly, he was soon off on another eastern tour, primarily to interview likely candidates. In the meantime, there were also family worries in Cloquet. Of particular concern was the health of Walter Driscoll, cousin Peggy's husband. Walter had inherited his father-in-law Rudolph's responsibility for Cloquet operations, and F.K. thought that Walter might be overly conscientious. "I imagine it is hard to keep away from the office and keep from worrying about things," he wrote to Uncle Rudolph. In any case, F.K. recommended to Peggy that she and Walter take some time off, go away to a place "where business matters will not be on his mind."

For himself, F.K. seemed to thrive with business matters always on his mind. At the moment, there were few distractions, what with Vivian and the girls vacationing in Florida. In addition to trying to resolve the Cloquet situation, he continued wrestling with the Rock Island Plow Company problem. And, as evidence that he was assuming greater family leadership responsibility, he attempted to interest F.E. in the subject of family investment. Shouldn't they be recommending purchases? He made clear his own preference: Buy stock in the Weyerhaeuser Timber Company. "I can think of no investment I would rather make in the summer of 1936 . . . assuming it can be bought at a price somewhere below $100 per share." Regarding the Timber Company, the directors of General Timber Service, Inc., had recently allocated $18,000 for chemical research at Longview, "the objectives being to get alcohol out of wood waste, to create wood waste into charcoal and to study the whole subject of wood preservatives." F.K. could not have known, but that decision put the Weyerhaeuser Timber Company on a collision course with Ed Davis's Wood Conversion Company. Finally, F.K. informed F.E. that he had been working "with your son, Fred . . . on a grandiose plan to better coordinate our group activities." F.E. likely smiled at that, smiled and said, "Good luck."

But those problems lay down the road. Of more immediate concern was the frustration of dealing with the Washington bureaucracy. "The Federal Housing Administration is becoming extremely technical and arbitrary in their handling of insurance under Title I," F.K. complained to the General Timber Service directors, bemoaning the "red tape." The fact was that most of GTS's problems resulted from the firm's own inexperience in the business of making loans, and more specifically, inexperience at the retail level. Even so, GTS was not faring badly. For example, in July, after reviewing some $175,000 worth of loans made in the Central Zone, only $40,000 were found to be questionable. In F.K.'s words, they were gradually finding their way around "and doing a better job all the time."

They were indeed. In June 1936, the Weyerhaeuser Sales Company shipped more than one hundred twenty-seven million board feet of lumber, the biggest month in its history. Although total sales were nearly $4 million, prices still lagged a bit, and they varied considerably from species to species. Douglas-fir prices were 94 percent of what they had been in 1929, while ponderosa pine was at 78 percent. Withal, F.K. admitted to feeling "much encouraged at the way things are going."

In fact, he was so encouraged that he and Vivian accepted an invitation from Minneapolis friend Totten Heffelfinger to join him on a fishing vacation at Minaki, Ontario, north of Lake of the Woods, where Heffelfinger had a cottage. They obviously enjoyed themselves, F.K. describing Vivian as a "most enthusiastic fisher woman," outfitted in overalls and an old straw hat. She did more than look the part, landing several big ones, "and the only thing she cannot do yet is take the hook out of the fish's mouth." F.K. recounted his own achievements for the benefit of Ed Davis. "I caught a 12½ pound pike after it had twice attacked the boat, also a 17½ pound muskellunge—so you can see we are no amateurs."

It was good that F.K. took some time off in August, for much work awaited his attention when he returned to his desk. First was the above-mentioned "grandiose plan to better coordinate our group activities." Second, and more immediate, was a plan for reorganization, or possible liquidation, of the family's holding company, the Timber Securities Company. Actual consideration of the question from F.K.'s vantage had begun at least two years earlier when he was studying the damage that the Rock Island Plow Company's indebtedness had done to his father's personal finances. Quite naturally, this led to a consideration of his own circumstances, present and future. And as he reviewed that, he thought increasingly of the Weyerhaeuser family's financial situation. To a very considerable extent, it involved their holding company.

The Timber Securities Company dated back to March 6, 1916, when it was incorporated under the laws of Delaware, replacing the Timber Loan Company, the original holding company into which Frederick's inheritance had been deposited. Timber Securities had continued over the years as the principal holder of the family's collective wealth, although accounts were individually maintained. This arrangement presumed a strength of togetherness and assurance of flexibility in times of special need, and for the most part it had worked well.

By 1934, however, the Timber Securities situation had grown worrisome, F.K. citing several contributing factors: "shrinkage of all values, excessive taxation, unwise investments, poor management in some cases, and debts acquired when values were high which must be met in a depression market." Worse, he felt that his cousins did not sense the urgency of the problem; he reminded them that what they failed to do would affect not only themselves and their children "but also the life of the Family itself as such."

Somewhere along the way, F.K. had learned to write an outline when attempting to analyze a work-related task. He approached the given topic by the numbers, and in this instance he listed three major problems. First, thinking specifically of his father's and the Davises' situation, F.K. noted the indebtedness of several branches to the Timber Securities Company. (When they spoke of branches, they referred to the seven children of grandparents Frederick and Sarah. But since the Hills had no children, there were only six branches in the third generation.) F.K.'s second point concerned management of the various properties and providing opportunities for those in the next generation. In his words, "It would be a major calamity for the Family to lose the services of those of its young men who have the ability to help in its business enterprises." This would become a constant apprehension. The third problem concerned the future of the Timber Securities Company itself:

> ... there is the danger of our failing to continue the financial unity of the Family in the Timber Securities Co. With the increase in our numbers, the ties that bind the third and fourth generations together will grow weaker. The members of the third and fourth generations, each with his or her own particular problems, are spread over the country far apart. Our children scarcely know each other and in many cases have never seen each other. A gradual drifting apart under such conditions is inevitable. A common financial bond like the Timber Securities Co. is the only kind of thing that is apt to hold this growing Family together.

As a step in the right direction, F.K. now proposed that Timber Securities issue 700,000 shares of $25 preferred stock, at the same time creating 300,000 additional shares of common stock that would be offered to younger family members for purchase. The advantages seemed obvious: Issuance of the preferred stock would allow for repayment of debts by those branches of the family, including his own, which had borrowed from Timber Securities. And the availability of common stock would encourage continued participation by members of the fourth generation. If they failed to participate, F.K. believed, the family's influence would be doomed. "If we are not jointly associated thru Timber Securities Co. we would probably as individuals soon have little voice in the conduct of affairs, and our Family would cease to be the dominating factor in the business." And business was only a part of the equation, indeed the smaller part. First came unity.

> Even more important . . . would be the weakening of the Family bond that in a sense perpetuates the traditions of Grandfather and Grandmother in respect to all the high principles of life that we have been taught. The Family association will always typify for its members the example, set by Grandfather and Grandmother, of Christian character, high moral life, and the economic virtues of frugality, industry, initiative, and respect for obligations. This is our most precious inheritance and one we should maintain at any cost.

Three months later, F.K. was pestering Uncle Rudolph on the same subject, although in this instance he concentrated on the indebtedness of family members to the Timber Securities Company, citing the advantage of repaying loans without sacrificing the basic equity of each branch in the company.

It is not clear just what the uncles thought of their nephew's proposals, but it is plain that there was no immediate response. Further, it is likely that F.E. and Rudolph, regardless of their reactions to the specifics of F.K.'s analysis and proposal, felt like the old bulls of the herd, about to be challenged. Given all the problems of 1935—deaths, strikes, and the kidnapping—it was understandable that any review of Timber Securities' health would receive short shrift. Nonetheless, at a family meeting in Cloquet on September 10, 1935, Timber Securities headed the agenda. But it was a piece of New Deal legislation—a new 1.5-percent tax on dividends received from corporations whose stock was owned by holding companies such as Timber Securities—that prompted the attention, not F.K.'s proposals. After some pro forma discussion, it was determined that Timber Securities would continue without change. Later in the meeting F.K. brought up his preferred-stock proposal, but it was simply referred to a committee. He left feeling discouraged. "It is hard to discuss these matters," he wrote to brother Phil, "simply because it is difficult to talk to anybody about them."

In the end, the question of whether the Timber Securities Company would be maintained wasn't settled by the family but by Congress. A surtax on personal holding companies was now law, and under its provisions income derived from a holding company would be treated the same as dividends received by individuals. Now it was F.E.'s turn to worry about family unity, and to complain about what he regarded as a lack of interest on the part of his nephews. That wasn't fair, at least not in the case of F.K. Indeed, he addressed a joint letter to F.E. and Rudolph in which he detailed a solution to the indebtedness of his branch to Timber Securities. The details were complicated, but the family leaders would offer a solution based on the worth of a share of Timber Securities stock at $50, which ended up being close to the final settlement, $46.55 per share.

In any case, there was no longer an advantage to family holding companies. Timber Securities was officially dissolved on October 24, 1935, when its $30 million worth of assets were distributed. F.K. continued to worry. "The most serious part of the problem," he reminded Phil, "is that what is proposed may break up the family unity and destroy the advantages of voting such a large amount of stock as a unit."

F.K. thought he had an answer, which he proposed to his uncles. First, however, he noted "appreciation for the wonderful support and spirit of the entire Weyerhaeuser Family in assisting Father and us, his children, [with] the settlement of his [Plow Company] obligations; and also for the great help given at the time of George's kidnapping." Now, what to do to replace Timber Securities Company? For beyond "cold-blooded" tax considerations, there were good reasons to have an entity like it on hand:

> I feel that the Family may eventually pay a terrible price for the tax saving it will secure through dissolution of the Timber Securities Company. The old story about the man who could not break the bundle of sticks but could break the sticks individually is borne out by our business experience of the past few years, which ended happily because we stuck together.

He then noted some of the likely losses, such as no longer having "large liquid funds" on hand to meet emergencies. And without the strength of togetherness, "the weaker ones" would suffer, the weaker being "girls without brothers, widows, boys without aptitude for business." He retained hope that they would "join forces again in a major way . . . it may prove hard to put Humpty Dumpty together again. This is not an argument against dissolving the Timber Securities Company, but it is a prophecy of what will happen if we are not careful."

There was a way out. An incorporated entity called The Bonners Ferry Lumber Company (and the capitalized "The" held significance) was on the books but had never been utilized. Now it proved to be the convenient depository for those stocks, bonds, and equities not readily distributed in the general dissolution of Timber Securities. These initially totaled about $9.5 million, and stock in the new holding company would be distributed according to pro rata ownership in the Timber Securities Company. Thus The Bonners Ferry Company succeeded Timber Securities as the retainer of some family monies but more vitally as the hub of joint involvements. It became, for example, the family office, and F.E. and Rudolph would continue to call it home. In addition, its board of directors, "composed of all the male members of the Family who are active in business," would meet frequently in St. Paul. As F.K. envisioned, "The new company would form the basis for a new kind of Family association that would . . . arouse the enthusiasm and interest of the younger men, and provide the basis for an efficient handling of Family business and make us all money." His expectations were on the mark. The Bonners Ferry Lumber Company remained in business for thirty years and assumed ever greater importance as its history lengthened.

ALLIED BUILDING CREDITS, INC.

CERTAINLY THE biggest event of the fall of 1936 was
Franklin Roosevelt's landslide victory over Republican
presidential candidate Alf Landon. For all of their wishful
thinking, the Weyerhaeusers were not surprised; perhaps
only F.E. felt utter dismay. F.K. had accepted the verdict as
a foregone conclusion. Now, at least, they could be fairly
sure of what lay ahead. The New Deal wasn't new anymore,
though that did not mean it was improving with age—not
according to those occupying the Weyerhaeuser offices.

But "that man in the White House" didn't deter them
from planning for a brighter business future. A year earlier, F.K. had informed F.E. that he and F.E.'s son Fred were
discussing some "grandiose plans," and, surprisingly, it was
Fred who introduced the subject. He had written F.K. a
serious critique of their circumstances, commenting on
"basic faults" in the Sales Company/General Timber Service organization. Fred cited three specific weaknesses: an
absence of stockholder initiative; a lack of consensus among
the stockholders; and minimal participation on the part of
stockholders in operations. In his response, F.K. sounded old
if not wise.

As to the first weakness, he simply thought of it as a fact
of life that all corporations had to confront. Stockholders
selected from among themselves individuals who would be
"best qualified" to deal with corporate problems. They, in

turn, would "employ the most competent management," contenting themselves with determining general policies. The second weakness, a lack of consensus among stockholders, was also to be expected. "I see no way to change this except by an actual merger, [and even then] we could never hope to effect a 100% group consciousness among stockholders." Finally, F.K. asserted, active participation should not be an objective, at least not in the sense of assuming responsibility for specific operations. That was properly a duty of management, and if owners disapproved of their managers, they could hire new ones. Nonetheless, F.K. agreed with his cousin that they could do better than they had done and that a merger of sorts seemed the likely answer.

Among the foremost concerns as the 1936 election neared was a modification of Weyerhaeuser Sales Company financing services in response to changes in the National Housing Act. The year before, at a special meeting of the General Timber Service, Inc., board of directors recommendations had been passed that the capital stock of GTS be increased in order to finance the formation of a mortgage company, that ownership of the mortgage company pass to GTS; and that GTS purchase Weyerhaeuser Sales Company's capital stock.

On July 23, 1936, a meeting was held supposedly to approve these recommendations. The result, however, was not as expected. A mortgage company was formed, but it became the property of the operating companies (that is, the lumber mills). Thus there continued to be no relationship between the mortgage company and the Sales Company, except that some individuals served as officers or board members of both organizations.

In a memorandum of September 18, 1936, F.K. once more called attention to what he saw as a problem, recommending that the Weyerhaeuser Sales Company and what was then called the General Home Financing Corporation be placed under the ownership of GTS. Citing supporting data in a recently completed study known as the Love Survey, F.K. noted that a financing or mortgage service was "entirely adjunct to sales and would not have been authorized on any other grounds." He also argued that their relative strength in the field involved coordination "with merchandising and other services so as to render to our customers a well rounded selling plan." In other words, he continued, "both Weyerhaeuser Sales Company and General Home Financing Corporation are instruments for the same end and should be controlled not only by the same people but by the same corporation."

He went on to point out how important it was for the two entities to speak with one voice, reporting the same information and complementing each other's activities. And it seemed clear to him that the placing of sales and financing functions under the umbrella of GTS would constitute "a logical first step in a broad plan of corporate coordination" that should be worked out during the next several years:

> The plan, put in its most brief terms, is that all corporations or properties having to do with sales and distribution, or with conversion of trees, lumber, or mill waste into other products, be owned in one place. To illustrate: One corporation, such as General Timber Service, Inc., would own Weyerhaeuser Sales Company, General Home Financing Corporation, all retail yard companies, the Eastern Distributing Yards now owned by Weyerhaeuser Timber Company, Twin City Lumber & Shingle Company, Rock Island Sash & Door Works, St. Louis Sash and Door Works, and the Wood Conversion Company.

F.K. had to appreciate that such a proposal would be considered revolutionary by many, starting with brother Phil.

In truth, F.K. had already truncated his original plan, circulated May 15. Like Uncle F.E. before him, he refused to believe that there might be no advantages inherent in a common ownership. Occasionally the separate organizations had acted in unison, but more often than not each went its own way, with little regard for the whole. "We are a group of separate institutions, with few common ties," he lamented, adding that a "stranger who is trying to become acquainted with our form of organization usually wants to know the name of the holding company or the parent company of the group and becomes quite puzzled when he finds there is no such animal." F.K. likened the "Weyerhaeuser Group" to "a deep sea invertebrate . . . which does not seem to be actuated from a single brain as in a higher form of life." Carrying the biological analogy forward, he described his purpose: "changing our type of organization from invertebrate to vertebrate, from a deep sea jelly-fish to a bird dog, or, if you prefer, to a race horse."

"We are a slow and cumbersome outfit," F.K. allowed, implying that the Weyerhaeusers' organization—or lack of same—made them so. It seemingly took forever to reach a decision. Eventually insights would evolve, "at which time we look back and wonder how much has been lost by our failure to do it before." He recognized the advantages of decentralization, "the development of initiative, competition, and the development of personnel." But there were also advantages to centralization, and his plan spoke to those: "placing the operating companies, the merchandising enterprises, and everything else, under the general control of one board and one executive, insofar as the setting of broad policies is concerned."

The GTS board met in mid-October and did as F.K. wanted, at least to the extent of approving consideration of the reorganization. He promptly informed Phil of the action, sending the complete package of materials "which I wish you would read." He also emphasized the importance of the change: "Having such a plan by any method without government insurance requires a large investment or the assumption of a big liability. If the necessity for this is not thoroughly understood I can imagine that you and others might think it unwise to do what we believe should be done."

Lawyer friend Laird Bell was the first to cast doubts, to which F.K. responded immediately. He did agree with one of Bell's points: Take things a step at a time, focusing initially on what was deemed most important. For F.K., of course, the first thing to do was resolve the financing problem. If they decided to do their own financing, "the simplest way to do it would be to increase the stock of the finance company and let the mills, or the stockholders themselves if they wish, hold the stock."

F.K. doubted they could negotiate a better deal with First Bancredit Corporation. The bank officials now proposed simply to loan the Sales Company or its successor organization money instead of instituting a complicated relationship. F.K. had no problem with this, but he thought it far better to do their own financing, without depending on First Bancredit or anyone else: "My whole position is that I sincerely believe that we need a finance plan because it will help sell our lumber more efficiently and because lumber as a commodity in the market needs the support of a good finance plan."

The sales meetings were set to begin in January, and F.K. had hoped to have the financing question settled by late November. Now, largely due to Laird's opposition—which meant opposition by the Laird-Norton family—he was far less confident of getting approval. The votes weren't yet in hand. Uncle F.E. informed Phil of the situation as he saw it. "If you are opposed," he contended, "the Weyerhaeuser Timber Company will not be a party to it and it will fail. If such is the case, then I think we would better give up our entire financing plan and get out of the whole installment selling business." That sort of assertion had become F.E.'s habit in recent years; there was little compromise left in him. Fortunately, however, it wasn't F.K.'s habit, nor would it ever be.

In fact, the result was a compromise and doubtless a wise one. It was agreed that they should organize a new financing corporation. But there were particulars still to be decided, some of which Laird Bell subsequently discussed with F.K. He noted, for example, that Laird's father, F. S. Bell, felt "the real test would come on the passing of credits, and that this should be done as a credit proposition and not as a sales promotion proposition." Indeed, the financing corporation would take shape as the Bells envisioned, both in terms of mission and organization. Officially named Allied Building Credits, Inc., it was to be entirely independent from the Sales Company, although all interested parties assumed that F.K. would be active in both. Laird, however, questioned such an additional involvement:

> I dislike more than I can say to see you saddled with another job. This financing job means more work than you could possibly save by any amalgamation of the service agencies. It seems to me that you are given all the mean jobs there are and that you ought to work to disentangle yourself from them. The Sales Company alone is a whole man job and I dread to see you further loaded down and driven. You have made a grand record with the job that you have tackled, but there must be a limit even to your patience and endurance.

So, circuitously, quietly, and in a manner unintended, F.K. accomplished almost everything he had hoped for in his "grandiose plan." Simply put, he became the "grand planner," president of Weyerhaeuser Sales Company, of General Timber Service, Inc., and of Allied Building Credits, Inc. At the same time, he willingly accepted the advice of others on most issues. The Weyerhaeuser organization would keep the Sales Com-

pany and the finance company separate, "except for the selection of dealers to whom the service is to be given," all the while preaching the gospel
regarding the advantages of installment buying.

As for the emphasis on credit, F.K. agreed that they owed it to their
own stockholders, and also to the banks whose funds they would use, to
provide the best possible management of the money loaned by the
finance company. Further, he planned to set up the corporation so as to
avoid "an unduly increased load for me or involve responsibilities for
which I am not competent," adding, "I fully realize my own limitations,
which are many." Withal, F.K. left no doubt of his satisfaction with the
progress that had been made. "I do sincerely feel that we have a big stake
in making this finance company a success and that it may materially sim-
plify our selling problem in years to come." Allied Building Credits, Inc.,
wouldn't disappoint, not in the short term anyway.

But not everything worked out as envisioned. It had become traditional for the Weyerhaeuser Sales Company to hold its general meetings
with personnel in January, which in recent years meant separate gatherings in the three zones, Eastern, Central, and Western. In the summer
of 1922, however, the Company had taken all its salesmen on a special
train to visit Cloquet and the western mills, to familiarize them with production aspects. F.K. recalled that trip with pride. "Nothing in the history of our Company ever contributed more to the improvement in the
morale of our men," or so he told the directors of GTS and the Sales
Company on December 16, 1936.

Now the time seemed appropriate for another such excursion. As F.K.
viewed the situation, they didn't need any more sales in the immediate
future. On the contrary, they faced the necessity of reducing orders if
they were to continue to give prompt service. So, all the elements seemed
to augur well for the trip. Salesmen on tour could not be selling; customers would understand that. As a result, they would achieve a healthy
reduction in business without having to explain their purpose.

The train would leave St. Paul on the night of January 4, visiting, in
turn, Cloquet, Coeur d'Alene, Potlatch, Lewiston, Klamath Falls,
Longview, Snoqualmie Falls, and Everett. The trip would conclude in
Tacoma, where meetings would be held on January 20.

The group departed on schedule, but almost immediately problems
developed. The train suffered various breakdowns, and the weather was

extremely cold. Further, many passengers suffered from the flu, with some twenty-five hospitalized at one time or another. F.K. caught the bug, too, but he managed to stay with the group. Conditions improved in Idaho, and by the time they reached Klamath Falls most in the party were back to normal. But by then the damage had been done, F.K. sadly reporting to Laird Bell that three had died, although only one death could be directly attributed to the trip itself. Despite the multitude of troubles, F.K. pronounced the excursion "a tremendous success," claiming it had done them all "a lot of good." In any event, no one proposed another such outing for years to come.

When F.K. had appeared before his sales groups at the Tacoma meetings, he apologized for reading his report, although in fact he always did so. In any case, his enthusiasm came through clearly. He began by reminding everyone that they had a much larger job than simply to sell lumber. They must also "properly express the ideals of the Company," and by that he meant not only the Sales Company but "our whole group." Then he spoke of objectives, those of the short term—turning "trees into the most money we can, in the most efficient and businesslike way we can"— as well as those of the longer term. They must always be working out ways to strengthen their "selling set-up." At the moment, this involved teaching their customers, the retailers, better merchandising: "Teach them the use of installment selling and make available to them our installment selling plan."

The second long-range objective he discussed dealt with improving the position of forest products in the marketplace. In the 1930s as today, finding substitutes for wood constituted a major concern in the lumber industry. Central to the competitive effort was lowering costs of labor by making construction easier, which was "part and parcel of our 4-SQUARE Plan and theory." And this was all related to the activities of Allied Building Credits, "whereby we have set up a standard of construction which we require if we are going to finance a house."

As I told some of the boys in the Western Zone last night, one of the reasons why we were so much interested in expanding and developing a finance plan for new construction was because we thought it gave us a chance to get our foot in the door of, "How is a house to be built," and have something to say about standards of construction to be employed and in the materials that are to be used.

His reasoning was rooted in an awareness that consumers were far more interested in the finished product than in the raw material. So, rather than discuss the technical aspects of lumber, salespeople should demonstrate how best to use it in the construction of farm buildings and small houses. First they developed a 4-SQUARE Farm Building Service, employing designs provided by experts at a number of agricultural colleges. This was followed by the 4-SQUARE Home Building Service, featuring plans submitted by noted architects. In both cases, the key was to use exact lengths and sizes in the construction, obviating the need for sawing.

But as 1937 wore on, little could be done to increase sales. The reversal seemed hard to believe. In December the worry had been overselling. Then, suddenly, there were few buyers. The next few months saw a return to recession, the term commonly used at the time. To many the term seemed a euphemism. F.K. and others had been extolling the benefits of installment buying, but credit opportunities couldn't assuage an alarming decrease in consumer confidence. He was already feeling the heat in early April, admitting in a letter to Laird Bell that they were "pretty much on the spot in so far as A.B.C. is concerned and feel that we have to put it over this year or else admit that we were wrong in the first place."

Inevitably, the return of hard times encouraged considerable finger-pointing. One of the first targets in the lumber industry was the tariff, specifically the Reciprocal Trade Agreements Act, which had taken effect January 1, 1936. Senator Charles L. McNary of Oregon, highly respected by most lumbermen, tackled the subject in an August 10, 1937, speech. He complained particularly about Canada's advantage within the British Empire. "It might well have been expected that the new reciprocity would work both ways," the senator observed. It hadn't. Canadian lumber had gained entry into the American market, but the agreement excluded "from any possible effect of its provisions all Canadian rights and benefits under British Empire trade pacts. The lumber industry of Canada may eat its cake and still have it." The trade figures seemed to support McNary's contention.

When confronted with questions not easily understood, such as the tariff, F.K., like brother Phil, commonly consulted Laird Bell. In this instance, F.K. sent Laird a copy of Senator McNary's speech. Laird responded quickly. He recalled a similar discussion little more than a year earlier with Phil. At that time, former chief forester Colonel Bill Greeley, now secretary for the West Coast Lumbermen's Association, had been arguing in favor of restricting Canadian forest-product exports to the United States. Laird disagreed then, and he disagreed now.

He began by noting one critical item that Senator McNary had failed to mention. "The extra tariff of $2.00 which Charles Dant, et al., succeeded in getting early in 1932, effectually excluded B.C. lumber from our market. This practically forced them to some line of action like the Empire preferential agreement. In other words, the situation is a beautiful illustration of what happens when we all get tariff minded. We exclude them from our market and they exclude us from other markets." Over the years, Laird thought, the lumber industry had fared pretty well without any tariff assistance. To prove his point, he claimed to have "repeatedly asked when the additional tax expired and nobody seemed to know surely, which seemed to me eloquent."

F.K. might agree in principle but not necessarily in practice. He likened Laird's position to that of the pacifist arguing against the maintenance of the military: "The first nation that does away with its army and navy is pretty apt to be scalped and the first nation that lowers its tariffs is apt to get hurt financially." In summarizing his position, he listed three essentials. First, he would support low tariffs, even to the point of free trade, "unless my country or my industry is discriminated against." Second, any time his industry was handicapped in its competition, he would expect his country to "protect me in the enjoyment of my natural domestic market." Third, free trade with undeveloped nations would inevitably affect the U.S. standard of living and was "inconsistent with artificial maintenance of high wages through unionization and legislation like the Wage and Hour Bill."

Laird would keep trying but to little purpose. He admitted that the answer to F.K.'s third point was "hard to express," even if it was something of a strawman. Sooner or later, nations had to trade. Japan was then a favorite example, "with their low labor costs." It might well be that the Japanese could put some American textile workers out of business by selling cheap cotton goods, but eventually they would also have to take in return, in payment, a product made in America, perhaps machinery.

So, while American textile workers might suffer in the short term, in the longer term American machinists might prosper; assuming gradual change, and allowing for adjustments, "That change would be all to the good." This wasn't the first time, nor would it be the last, that Laird Bell found himself almost alone in defending White House policies to his Weyerhaeuser associates.

Actually, F.K. appreciated Laird's 1937 efforts. "I would like to keep up the argument," he replied, "for the purpose of getting myself educated on the subject." Of greater immediate concern, however, was the declining market. He now expected to sell no more than three thousand carloads in October. Occasionally, however, he could look ahead with slight optimism. Specifically, he predicted "a gradual pick-up towards the middle or last of the year," consistent with economists' forecasts, which "probably means that it is not going to happen at all." In response, Laird offered encouraging words. While acknowledging that everybody was "talking blue," he reminded F.K. "that the crowd is almost always wrong, and I cannot believe that we are starting down a long hill."

F.K.'s pessimism increased as the year's end approached. He expected little in the way of "tangible results" from the Roosevelt administration's new tax laws and thought they might have to endure "the agony of liquidating some part of our labor costs before the machine will again begin to function." But as usual, Laird wasn't giving in to the blues, reasoning that expectations were simply a little too high. Ensconced in his Chicago office, he doubtless had studied the reports more carefully than most, and he found the figures downright encouraging.

That may have been overly optimistic, but it would become clear, when the dust had settled, that Laird's analysis was close to the mark. A good deal of their disappointment with the economy in 1937 had more to do with expectations than anything else. Sales for the calendar year 1936 set records for the Weyerhaeuser Sales Company. Shipments totaled 1,332,899,000 board feet, an increase of more than one-third over 1935. And aggregate sales for 1937 were 1,225,007,000 board feet, considerably below the estimates but only about 110,000,000 feet behind the 1936 totals.

Perhaps Sales Company general manager Harry Kendall offered the best assessment. He reminded F.K.—or more likely informed him—that the ancient goddess of business was Fortuna, often depicted holding a wheel, which some scholars claimed symbolized the business cycle. If true, then they should worry less about eliminating the business cycle than about how best to deal with the changes that were inherent in it. In that regard, recent events had certainly offered a challenge. "The year 1937," Kendall observed, "was a complete business cycle," beginning at a peak and then declining precipitously until the bottom was touched. Kendall and others assumed that they were on the way back up, but they would be disappointed. Markets failed to improve in 1938. Demand continued to slow, and prices fell. The Depression had taken a while to set in, and now it was taking a while, a long while, to abate.

How had Allied Building Credits, Inc., fared in its second full year of operation? Not well, at first glance. In the spring, F.K. had acknowledged he felt that he was on the spot, that unless ABC performed close to expectations in 1937, they might as well admit that they had been wrong about the wisdom of establishing it. When the figures were totaled, ABC counted losses of more than $150,000. But he knew, and several others understood, that this figure told only part of the story. Had the affiliated companies sold more lumber because of ABC? That was the critical question. Cousin Ed Davis was a firm supporter. After noting Uncle Rudolph's lack of enthusiasm, Ed observed to F.K. that ABC had "helped Wood Conversion Company sell some of its products and I feel we ought to do something to help you." Specifically, that meant voting to increase ABC's capital stock to $2 million, up from $1.275 million. In requesting that the operating companies subscribe to their shares, F.K. spoke with undisguised excitement about ABC's prospects. Thus he wrote to brother Phil, "It seems to me that this Company may grow to very large size and be not only a great help in the sale of our lumber but a good investment all by itself." He even wanted the Weyerhaeuser family to take the portion of the share that Potlatch Forests had declined.

Phil reluctantly agreed to Weyerhaeuser Timber Company participation, but he wasn't the least bit interested in any personal investment. He should have been: F.K.'s optimism would prove to be well placed.

THE DEPRESSION ENDS, FINALLY

FEW PEOPLE find the subject of selling lumber inherently fascinating. Lumber is one of those taken-for-granted, everyday commodities that are often assumed to sell themselves. That was as true in the late 1930s as it is today. It must have become tiresome for F.K. and his colleagues always to be justifying their efforts, or more precisely, justifying the overhead costs of selling. Ed Davis was sympathetic, at least to an extent. For example, when F.K. and his colleagues began promoting the 4-SQUARE Home Building Service—this in addition to the 4-SQUARE Farm Building Service—they doubtless heard a good many sighs in response. Ed predicted as much. "One of your chief difficulties," he warned F.K., "will be to have the 'small house' injected into discussions at various intervals. This subject reminds me of advertising—everybody knows all about it."

Well, they did and they didn't. Operators like Phil maintained that the crucial part of the process involved turning trees into lumber as efficiently as possible, while others, like F.K., faced the myriad problems and uncertainties of moving the product. It was anything but easy. Competitors were numberless, and, increasingly, the competition wasn't made up solely of those who dealt in lumber. Builders, then as now, had a variety of choices when it came to materials. So, beginning with advertising efforts in the years immediately following World War I, the Weyerhaeuser-affiliated operations searched for an advantage.

Early on they had decided to concentrate on retailers rather than wholesalers. That skipped one step in the process, but simply selling to a retailer did not solve the basic problem. As long as lumber remained in the retailer's inventory, little had been accomplished beyond moving it from mill to yard. The retailer would not reorder until he had sold his first shipment to the consumer, the builder. And it was upon these subsequent shipments—retail purchases—that the mills depended. The process wasn't a matter of a sale but of continuing sales, of creating a flow of products from mills to users.

Thus how to increase the flow out of the retail yards was not only of interest to the retailer but also of primary concern to the producer, in this instance to those who labored for the Weyerhaeuser Sales Company, beginning with F.K. Granted, overall demand for lumber depended on the economic health of localities and the times. Beyond that, however, there lay a challenge: Could Weyerhaeuser create a preference—first for wood and second for *its* wood? Clearly the advertising program in general and the two building services in particular assumed that was possible. By helping the retailer find prospective buyers, Weyerhaeuser was simply encouraging the flow and in the process establishing long-term relationships.

Part and parcel of that process was the facilitating of installment buying, which is why F.K. had envisioned a single agency encompassing advertising, sales, and financing. While that hadn't yet been achieved in an organizational sense, the fact that he oversaw each of the efforts ensured coordination.

Title I of the National Housing Act expired in March 1937, at which time Allied Building Credits, Inc., announced its own independent Installment Note Plan. Borrowing from four banks—the New York Trust Company, Continental Illinois, the First National of St. Paul, and the First National of Seattle—ABC offered loans at a lower rate and for longer terms than most others in the field, and the early response suggested that this approach was not only popular but fiscally sound as well. Although, as noted in the preceding chapter, ABC's net loss for 1937 exceeded $150,000, F.K. could hardly have been more enthusiastic regarding the future.

Accordingly, he had written to brother Phil soliciting his support for the family's assumption of that portion of ABC's increased subscription that Potlatch Forests had declined. "Personally," he wrote, "I look upon this Company [ABC] as a very attractive field for investment and would be glad to see the members of our family, either in Bonners Ferry, in the various trusts, or as individuals, take the whole amount." He sent copies of the letter to uncles F.E. and Rudolph and other relatives, in hopes of gaining their support as well. But interest was tepid at best; had F.K. looked over his shoulder he would have found few followers.

While reluctantly committing the Weyerhaeuser Timber Company to its portion of the new subscription, Phil observed that with "so many doubtful things on the horizon I would prefer to put no more money into stock than was necessary to provide the tools for the immediate job." Rudolph, still serving as president of Potlatch Forests, Inc., felt a bit guilty about his company's begging off its share of ABC's increased capitalization. Accordingly, he took seriously F.K.'s suggestion that family members consider purchasing the available shares, the difference. In this he received no encouragement whatsoever from John Musser, officially secretary-treasurer for ABC. Musser and F.K. normally marched in step, but not this time. In his reply to Rudolph, Musser emphasized the importance of the operating mills being ABC's only shareholders. "The interests of the mills and of A.B.C., Inc. are identical," he noted, that of assisting the Weyerhaeuser Sales Company to sell more lumber over a continuous period. Now, were they to permit individuals to purchase ABC stock, it was "conceivable that the stock might fall into the hands of an individual who had no interest at all in any of the mills." He would naturally consider his purchase solely as an investment. Inevitably that would result in a change of policy, ABC being run as a finance company, with less consideration given to providing "the maximum service possible to builder, contractor, dealer, and, especially, to the mills." And so the debate continued.

This wouldn't be a fight to the finish, as far as F.K. was concerned. He had admitted that he was somewhat inclined to get overly optimistic in matters such as this, while still contending that "it seems to me like an excellent investment if we can assure ourselves of good management and are not too impatient."

F.K.'s proposal regarding possible purchase of ABC stock by Weyerhaeusers reflected concerns he had been harboring for some time. Earlier, prior to a family meeting in mid-September, he had shared some of his thoughts with F.E. The uncle may not have entirely appreciated his nephew's unsolicited advice, but he got it anyway. The first item on F.K.'s "agenda" was the handling of individuals' investments and the various family trusts. He also hoped they would discuss the effects of recent legislation affecting the trusts and their new holding company, The Bonners Ferry Company. Further, he wished to encourage greater participation "in determining the policies of the companies in which they are interested." What may have bothered F.E. most, however, was F.K.'s final suggestion, that family meetings should "be devoted to the more important matters . . . and that the discussions be held close to the point so that no time will be wasted."

Family meetings were important, no doubt about that, but suddenly they seemed less so. At long last, Walter and Peggy Driscoll had taken a lengthy vacation, sailing to South America on what would prove to be a fateful journey. Walter died in Brazil on January 30, 1938, leaving two young sons, Walter John and Rudolph.

Before Walter's death, F.K. had been wrestling with lesser family problems and not just agendas. First, he wished to do as he preached, provide business opportunities for younger cousins, starting with F.E.'s son Fred. Second, F.K. hoped to resolve a frustrating office matter involving an old friend and colleague, George F. Lindsay. George was the son of James E. Lindsay, partner in Lindsay & Phelps, a Davenport, Iowa, lumber firm. The Lindsays had been longtime associates of Frederick, and George subsequently formed a close friendship with F.E. and Rudolph. Now, however, it seemed to F.K. that George was causing unnecessary problems. F.K.'s suggestions were, first, that Fred replace Lindsay on the General Timber Service board, "although it might hurt Mr. Lindsay's feelings," and second, that they get Lindsay moved out of the family office, arranging for "a nice office somewhere else that the family as a whole would pay for." What most irritated F.K. was a recent news report to the effect that "Mr. George F. Lindsay, a Weyerhaeuser executive, has been to Washington conferring with different departments of the Government on the subject of his survey of the Small House Building problem." F.K. had been asked about the survey, "and to be perfectly frank we have been very much puzzled as to how to reply." In short, Lindsay was an embarrassment, and F.K. now asked F.E. for permission to act.

The response was interesting. F.E. was in an excusing mood, observing that George had meant no harm, that he simply didn't understand the procedures necessary in a large organization. While F.K. had every right to be annoyed, F.E. conceded, loyalties had to be respected. He knew that his nephew understood; F.K. was always tactful. Thus the uncle took a benign approach, suggesting that perhaps F.K. was irritable because he was tired and in "need of a long rest. This truly is more important than trying to hold George in leash."

F.E. doubtless knew that plans for a month's vacation in Daytona Beach were already being made. F.K. subsequently claimed to have had a "nice rest" there. He also landed a "tremendous tarpon," an event, he informed brother Phil, that would provide "quite a story!"

Phil would hear the story told in person; F.K. was heading to Tacoma, soon to be his brother's houseguest. But, as usual, pleasure wasn't allowed to interfere with business:

> I am planning to go West with Horace Irvine and Nesbit Tate, via the Great Northern, arriving in Tacoma about 9:30 Monday morning [April 25]. Will check my bags at the station and go up to the office to attend the Public Relations Committee meeting of G.T.S., which I hope you will also find time for. The Sales Company meeting comes on Tuesday and after that the week will be pretty much in the clear, except that we want to meet Leonard Hammond and his crowd in San Francisco the following Monday and Tuesday, after which I have to skip home as fast as possible in order to be here on the 6th and 7th for a mass meeting on the subject of our mortage business [ABC, Inc.]. Then we have the Pine Tree [Lumber Company] meeting on the 10th and The Northwest Paper Company meeting on the 11th.

The reference to a Public Relations Committee meeting deserves comment. This department had been organized a year earlier, in the spring of 1937, with three main initial purposes: first, to keep current with the activities of various relevant national and regional organizations and associations, such as the National Lumber Manufacturers Association, the American Forest Products Industries (whose ostensible goal was to improve forestry practices), the National Association of Manufacturers, the U.S. Chamber of Commerce, and legislative and governmental agencies; second, through its chairman, I. N. Tate, to determine "policies and programs affecting public relations"; and third, to serve as a "coordinating agency for such matters for our group." For GTS, public relations would become a vital concern.

A major disappointment simmered, involving research conducted under the GTS umbrella. In August 1938 F.K. attended a Longview, Washington, meeting with Phil and others from the Timber Company along with C. L. "Bill" Billings of Potlatch, at which he declared that "considerable headway was made in organizing our Research work for the future." Maybe so, but subsequent "headway" didn't come easily.

F.E.'s son Fred assumed the chairmanship of GTS's new Research Committee; its members, besides F.K., were Ed Davis (representing the Wood Conversion Company), Bill Billings (Potlatch Forests, Inc.), Stuart Copeland (Northwest Paper Company), and Robert Bunson Wolf (the Weyerhaeuser Timber Company's manager of pulp operations). Also serving were Clark Heritage, director of research for Wood Conversion; Ray Hatch, director of research for the Weyerhaeuser Timber Company; Neil MacKenzie, director of research for the Weyerhaeuser Sales Company; and Sales Company general manager Harry Kendall. One might well infer what soon would become a real problem: too many cooks in the kitchen.

At an early meeting, Fred described four lines of scientific work, three of which fell into the category of research. The first was fundamental, or what some would call pure research, "without particular regard to its economic value." The second was new product development. The third was research aimed at improving products already being manufactured. And the fourth was "Manufacturing Process Control." F.K. explained his reasons for supporting a general research effort, noting that in twenty-five years the highest return the Weyerhaeuser Timber Company "had realized in any one year was 5% of the value of its capital investments." This suggested a dire need for a research program whose major objective was increasing the value of products "manufactured out of each acre of productive woodland."

F.K., with the assistance of Neil MacKenzie, soon offered specific recommendations for projects "aimed at the development of improved lumber products and improved application of those products." Initially these numbered twelve and included subjects such as better utilization of log-grade dimension, plywood, laminated roof structures, and simplified design for houses. But with so many individuals involved, who should be doing what? F.K. wasn't certain, although he had given the question some thought. They already ran a small laboratory in St. Paul, sufficient to study a few projects. Others would be contracted elsewhere, some at the Forest Products Laboratory in Madison, Wisconsin, and some at Iowa State College in Ames. Because of the availability of materials, plywood research would logically be the province of the Longview research lab, and the work of fabricating wide boards by gluing narrow boards together would "no doubt best be handled at Lewiston [Idaho]."

Foreseeing a research budget of between $25,000 and $35,000, F.K. indicated that he would seek the larger amount "and then spend money carefully, only so long as the particular project appears worth while." He initially requested $35,000, also recommending that MacKenzie, then with the Merchandising Department of Weyerhaeuser Sales Company, assume an overall research-management responsibility, with research activities "entirely divorced from the Merchandising Department or from any other present activity."

Difficulties surfaced almost immediately. To begin with, although MacKenzie was a logical choice to head the effort, there seemed no one available to replace him in the Merchandising Department. But that was a minor problem. Indeed, F.K. would resolve it simply by eliminating the Merchandising Department of the Sales Company and creating a new section, the Engineering/Research Department of General Timber Service, Inc., with Fred Weyerhaeuser in overall charge and MacKenzie as director of research.

A more basic and long-lasting problem was the absence of focus and general enthusiasm. To say that the research program floundered would be an understatement. For example, one of the early potential projects was development of a wood-fireproofing process; immediately, some questioned whether there was a demand for fireproofed wood. Thus the committee recommended that they merely initiate a market-research project, a feasibility study as it were. The research would have to wait. Projects that involved gluing were high on the list, beginning with plywood. Here F.K. was and would continue to be a champion, but brother Phil expressed little interest. And when F.K. suggested that Potlatch undertake plywood research, "the general reaction was that if the Weyerhaeuser Timber Company did not think it advisable to manufacture plywood on the Coast, why would Potlatch Forests, Inc., consider it." And so it went.

Everything depended on one's point of view. Where Phil envisioned the need to concentrate on familiar tasks, improving forestry practices and logging, and sawmilling efficiencies, F.K. scanned the horizon for new marketing opportunities. The same was true of Sales Company general manager Harry Kendall. He was as enthusiastic about the possibilities of research as F.K. When Kendall looked back at 1938, he regarded the commencement of the research program as "the most important event." The "long anticipated general building boom" had not developed, and they had been left with the question of what to do. The answer was "easy to find: 'Substitute boards,' plywoods, and hard materials, which during depression years had been vastly improved, [and] were taking an increasing share of lumber's market."

If Kendall and F.K. were disappointed in the early results of the research program, they had to be slightly encouraged by the performance of Allied Building Credits, Inc., this in spite of continued hard times. As noted, the recession that laid them low in 1937 refused to go away. In fact, total lumber sales for the period declined slightly, from 1,225,000,000 feet in 1937 to 1,176,614,000 feet in 1938. But surprisingly, ABC enjoyed a profit in 1938. Granted, it was a small profit—not quite $37,000—but that was surely an improvement over the previous year's loss of more than $150,000. In retrospect, F.K. considered 1938 a fortunate year "because it enabled a new company, offering a new type of financing, to learn from its own experience what effect a business depression would have on its volume delinquencies and credit losses." In short, they were learning with their feet to the fire.

One thing was certain. F.K. had put together a competent and efficient organization, in his words "possessing the experience, skill and personality required and one which is capable of expanding to whatever extent future conditions may require." They were not only eager for better times, but they were also advantageously situated. And better times were at hand. In 1939 Weyerhaeuser Sales Company shipments totaled 1,476,936,000 feet, an increase of nearly 20 percent over the previous year. The corner was finally turned.

WORRIES NEAR
AND FAR

LITTLE BY LITTLE, F.K. had been assuming more responsibility. In the business arena, his increasing presence was nothing new; it had been developing over two decades. But in a family sense it was. He celebrated his forty-fifth birthday in 1940. His two daughters would soon be teenagers, and others in the extended family looked up to him much as he had looked up to F.E., and F.E. to father Frederick. F.K. not only understood his role; he accepted it cheerfully. But the torch wasn't easily passed.

The previous summer, he had taken pains to arrange an outing for nineteen family members on northwestern Wisconsin's beautiful Brule River, coincident with a July 8 family meeting in St. Paul. They would leave St. Paul en masse early Saturday morning, driving to Cloquet, where they would spend the night. "It is hoped," F. K. wrote, "that Mesdames Davis and Driscoll will allot sleeping accommodations on porch swings, dining tables, or any other flat spots available." The next day they would proceed to Lake Nebagamon and eventually on to Stone's Landing, a site familiar to many canoeing enthusiasts, and he advised that "all survivors should be washed ashore at Winneboujou between 5:00 and 6:00 o'clock in the evening." It was a grand event for the participants, eleven adults and eight children, a fine installment in the continuing effort to maintain family esprit de corps.

Distant events began to intrude, however, as Germany and Japan precipitated troubling incidents. "The threatening of a European war has everybody jittery," F.K. observed in an April 1939 letter to Phil. "Most of the wise people still think there will be no war," he continued, "but I doubt whether their guess is better than anybody else's." He hoped that things would settle down so that business, which was "just fair," might be given the chance to enjoy "a very fast pick-up." The undeniable truth, however, was that war preparations provided just the sort of economic stimulus that had been missing. What New Deal legislation failed to accomplish in terms of fiscal recovery no longer mattered. Just as the forest-products industry had suffered along with everybody else during the Depression, so would they all prosper as the populations armed themselves. It was a sad state of affairs, and it only got sadder. On September 1, 1939, German troops invaded Poland. Despite the predictions of F.K.'s "wise people," World War II was a fact, though Americans were not yet on the battlefields.

In January 1940, F.K. had his usual series of meetings across the country, ending in Tacoma. And in mid-February he was preparing to leave the Minnesota winter behind, heading for Jupiter Island on Florida's Hobe Sound for what he hoped would be a month's vacation, "unless something comes up that makes my return necessary." Over the years, Hobe Sound would become a home away from home, the favorite getaway. In this instance, F.K.'s vacation plans were disrupted less by business than by the flu bug. He was laid low and spent some ten days on his back while Vivian and the girls enjoyed the sun and sea. Uncle Rudolph surmised that F.K. brought it on himself. "You had a pretty strenuous six weeks before going to Florida and am not surprised that you ran up against difficulties."

F.K. soon recovered and didn't return to St. Paul until April 1. All in all, he reported to F.E., the vacation had been "very enjoyable," claiming he had "never felt better." F.E. welcomed the news while expressing concern about his nephew trying to do too much. After noting the obvious—"The number of men in our family is small and we have a big business to manage"—he added, "Don't think that I am trying to tell you what to do." As for business, F.E. took the usual dim view, worrying about "what tomorrow will bring forth in the New Deal."

Actually the 1939 reports were encouraging, Harry Kendall announcing record shipments by the Sales Company mills coupled with "the lowest cost per M feet since the Company broadened its activities in 1934." Prices were not quite up to expectations, but there was no cause for complaint. Still F.K. worried along with F.E., mostly about the future. When he spoke of the future, increasingly it had to do with perceived threats to capitalism.

In this regard, F.K. was quite the opposite of brother Phil. He was the activist while Phil, for whatever reason—maybe metabolism—was willing to accept things as they came. A case in point was F.K.'s July 5 memo "To my Associates" in ABC, GTS, and the Weyerhaeuser Sales Company. "I am sending you the attached reprint from the *Omaha World-Herald,* of June 14, 1940, because I believe it states the basic problem of our country at this time." The article was entitled "When France Awoke," and it quoted excerpts from a report written by Édouard Daladier and Paul Reynaud, the former and present French prime ministers, respectively, in November 1938, when France officially recognized the dangers of Nazi Germany. The gist of the report was that the French found themselves in peril because "of the continuous deterioration of economic activity" in their country. At the base of the problem was a deterioration of the capitalistic system:

> In every field where activity might be reborn enterprise has been restricted and discouraged. The creative spirit and the willingness to take risks have been weakened. This—let us not fear to say it!— is the root of the evil, for it adds a sort of moral abdication to the material difficulties. . . . The state must do its utmost to restore the doctrine of risk and profit as well as that of work and output.

Whatever the merits of Daladier and Reynaud's assessment, their words had no effect on the outcome. The Sitzkrieg, or Phony War, ended on May 10, 1940, with the German invasion of the Low Countries. The *Omaha World-Herald* reprinted the report excerpt a month later, on the very day German troops marched into Paris. The French were in a desperate position, pleading for American intervention.

France would fall before the end of July, but America did not hurry to respond. President Roosevelt bombarded Congress with requests for an increase in the military budget. Finally, on July 19, he signed the Naval Expansion Act, which, on paper, would increase tonnage by 70 percent. But the legislation that truly focused everyone's attention was the September 16 passage of the Selective Training and Service Act, the first peacetime conscription in U.S. history. This required registration of all men between the ages of twenty-one and thirty-five and the drafting of 1,200,000 for twelve months' training. Immediately, managers like F.K. had to deal with an entirely new problem, developing a policy for employees who were drafted or who enlisted. He recommended that the company agree to pay life-insurance premiums for up to one full year for those who entered military service in 1940. Also, in accordance with the new law, they would reemploy those who returned from military service. Beyond that, F.K. allowed that each Weyerhaeuser company could "exercise its own prerogative of making special arrangements," although this flexibility was not to be announced.

Suddenly, the conducting of business was incredibly complicated and promised to become even more so. What businessmen dislike above all is uncertainty, and surely uncertainty characterized the world in the fall of 1940. Some subjects could be addressed directly, and F.K. did so in terms of Sales Company management. In a mid-October memo to the salesmen, he noted the growing complexity of affairs. "The problem of keeping in close touch with the many and varied activities is, in fact, becoming impossible." He cited examples: "Price and stock control, setting of financial and sales budgets, merchandising, sales promotion, advertising, finances, credit and accounting, direction of sales functions, mill contacts, distributing yard operations, market studies, policies and contacts with affiliates, et cetera." General Manager Kendall needed help. Accordingly, Luther H. Atkinson was appointed director of marketing, effective October 12.

While F.K. could appoint his company's director of marketing, he couldn't elect his country's president. Wendell Willkie had inspired enthusiasm among the Weyerhaeusers as he did among Republicans across America. In an optimistic spirit, F.K. addressed a letter to "Dear Fellow Citizen"—to employees, colleagues, and friends—reminding them of the importance of voting. "It is absolutely essential that you and every member of your household, of voting age, go to the polls and vote his or her honest convictions on Election Day, Tuesday, November 5th." But Willkie proved no match for "the Champ." It didn't matter that a third term was unprecedented.

F.K. was disgusted. Would there be no end to FDR's reign? Within a week, F.K. proposed initiating monthly or semimonthly meetings of all employees of the various St. Paul operations, "including F. Weyerhaeuser Company, Weyerhaeuser Sales Company, General Timber Service, Inc., Allied Building Credits, Inc., Wood Conversion Company, Thompson Yards, Inc., office employees of Twin City Branch, and any others I may have forgotten." The new auditorium at the *St. Paul Dispatch and Pioneer Press* was available free of charge. They would meet during the noon hour, with attendance voluntary. As for the subjects to be discussed, F.K. confessed his motivation: "The late national election has taught me one lesson if no other, namely, that the majority of the American people have no adequate understanding of the laws of economics or finance. The only way of avoiding an eventual national collapse is through the process of education, which, I believe, every business should start immediately." True to his word, he called the first meeting for December 1, promising regular meetings thereafter, if they were found to be "interesting and worthwhile." One could have foreseen the results, and had he been consulted, Laird Bell would have correctly predicted the outcome. F.K.'s view of the world was not universally shared, not even within his own organizations. And, in the end, politics were rightfully one's own business.

But failure on one front didn't mean inaction on others. Heading F.K.'s list of things to do was the mounting of an intensified public relations effort on behalf of the entire lumber industry. While many had recognized the need for such an effort, the issue was specifically raised by the National Lumber Manufacturers Association (NLMA). Its directors had met in November 1940 and appointed a committee of four—R. C. Winton, Leonard Carpenter, Corydon Wagner, and F.K.—to study the possibility of organizing a public relations program and to make recommendations to the NLMA board. Those recommendations were initially rather vague, largely because not enough was known about the subject. It was decided to survey public opinion in order to determine just "what the public thinks about the lumber industry, its practices and policies and about U.S. forest resources and problems." Then in February, F.K. met with Phil and Roderic Olzendam, the Weyerhaeuser Timber Company's public relations expert, and they agreed on several points. The most important was "a tremendous need for a substantial program to improve the public relations of the lumber industry," allowing that such a program would cost a lot of money, some $250,000 over three years, and that the Weyerhaeuser companies should be prepared to finance one-third of the total.

Progress was slow, but F.K. kept stressing "the contribution which the lumber industry is making towards the defense program," along with the eternal themes concerning the future supply of forest products. He hoped for a "thorough discussion" at the annual meeting of the Weyerhaeuser Timber Company in late May. If F.K.'s public relations effort lagged, however, everything else the world over seemed to be happening at once. Lend Lease was now the law of the land, and American ships had begun escorting Allied convoys in the North Atlantic. On June 22, Germany launched the biggest invasion in history, attacking the Russians along a front stretching nearly two thousand miles. Meanwhile, war raged across the deserts of North Africa. Responding to British requirements there, the Weyerhaeuser Steamship Company ships became directly involved in the summer of 1941, transporting supplies via the Red Sea.

It must have been hard to concentrate on matters close to home, but F.K. had no choice. His cousin Fred was creating problems that could not be ignored. Fred was still ostensibly in charge of the research program, and it was here that his expectations exceeded reality. Although no problems were welcome, those involving family members were clearly the most difficult.

Fred circulated a memorandum dated June 28 that detailed his thinking on the future of the Engineering/Research Department program. Initially, F.K. indicated little sympathy with Fred's complaints. In a July 2 letter he never sent, F.K. noted Fred's contention that certain "bottlenecks" existed that frustrated the overall effort. While acknowledging that he wasn't sure "just what is in your mind," F.K. proceeded to state some "obvious" facts. For the most part these dealt with commitment to the program at every level, including the shareholders, who were willing to support "a research program just as large as can be justified." F.K. also reminded his cousin that he had urged him to study other research facilities and to use their experience in considering ways to expand "our own research program." Had Fred visited the Forest Products Research Laboratory in Madison? And how recently had he toured the western mills? Wasn't Fred depending entirely too much on Neil MacKenzie? "Does this give you a chance to have a broad enough personal understanding of our research program in all its aspects?"

In short, F.K.'s reaction was akin to "Heal thyself," asserting that the bottlenecks were simply "mental hazards which you and Neil have created in your own minds." Stop complaining, and get to work. "It seems to me that it is now up to the Research Department to show whether or not it can justify itself. If it can not, I think we have the wrong men in it." The message was abundantly clear, but, as noted, the letter was never sent.

Ed Davis's response to Fred's memo was considerably milder, sent to F.K., not Fred. Ed cited two missing links. First, Fred had inquired, "What are we shooting at?" That answer, Davis contended, should be coming from the field, taking into account deficiencies in finished products or need for new products. If the salesmen were unable to provide that sort of information, they should hire some sales engineers. The second missing link concerned Fred's last step, "commercialization," a misplaced worry. Fred should "go on the assumption [that] if he develops something good, that something will be done about it."

By mid-August, F.K. had reflected sufficiently on the problem and so offered his "carefully considered conclusions" in a letter to Fred. Despite the expectation that the Weyerhaeuser Sales Company would sell some $60 million in 1941, their research efforts had been "pitifully small and insignificant, particularly in the face of the losses of markets which lumber has sustained in every direction during the last thirty years." He then listed recommendations for improving their program. They needed a positive approach; and they all had to recognize "that some money will be spent on projects which will not bear fruit." Of course. The next item, however, would rankle Fred. F.K. recommended that they hire a new director of research, replacing MacKenzie. "The first step to setting up and carrying out this program would be finding an individual having a background of training and experience, plus the necessary executive qualifications, for successfully carrying on the activity under your direction."

Fred's rambling reply filled six single-spaced pages, and F.K.'s notations provide an indication of his impatience. He wasn't satisfied, and Fred offered little in response. In short, the cousins seemed to be at an impasse. Thus F.K. carefully prepared a memorandum to F.E., Fred, Ed Davis, and Walter S. Rosenberry, Jr., "To be presented at conference in F. Weyerhaeuser Office on August 26, 1941." First, he noted that in June "a difference of opinion has arisen between Fred and Neil MacKenzie on the one hand, and Luther Atkinson and myself on the other" concerning the Engineering-Research Department of General Timber Service, Inc.

Given the circumstances, it appeared necessary to have "a fair and friendly discussion of the whole matter"; F.K. trusted that they could debate the questions "on a purely business basis." He then provided a history of the matter:

> It has been my feeling for many years that the Weyerhaeuser group of Companies needed almost beyond any other one thing, a substantial and well-directed research program aimed at the development of improved forest products and better utilization of mill and forest waste, the final objective being the greatest possible efficiency in the utilization of forest crops. The magnitude and importance of this job seemed to me to justify the expenditure of time and effort by a member of our family. Consequently, I have felt for at least six years, and feel today, that the development of a comprehensive research program is a job which Fred might well find worth his utmost efforts.

But why call a family gathering, especially if the questions were to be resolved "on a purely business basis"? F.K. explained, "I feel that our family should first consider a matter of this importance so that we may stand together." Above all, he wanted the research program to succeed under Fred's leadership, but he also believed that "the activity will not be a credit to him nor a profit to the Company unless certain changes are made." In the end, however, he would do as his family directed. "My uncles have always been fine to me in every way so that the least that can be expected of me is to do as well by my cousins when the opportunity comes." It wasn't easy.

The list of deficiences was long. F.K. noted "undue concern" with those "bottlenecks," the lack of a technically trained director (MacKenzie was "not a trained engineer nor has he had any previous research and laboratory experience"), and the many resultant weaknesses, such as "a failure to visualize all the possibilities for the solution of a problem and to organize the scientific approach to such solutions." Then there were general inefficiencies, from "a lack of resourcefulness and imagination" to an absence of completion dates and progress reports.

The discussion took place as scheduled, but nobody left happy. Still, perhaps the air was cleared. In a subsequent confidential memo to Fred, F.K. detailed their "tentative understanding." He began with what should have been unnecessary: "As Executive Vice President of General Timber Service, Inc., you are responsible to me for the direction and supervision of all departments, and I, as President, am responsible to the Board of Directors." In order to resolve that inherent problem of too many cooks (the correlation of the GTS Engineering/Research program with that of the general Weyerhaeuser group), F.K. proposed a committee consisting of himself, Fred, Phil, and Ed Davis, who would ensure that there was "no overlapping of work done in different places and that all desirable fields for investigation are being covered." Fred was also directed to develop a list of possible projects; those approved would be undertaken. In addition, the director of research would also submit a project report every two months for review by the committee.

That committee would also consider market studies conducted by the Weyerhaeuser Sales Company, F.K. promising that he would personally serve as "contact man" between the Sales Company and Engineering/Research. For the moment, he gave up on his effort to replace MacKenzie. "It is my sincere hope," F.K. concluded, "that the present personnel in the department will prove adequate and competent to carry on the work successfully." And so it stood, for a time at least, notwithstanding his skepticism.

F.E. and Rudolph visited Tacoma in late summer, updating Phil on recent St. Paul developments. In Phil's words, "F.E. indicated, without rancor, that he felt his son Fred had been slighted in something which went on in St. Paul with regard to his research program." Phil sympathized with F.K. "in your problem," also expressing frustration of a similar sort, "being unable to get down to brass tacks with Ed Davis" on a research program. At this point, Phil was hoping that Ed's Wood Conversion Company would merge with the Weyerhaeuser Timber Company, thereby combining their research efforts. That, however, was not just premature. It would never happen. In this instance, F.E. was a supporter, and he even went so far as to suggest that it might be a good idea to move the GTS program out west, too. "I don't have much idea about that," Phil added, "but thought I would repeat it to you because it might offer an out if you feel that progress under the present setup has been too slow."

In his response, F.K. allowed that there had been "considerable discussions" about the management of the research activities, admitting that he had likely offended both F.E. and Fred. "This was, of course, not my intention," and he still hoped "some good may come out of it all before we are thru," adding, "I would be sorry to have Fred sever his connection with the Engineering-Research work because that is the one phase of the affiliated activity that interests him enormously." Their only substantial difference involved management, "the type of talent in immediate charge of the laboratory work."

Fred's responsibilities in research had seemed important, but clearly they were not vital in the total scheme of things. F.K. could legitimately worry about family and greater utilization of trees and the future of the overall industry, but all that paled before world events. The traditional Christmas letter from famed German forester Dr. Carl Schenck underscored that fact. Writing on the last day of November, Schenck observed, "Christmas! We shall not have much of a celebration in Lindenfels because it is impossible to think any thought which isn't paralleled by that of war." A week later, Pearl Harbor.

WAR ONCE MORE

FOR MANY Americans, including Vivian, the war effort was under way long before the Japanese attack on December 7. Notwithstanding Willkie's 1940 defeat, Republicans the country over enthusiastically registered their support, Vivian prominent among them. She managed an eighteen-state Republican women's organization, and her disappointment in the election results didn't diminish her zeal. In the spring of 1941, she decided to be actively involved once more, not in politics per se, but in the American Red Cross. Vivian volunteered her services to the St. Paul chapter, immediately finding herself chairman of public relations and thereafter vice-chairman of the chapter. It was no small job; the chapter quickly grew to some twenty thousand workers. And they were doing real work, running a blood-donor center, hosting the canteen, and many other important home-front activities.

F.K. was proud of his wife. He probably didn't even take exception to a piece in a St. Paul paper suggesting that the Red Cross could use Vivian "advantageously as its poster girl," the columnist adding, "I don't know anyone quite so attractive in uniform." As for F.K., he was busier than ever, implementing fundamental changes within the Sales Company. He had determined that it needed to increase its working capital by $300,000, and a new contract had been prepared by Gus Clapp that would allow "a fair return upon its operations and should permit to holders of its stock a fair return upon their investment." The additional capital would be raised in proportion to stock ownership, from the 33 shares owned by the Northwest Paper Company to the 333 of Weyerhaeuser Timber Company, with assessments ranging from Northwest's $9,900 to Weyerhaeuser's $99,900. The change was authorized on December 16.

Thus 1942 would be the first year in which the Weyerhaeuser Sales Company purchased all the lumber and wood products produced by the contracting companies. That purchase price, fixed by the contract, permitted a gross profit to the Sales Company "equal to the sum of the operating expenses, cash discounts allowed, sales allowances, bad debts, etc., allocable to contract operations, plus 5% of said operating expenses." For the year, the net profit amounted to some $97,000, or 0.108 percent of sales, after providing $211,437.96 for income and excess-profits taxes. In 1943 net profits increased to $143,000, largely because excess-profits taxes were eliminated by investing capital for tax-credit purposes.

Federal taxes were among the chief factors to be adjusted to in doing business during wartime. In his March 31, 1942, report Sales Company general manager Kendall, reflecting on the recent past, observed that the company had altered its "carefully laid plans overnight to meet new conditions." Indeed, the previous year had been one that lumbermen would not forget. The same proved true of 1942, a year Kendall would describe as "the most unusual and perplexing in the industry's history." And it wasn't the Sales Company personnel who deserved credit, for selling was no problem. Credit belonged to the mills. What would be known as the "miracle of production" wasn't limited to the arms and machines of war. Farmers and laborers of all sorts, including lumber workers, contributed mightily. Throughout, one of F.K.'s concerns was that they seek new ways to help in the war production effort. "With or without the assistance of representatives of the government," he advised cousin Fred, "we should aggressively contact fabricators, particularly during the industrial flux of this war period and suggest to them articles which they might profitably manufacture of wood that will take the place of critical materials needed for war purposes."

Most people take wood for granted—until a shortage develops. And so it was as the war commenced. But soon the importance of wood was recognized, and fears regarding shortages were expressed, especially by those unfamiliar with the facts. It was estimated that nearly five billion board feet of lumber would be required in 1943 to substitute for critical metals. How much is five billion feet? Bill Billings, general manager of Potlatch Forests, Inc., tried to give some idea in a talk before the Lewiston, Idaho, Chamber of Commerce. The giant Clearwater plant, which they knew as a neighbor, could produce only one-twentieth of that amount in a year, working two shifts. Billings began to list examples of the wartime need for wood products:

> As boards and timbers, wood is being used to fashion torpedo boats, barracks, landing barges, bridges, wharves, mine props, scaffolding, concrete forms, assault boats, ship interiors, truck bodies, Army lockers, Army cots and stretchers, bunks for Army and Navy alike, pontoons, anti-tank barriers, interior lining of tanks, charcoal for gas masks and production of high grade steels, wood wool spun from Redwood bark, airplane propellers.

And there was more, much more. The Herculean task was made all the more difficult by a declining labor force, as men left forests and mills for military service. In the face of the challenge, Billings and his colleagues were angered by continued talk of a lumber shortage. As he put it, "To say there is a shortage of lumber is about as helpful as saying that Custer was short of soldiers on the Little Big Horn." If there was a shortage, it was because of unprecedented demand.

None felt the pressure more than F.K. and Sales Company personnel. Luther Atkinson, Kendall's new assistant, brought enthusiasm to his responsibility as well as some definite ideas, many of which focused on the familiar research disappointments. He communicated directly with Fred Weyerhaeuser, recommending ways in which they could develop "a better, more clean cut and effective working basis" between Fred's group and the Sales Company. The principal suggestion was that they "wipe the slate clean and start from scratch." Further, Fred was advised to expect that mistakes would be made but also to realize that these were simply "the result of good intentions to get the job done."

To a degree, F.K. appreciated aspects of the changing circumstances, particularly as they seemed to encourage a greater emphasis on research. That, however, rekindled old frustrations. On March 4, F.K. called Phil's attention to an article in that month's *Fortune* magazine that discussed, among other matters, the possible use of plywood in airplane manufacture. That prompted F.K. to wonder whether the Weyerhaeuser Timber Company might hire an engineer specifically to work with companies that were "adapting wood to their purposes." He also noted Standard Oil of California as being "tremendously interested in devising oil containers" possibly made of wood.

Phil's response to his brother's "March 4 bombardment" was anything but encouraging. He could well imagine that many industries would "welcome assistance in seeking substitute materials," especially materials as cheap as lumber, but wouldn't they be "splattering [their] shot pretty widely" if they were to undertake very much, "especially for such things as oil drums or the myriad things which we can all think of which would involve technical processes entirely outside of our sphere?"

And the differences continued. F.K. later suggested that they consider the possibilty of building wooden ships, and Phil again shook his head. Wooden ships or wooden planes, it was all the same. Phil watched helplessly as men left the woods and mills in droves. "Our work force is daily being depleted," he reminded his brother, "and we know there are shipyards already built in the territory to take additional ten thousands of men—many away from us." His immediate problem was to produce needed lumber with the available workers.

Another proposal from St. Paul rankled. Over the phone, F.K. recommended that they might begin purchasing retail lumber stocks on behalf of the government, "using our money and retaining 2% for the service." Again, Phil wasn't interested, at least not initially. "If help is needed to locate the retailers and the stocks," he countered, "give the help and give generously of time, effort, and telephone calls, but don't put our money into the situation and don't let it be said afterward that we became government contractors and stepped into a sphere entirely outside of our own to make some money." He also apologized for sounding "very testy" on the phone, "probably because you were telling me more at one time than my absorptive faculties could take."

But in this instance it was too late to back out. F.K. had already made commitments to purchase twenty million board feet for midwestern defense projects. The Army refused to deal with lumber retailers directly, convinced that price-fixing would substantially increase costs. The plan seemed simple enough. The Sales Company would help locate the lumber, secure bids, and then take those bids to Washington for approval. While this involved interim expenses, the Sales Company would "not be in a position of being a contractor in the matter." F.E. had given his approval, indicating that they should be sure not to buy from Rock Island Lumber or Thompson Yards without notifying the government that these were affiliated companies "and also being sure that their prices were at least as low as the average." F.K. concluded his letter to Phil on a patriotic note: "As you know, we have been trying to help the government in every way and this seemed to be one of those things we could do efficiently with comparatively little risk."

Phil much preferred to concentrate his efforts, and at the moment he felt quite busy enough without assuming any new undertakings. The first concern continued to be manpower. The second was construction of the $100,000 research laboratory at Longview. Back in St. Paul, Fred Weyerhaeuser still tried to figure out the boundaries of the various research programs. "Our work," he surmised, "focuses on the problems of the lumber business as such, whereas your work [Weyerhaeuser Timber Company's] is more of a pure research type," he wrote to Ed Davis in April 1942. Phil also wasn't much interested in boundaries. In his statement to John McClelland, editor of the *Longview Daily News*, he described the program of the Development Department as being "concerned with all technical fields dealing with the utilization of the standing forest, which may be broadly classified into structural products, fiber and fibrous products, chemicals and products therefrom, and plastic materials."

In March they applied to the director of priorities of the War Production Board for permission to construct the research laboratory. Approval was granted in May, with groundbreaking on June 4. It was also noted that "close integration of development activities at Longview and those of the Wood Conversion Company at Cloquet will be maintained." Clark Heritage, now Longview's director of research, would retain his position as technical director of the Wood Conversion Company, but there was no mention of Fred Weyerhaeuser or St. Paul.

It is curious how the most unexpected happenings can affect plans, rearranging priorities. The threat of war was real along the American coasts in 1942. On June 7, Japanese troops landed on Attu and Kiska in the western Aleutians. This would be the only occupation of North American territory, but of course nobody could know that at the time.

Then on June 22, a Japanese submarine lobbed a few shells at Fort Stevens, Oregon, without effect. With forests and mills to protect, Phil and other western operators wondered about the need for war-risk insurance. Typically, however, he wasn't too concerned, at least not about remote places such as Klamath Falls. "I have figured that as long as we were dealing with Uncle Sam, probably the coverage would remain open, even if some bombs fell on the Pacific Coast."

He was right. But none could have predicted when and where fire would strike. On July 2 the boiler room of F.K. and Vivian's 294 Summit Avenue home erupted in flames. Damage to the basement and living room was extensive, initially estimated at $5,000. Eight firemen were overcome by smoke, two briefly hospitalized. Fortunately, the firemen were fine. As for the house, it would be repaired.

News of damage of a far worse kind was relayed just a few days later. The Weyerhaeuser Steamship Company's SS *Heffron* was torpedoed and sunk off the coast of Iceland on July 5, while serving in the Murmansk trade.

Meanwhile, the St. Paul office continued to perk away more or less as usual, combatting an endless string of demands and distractions. F.K. must have felt under the gun, wishing that Tacoma—and Phil—were more accessible. That surely was the case in late July. Robert Bunson Wolf, manager of the Weyerhaeuser Timber Company's Longview pulp operations, paid a visit and shared his worries that pulp mills might be closed down so as to divert hemlock logs to the sawmills, this to help meet the government's urgent need for lumber. F.K. wished that Wolf had stayed around because the very next morning a writer from *Fortune* magazine dropped in along with Dr. Egon Glesinger, the two working on an article that focused on wood as the material of the future. What most interested the visitors was current research efforts. As F.K. described to Phil, he walked them through Fred's "little laboratory here on the 23rd Floor and finally, in desperation, got hold of Ed Davis because they kept insisting on knowing something about our Longview laboratory."

F.K. came away from the impromptu meeting convinced that if they wanted to experiment with making alcohol from wood waste, they could probably obtain approval for the plant construction and perhaps receive government financing as well. In any case, why not sit down with Wolf and consider the situation, perhaps even inviting "our friend Glesinger out West and trying to absorb some of his ideas?" With that, F.K. himself headed west for a Sales Company gathering at Glacier National Park. Phil was enthusiastic about the results: "Every one got reoriented, reacquainted, and had a little fun besides."

That meeting, however successful, didn't make everything right. In one of his most revealing observations, Phil responded to F.K.'s earlier recommendations on research, specifically as concerned production of alcohol from wood waste. R. B. Wolf was called to Washington, D.C., and alcohol was one of the subjects on his agenda; so that step had been taken. Now, would a visit by Dr. Glesinger "inspire us to greater promotional efforts along certain indefinite lines?" Phil was predictably less than enthusiastic, explaining, "Whereas you have dubbed yourself the 'exciter' of the outfit, I sort of imagine myself fitting into the roll [*sic*] of the 'debunker.'" Admitting that he didn't know enough "to debunk Dr. Glesinger," he could inquire just what F.K. had in mind. "We have no hesitation whatsoever to put money, energy, and what-have-you into any new development which bids fair to fit into our picture (currently to serve the war effort) and do not, as I see it, need to be punched up along those lines." What constantly concerned Phil was that they could overstate progress and promises; in this regard he had plenty to worry about right in Tacoma. Rod Olzendam was the Timber Company's public relations head, and he was proving difficult to control.

Public relations was a subject of growing concern, and, as had been the case in World War I, it seemed likely that the Weyerhaeuser Timber Company might be singled out by public officials and even industry colleagues for more than its share of abuse. Back in the spring of 1942, F.K., with some reluctance, accepted appointment to the Softwood Loggers and Lumber Manufacturers Industry Advisory Committee, one of many under the aegis of the War Production Board. At the time he wasn't sure just how important the committee might be, but it seemed best that they "should at least know what was going on." Phil agreed, happy that it was F.K. and not himself who would be spending time in the other Washington.

But F.K.'s presence didn't eliminate problems. As the summer of 1942 wore on, lumber became an increasingly scarce item. Part of the dilemma involved an inadequate labor force, an undeniable fact. Another aspect, however, occasioned numerous opinions. F.K. endured an uncomfortable week of committee discussion in mid–August, hearing reports of "a great deal of feeling on the coast against the Weyerhaeuser Timber Company on account of its policy of buying logs on the open market, while other mills are suffering for lack of log supply." In light of the shortage of lumber, and the accompanying unfortunate attitudes, he inquired of Phil whether the Timber Company should "abandon its log buying program for the next four to six months and to increase the rate of cutting on its own timber."

Phil's answer came as no surprise. He knew who the complaining parties were, small operators lacking timber of their own and, motivated by the possibility of big profits, always in search of logs from any source. The "talk about us being an octopus" was expected, and he also anticipated that some logs would be "arbitrarily" taken away from the Timber Company. So be it.

> The best we can do, as I see it, is so to use our production and facilities as to aid the war effort regardless of whether in so doing we assist our competitors or not. We are at Longview now engaged in a selective logging program, going way back to get noble fir and airplane stock. As far as I know, this will go through our Longview plant, because that plant is functioning better on airplane stock than any other plant in the industry.

The log buying largely involved operators utilizing Weyerhaeuser timber convenient to their mills, a practice akin to trading. Phil estimated that were they to follow F.K.'s suggestion, production would decrease by one-third, "which I do not believe would be in the best interests of the war effort."

F.E. had been included in the debate, and he quickly took Phil's side, noting that they had colleagues in Washington, D.C., who didn't understand the western situation. "Like most things of this kind," he began, "one easily magnifies possibilities of trouble, but I am surprised to learn how little some officials of the Sales Company know about our operating facilities at our coast mills and our ability to take care of urgent demands upon us as compared with small mills." As he continued, he cited the danger of someone in the sales organization suggesting that the Timber Company should not be buying logs on the outside and others accepting that as a knowledgable opinion. Although F.E. didn't mean to imply that F.K.

was personally guilty, clearly F.K. was in command, ultimately responsible for those who could be at fault. Phil agreed, but tactfully, accepting a portion of the blame. "Maybe we have been neglectful in keeping [Phil] Boyd and [Ray] Clute aware of all sides of our problems," until recently simply considering them to be sales representatives doing a good job along that line. Probably a direct approach was in order, with either Phil or Charlie Ingram going east for a face-to-face discussion.

To compound the problem, at the very time Weyerhaeuser was being excoriated for buying logs, Phil was considering several attractive opportunities for buying timber. The first was a tract of Northern Pacific timber around Spirit Lake, Mount St. Helens, in the heart of Weyerhaeuser-owned lands. F.E. doubted that any others would bid, but one never knew. More important was a Long-Bell tract in the Klamath Falls district, amounting to 87,000 acres. On December 16 they agreed to purchase at a rate of $6.00 per thousand board feet, with an additional 43,500 acres of cutover lands at $1.25 an acre. Final settlement awaited results of a joint cruise, but there would be no give on the specifics. Phil's memo announcing the deal suggested facetiously that it would demonstrate "how poor a trader I am." There was a curious precedent for the negotiations: John Tennant of Long-Bell had "gleefully quoted Mr. George S. Long" on the occasion of the original sale of lands from Weyerhaeuser to Long-Bell: "This is our price—it is a fair price and we will not deviate from it." F.E. allowed as how the quote seemed in keeping with his memory of that occasion.

F.E. had time to reminisce, and Phil could concentrate on the tasks at hand. Meanwhile, F.K. raced about picking up the pieces, most of which seemed scattered over the Washington, D.C., landscape. As the war continued, worrisome new laws and agencies came into being. One such law was the Renegotiation of Contracts Act, drawn up, according to F.E., in language confounding interpretation and "one of the most dangerous of recently enacted laws." In short, it was a subject for lawyers.

F.K. did his best to prepare. No legal committee existed, but the Executive Committee of General Timber Service, Inc., could assume the responsibility for "determining group policy with respect to legislation proposed or wanted." The committee would ordinarily employ Charlie Briggs or a member of his firm for "advice and may on occasion use him on Washington missions." Gus Clapp also was available, both to the Timber Company and the affiliated companies as needed. The lawyers would indeed be busy: The first renegotiation conference was pending, now scheduled for January 15, 1943.

It had to seem unjust at times, finding oneself wrapped up in fiscal and legal machinations while soldiers and sailors the world over suffered terribly. For Americans the war was now more than a year old, with no end in sight. But hope glimmered. The Russians mounted a winter offensive in relief of Stalingrad, and Allied troops were advancing in North Africa. And in the Pacific, Americans achieved bloody success at a place called Guadalcanal.

No ONE IN HIS right mind enjoys red tape, but the wartime problems confronting the federal government appeared unavoidably complex. And, all things considered, the tax and control efforts were working amazingly well. The "miracle of production" was a result of combined efforts, public and private. The public concerns were, first, that production be geared to meet defense needs, in terms of manpower, resources, and plant capacities. At the same time, citizens needed some assurance that their dollars were not being squandered, that since the demand for many materials was limitless, wages and profits would not be excessive. Federal tax policy during the period naturally reflected those concerns, beginning even before Pearl Harbor with the revenue act of June 25, 1940. This law set the pattern, decreasing personal exemptions and increasing tax rates. The same held true for corporations, with progressive taxes topped by an excess-profits tax. It seemed only fair. But among the more interesting features touching on war contracts were the renegotiation clauses, which provided for review of contracts should actual costs prove to be lower than estimated. And since, in the case of the Weyerhaeuser-affiliated operations, the Weyerhaeuser Sales Company was now the sole distributor—seller—it was Sales Company personnel who were the chief negotiators.

F.K. and Phil served as team managers, of course, and it was they who puzzled over the best organizational answer to problems—problems that would only grow more complicated. Quick response and flexibility were consistently their priorities when it came to Timber Company and Sales Company coordination and cooperation. In the spring of 1942, they discussed Sales Company organization, particularly that of its board of directors. At that time, the various mill managers participated reluctantly, convinced that their opinions mattered little if at all, that they were mere rubber stamps for whatever the owners—the actual stockholders—wanted. They were probably right. F.K. and Phil thus recommended that the board be changed, eliminating the so-called dummy directors.

Initially, F.E. appeared to be in agreement, but as F.K. reported in mid-April, "He seemed to have changed his opinion rather strongly." F.K. asked that his uncle discuss the matter with Rudolph and "that together they attempt to come to some conclusion." He also urged Phil to write F.E., "as I think that your views would have a great deal of weight with him."

Phil did as requested, beginning by noting that the "outstanding principle" honored in the affairs of the Timber Company "has been the delegation of authority to the greatest possible extent." But that principle had apparently been violated within the Sales Company, at least with regard to its board of directors, on which the mill managers saw themselves as "yes-men." They would all feel better, Phil contended, if the board were reorganized, "composed of active shareholders primarily, to whom there will be no hesitation in disclosing all actions taken." The mill managers could then serve as an advisory group, and he believed they would "respond more heartily."

While F.E. wasn't convinced, neither was he willing to challenge the brothers united. He also had no intention of serving on the board himself, although he allowed that Rudolph wanted to be elected. F.E. couldn't imagine that the stockholders would be of much help and suggested the possibility that F.K. "has not given his mill manager directors the opportunity, which he should, in fact, have encouraged, to express themselves about sales policies." In truth, F.K. was the most democratic of managers, and none hesitated to offer opinions by reason of intimidation. Indeed, it is hard to understand F.E.'s criticism. The mill managers were far happier simply complaining about sales personnel and policies than becoming involved themselves. The effort to include them in the decision-making was akin to "put up or shut up," and it hadn't worked. They weren't salesmen, and they didn't want to be salesmen.

In any case, the reorganization took place. There would be a new board of twelve, composed principally of stockholder representatives. There would continue to be an executive committee of five "living in or near St. Paul, who will be most easily available for frequent meetings."

And there would be an operations committee—this instead of the proposed advisory committee—with functions "similar to those performed by the Board of Trustees in past years, except for certain basic financial or policy matters."

This natural, perhaps inevitable, division between production and sales was not the concern of F.K. and Phil alone, although they manned the front lines. Laird Bell called attention to the problem in a thoughtful letter of July 9, 1943. He noted the problems others had been wrestling with for years, that "the whole organization has been defective in that the ordinary machinery for maintaining a balance between the conflicting interests of production and distribution is lacking." There was "no single place . . . where these two interests [could] meet and thresh out their conflicting problems"—which is exactly what F.K. had been trying unsuccessfully to resolve with the mill managers serving on the Sales Company board. What impressed Laird, and should have impressed others as well, was that the thing worked in spite of itself. While it was "still true that the salesmen think the mills dominate the sales policy and the mill men think the Sales Company does," it was a credit to both—and a credit to F.K. and Phil—that in the end, they got the job done.

As early as 1943, postwar planning took on increased significance. Perhaps his Chicago vantage provided Laird with some perspective. In any case, as he looked at the situation, he was not convinced that those doing the planning had their priorities in order. Weren't they overemphasizing the importance of distribution? While he understood that those in the St. Paul office did not wish "to be charged with invading the province of the mills," shouldn't they be talking more about "the production aspects of planning"? And that would lead to a conclusion that "the best postwar planning we could do is the development and improvement of our logging and manufacturing facilities." This in turn meant "planning to put out the largest possible amount of lumber at the lowest possible cost. Prices may go down and wages not; we want to be among the few that can survive under those circumstances." He concluded with a truism: "[P]rice is . . . the best sales help."

Laird, of course, enjoyed the luxury of having to think about lumber only now and then. F.K. thought about little else. He fretted, though that was not apparent to most of his colleagues, his worry always focused on improving the situations for which he bore a major responsibility. Sales would again be his greatest concern, but in 1943 that was hardly a problem. Thus F.K., when he tired of planning, could turn to other matters, such as research and public relations.

I. N. Tate, who had been in charge of public relations, left the Sales Company early in 1943. Tate's departure provided an opportunity. Why not replace him with someone knowledgeable about forestry, since that was obviously going to be a major subject of future concern and debate? At the annual meeting of the General Timber Service, Inc., F.K. was authorized to appoint a committee to consider such a possibility, and for that purpose he called upon cousin Fritz Jewett and the Timber Company's forester, Clyde Martin. A recommendation was immediately proposed by Martin: S. R. Black of San Francisco, a graduate forester with considerable experience lobbying in the California legislature. And Rex Black it would be, although his hiring was delayed for many months. But Black proved worth the wait. F.K.'s memo to Black outlining his responsibilities is of more than passing interest. Besides assisting officials of the affiliated companies, F.K. wrote, Black was expected to seek the cooperation of representatives of the numerous industry and business organizations in which the companies were interested: the Western Pine Association, West Coast Lumbermen's Association, National Lumber Manufacturers Association, American Forest Products Industries, Inc., National Association of Manufacturers, and the U.S. Chamber of Commerce, to name a few. Still, the main objective of the job was "to promote conditions conducive to the maintenance of profitable free enterprise for American industry and for the forest industries specifically." In that connection, F.K. emphasized the danger of excessive taxation. "The imposition of taxes, so burdensome as to destroy private initiative in forest ownership or the economic reason for maintaining and reproducing the forests should not be permitted."

To no one's surprise, taxes were of fundamental concern when F.K. and his colleagues began to think about postwar America. Needless to say, F.K.'s views were conservative in the extreme, at least by later definition. Naturally, he advocated radical reduction in federal expenditures, with the elimination of deficit financing. And he held that taxes ought to be a shared responsibility, "equitably distributed so that every voter may be tax-conscious." He also argued that "the ultimate top rate" of corporate taxation should be 30 percent, with no personal exemptions "so as to get the widest possible tax base." Few things excited F.K. more than federal tax policies, and seldom did his views prevail. Unlike his uncle F.E., however, he took his string of defeats in good spirit. But he didn't suffer silently.

One area of federal involvement about which he felt hopeful had to do with postwar housing construction, particularly the need for federal standards. He thought that in this instance, Weyerhaeuser enjoyed "an opportunity to bring considerable influence to bear upon the course of national thinking and action." Still, the odds were against any such influence.

He reviewed the situation with care, even to the point of studying the writings of economist J. M. Keynes, noting what the administration had accepted in terms of Keynesian theory, and also crucial additions, the "contempt for thoughts of restraint in government financing [and] increasing hostility to private management as well as ownership." F.K. proceeded to enumerate threats posed by the New Deal to the national welfare: "Free enterprise, representative democratic government, and civil and religious liberties go hand in hand and are actually inter-dependent. They are the three legs of a stool all of which must function if the stool is to stand up. When free enterprise dies so will individual liberties cease to exist." The stakes were overwhelmingly high, and they should be opposing "as vigorously and effectively as possible the entry or continuance of Government in any field which private initiative can handle." Rex Black would obviously have a big job, but of course he wasn't to serve alone.

One avenue of influence was representation on various key councils and agencies. F.K. himself served on the board of trustees of the National Lumber Manufacturers Association and also was a member of the administration committee for American Forest Products Industries, Inc., the public relations arm of NLMA. In addition, he chaired the Forest Industries Council, representing the entire forests products industry, and he belonged to the Producers Council. He was in the midst of advocating the election of Bill Billings as president of the NLMA to replace Marc Fleishel, at the end of four terms. Fleishel had done an adequate job, but he represented the southern industry's point of view. In F.K.'s opinion, Billings would be a decided improvement.

Visible representation did not always work to advantage, however. That was made abundantly clear in early September when the Weyerhaeuser Timber Company was charged with controlling Sitka spruce production, this being a crucial material in building the British Mosquito bombers. The "details," featured in Drew Pearson's widely syndicated "Merry-Go-Round" column that month, charged that Phil Boyd (of the Weyerhaeuser Sales Company), recently appointed head of the lumber division in Donald Nelson's War Production Board, had attempted to influence decisions, and that Arthur Upson, previous lumber division head, had termed Boyd's actions "ill-timed and ill-advised." The entire affair was ridiculous, reminiscent of similar charges made in World War I, but there they were for all the world to see. F.K. must have felt a bit nostalgic for days of long ago. Certainly he remembered his experiences as a bomber pilot more fondly than the thankless tasks of supplying the materials for war.

Meanwhile, he prepared an agenda for the next meeting of General Timber Service's Executive Committee. But that, too, would prove disappointing. The second item asked for an "official determination of attitude towards postwar activities by the Government in the housing field," and while all agreed in principle, the specifics of action were elusive. The final item, number 11, calling for "approval of group policy on research," was equally frustrating. F.K. and cousin Fred simply could not agree, and the longer the debate continued, the more rancorous became their disagreements.

With no clear decision by the Executive Committee, F.K. and Fred tried to resolve the problem through an exchange of memos, but to no avail. Fred became convinced that the days of his independent research effort within the General Timber Service, Inc., were numbered, with F.K. apparently favoring a closer connection between research and the Sales Company. Additional memos seemed unlikely to be helpful.

But beyond the St. Paul offices, worries of a larger sort placed matters in perspective. The coming holidays offered hope around the world, and F.K. used the occasion to write in his own hand a note to "my business associates":

The Christmas of 1943 will be long remembered by us first because of the terrible travail and suffering which the war is inflicting upon the world and second because of the hope for the future which the anniversary of Christ's birth symbolizes for us.

The road ahead looks brighter for our country and for us than it has for many years. The storm of war is abating and the sunrise of returning world sanity is beginning to show in the east.

May this Christmas bring to you a renewal of your faith in God, of confidence in yourself, and of belief in the future of our country.

THANKLESS TASKS

As his fiftieth birthday approached, F.K. found himself looking to the past with increasing interest. In December 1943 he learned of the pending retirement of a longtime Sales Company employee, R. E. "Jack" Irwin. Jack's lumber experience began in the late 1880s, when he worked with Robert L. McCormick and the North Wisconsin Lumber Company in Hayward. As a personal favor, F.K. asked Jack to compose "a resume of those experiences with some references to the personalities and events," adding, "We lived through some of the interesting ones together, which I will never forget."

Jack would try his best, but memories don't automatically translate into text, and so it was in this instance. The words simply didn't come. He apologized, citing health problems. He clearly missed the business associations, especially the likes of F.K. Irwin could only assert that if F.K. would continue "as a guide to the conduct of the business one will feel the organization will continue to hold its high place in the industry." Jack considered the succession from grandfather to father to son to be as unusual as it was important. "So few of our large industries seem to be able to hold the succeeding generations of their original stockholders interested in the business." It *was* unusual. It could also be a mixed blessing.

But with so much history happening in early 1944, few had the luxury of backward glances. F.K. was an exception. Watching the thousands of young men marching off to war, he had to recall the experiences of his own generation. Now, of course, his responsibility was on the home front, and he would again give his all. So, too, would Vivian, although she had removed herself from the main action the previous June, resigning as Red Cross vice-chairman in charge of volunteer departments. She hung up her uniform with a feeling of real accomplishment; she had served long and with distinction and left behind a healthy organization with more than twenty thousand active volunteers. Her departure was certainly justified—after having worked up to six days a week for three years, she wanted "to devote more time to home and family," as she was quoted in the *St. Paul Dispatch*. Both daughters were nearly teenagers and doubtless had need of a mother's attention. The fact was, however, that Vivian, like so many American wives and mothers of World War II, never quite went home again. Her involvements changed, but they didn't cease. Immediate on her agenda was service with the St. Paul Women's Institute Board. And 1944 was another election year, so there would be politics aplenty.

In the meantime, obviously wondering what the future held, F.K. reflected on the status of General Timber Service, Inc., which had started doing business in 1932. Somehow, it seemed longer ago than that. The initial activities had included auditing, traffic, merchandising, and engineering, along with legislative and trade association work. Over the years responsibilities shifted, but by the end of 1943 they were nearly the same as they had been ten years earlier.

Now F.K. reviewed the purposes originally envisioned for GTS, as stated in its Certificate of Incorporation.

These are: (1) to furnish management service of every kind to business enterprise, (2) to supply advice and service with respect to advertising, auditing, transportation, insurance and laboratory and other research, (3) to undertake and assume the supervision and management of business enterprises, (4) to make surveys, appraisals and investigation of properties and businesses, (5) to acquire and hold inventions, patents and trademarks, (6) to undertake the supervision or construction of plants, factories, railroads and operating and transportation facilities, (7) to engage in the insurance business, (8) to buy, sell, and deal in goods, wares and merchandise, (9) to own and operate ships, (10) to purchase, sell or hold stock and bonds.

In short, little fell outside the province of GTS. But as F.K. observed, although the charge seemed all-inclusive, it was never planned that GTS "would carry out all of the functions outlined." Rather it would formalize the activities previously managed by the F. Weyerhaeuser Office and by Weyerhaeuser Forest Products, including auditing, traffic, merchandising, and development engineering. It was expected to be a policy-making organization in terms of offering a Weyerhaeuser position on "national association matters or with regard to general legislation." Then, somewhere along the line, GTS inherited a responsibility for helping sick businesses, of which there had been many—Potlatch Forests, Inc., the Northwest Paper Company, the Boise Payette Lumber Company, and the Rock Island Plow Company, to name the most obvious.

Over the years, F.K. thought, GTS had done pretty well. And he looked ahead to future services, realizing that the particulars would change with conditions. The group would continue to have need for GTS or something like it, though he suggested the likelihood, after the war, of some other activities being resumed or added: marginal cost studies, budget controls, interviewing and hiring of personnel, economic research, trade relations, and insurance, "a real department with trained personnel." One motivation for such analysis was the hope that cousin Fred might assume greater management responsibility within GTS. Fred would try, but as had been the case with research, the thing proved unwieldy, to the point of being amorphous.

Procedures were put forth, and in a February 1 memo F.K. outlined the agreement. He and Fred would meet with the heads of GTS departments on the first Monday of each month, beginning February 7, for a thorough discussion of GTS affairs. The department heads would report to Fred, as the executive vice-president of GTS, and he would have "full responsibility for their direction." But F.K. had a couple of recommendations. First, he advised Fred to find an industrial engineer who would "diagnose troubles in present affiliated Company activities [and] assist in the commercialization of new products." Second, he directed Fred to organize an insurance department as soon as he could find the necessary personnel.

Trouble awaited on both fronts. While working to position Fred, F.K. also tried to lay some groundwork to make the tasks easier. He wanted once again to establish closer contact between the mills and GTS's product-development efforts. But one suggestion backfired, that the Weyerhaeuser Timber Company delegate a single individual with "the responsibility for making all decisions regarding commercializing of developments." Brother Phil's response was clear enough. "What the h— are we here for? Why have an engineer, a general manager, plant managers, officers, executive committee, directors, etc., if it's as easy as that? I suspect you of insinuating that the reason more developments haven't taken place is because Weyerhaeuser Timber can't make up its mind. . . . Well, 't ain't so!" And he concluded, with some advice. "Better make a New Year's resolution: Write no letters during the holidays."

F.K. claimed to have been misunderstood. "My real intent," as he explained to Bill Billings, "was to suggest that the Weyerhaeuser Timber Company needs one individual in the general office to ride herd on all product development interests of the company and particularly to form a point of contact for our St. Paul program."

By midsummer F.K. seemed ready to admit defeat on the subject of GTS research. On July 24 he circulated a "new Memorandum on Company policy regarding certain phases of Research." While it was general in the extreme, clearly he saw little hope. In his words, "It seems to me rather a waste of time to do anything more," and he complained, "You experts simply don't agree on this subject."

Fred had enjoyed no success on the insurance front either. He blamed the corporate setup, specifically the two sets of stockholders, Class A and Class B. The Class A stockholders represented the actual owners, the families; but they did not directly represent the clients, the Class B stockholders, the mills. "This required that G.T.S. take two steps to accomplish any function, first prepare its facts for the directors' approval and then undertake to secure the cooperation of the clients." Impasses were inevitable insofar as GTS had neither a board (with few individual exceptions) capable of reflecting a client viewpoint or any means of meeting collectively with client companies to institute and carry out cooperative programs.

It was a mess. Again, GTS may have made good sense in theory, but practice seemed to prove otherwise. General Timber Service research would limp along, eventually entering the prefabricated-house business, but it was forever a headache and a disappointment, perhaps in the end only confirming decentralization as the abiding principle.

Another apparently endless nuisance involved industry differences with government agencies, particularly the Forest Service. Lyle Watts was the new chief of the Forest Service, a zealous advocate of cooperation between the public and private sectors to achieve greater efficiencies and better forestry practices. But what Watts termed cooperation, many, notably F.K., termed interference. Central to the controversy were suggestions dating back to the Copeland Report of 1933, which included recommendations that the federal government purchase annually $50 million worth of private timberlands. In addition, federal regulations would be imposed on the logging of private lands. F.K. and many colleagues viewed this as the proverbial camel's head in the tent. Phil, responding to a query from Colonel Greeley of the West Coast Lumbermen's Association, stated his fears plainly. Greeley had specifically inquired as to whether the State of Washington should spend some research monies on pilot plants. Phil responded, "If the state or federal government got that far in the business of production, soliciting business, etc., I see no other end than government ownership of producing units."

F.K. continued to believe in the effectiveness of a positive stance on the industry's part. He had corresponded with Earl W. Tinker, formerly of the Forest Service, now executive secretary for the American Paper and Pulp Association. Tinker held little hope that the Forest Service would alter its objective of federal regulation and of federal ownership of timberlands, although he also felt that the secretary of agriculture "might exercise a restraining influence."

Phil didn't trust Tinker, but F.K. did—almost, anyway—acknowledging that he had made "quite an effort" to get the paper and pulp industry committed to the American Forest Products Industries (AFPI) program. He believed that they were "getting some place." F.K.'s position was summarized in a letter to Tinker:

In spite of these apparent difficulties, I feel our program should be carried on aggressively, that it should be made a positive program (for instance, to improve fire protection or forest practices), rather than a negative program and that we should not lose sight of the main objective of stimulating improvement in private forestry so as to provide a sound argument against Federal regulation and large Federal acquisition of timber lands.

A major problem for the industry in the debate with the Forest Service was that its public voice seemed so fragmented, as did its solicitations of funds. F.K. tried mightily to bring order out of chaos, but the effort was akin to pushing a string. To begin with, there were the National Association of Manufacturers (NAM) and the U.S. Chamber of Commerce, the two largest pro-business associations. In more recent years, NAM had established a public relations program, the National Industrial Information Committee (NIIC), whose primary purpose was to extol the virtues of the private enterprise system. As for the forest-products industries themselves, they had organized AFPI, the public relations arm of the National Lumber Manufacturers Association (NLMA), and it was to this organization that F.K. contributed considerable time and energy. In his words, AFPI's objective was simply "to encourage the forest industries to do a better job of fire protection and growing trees and to tell the world about it." Then there was the Forest Industries Council, which F.K. chaired, organized to coordinate policies and activities of the American Paper and Pulp Association, the National Lumber Manufacturers Association, and the American Pulpwood Association. It was indeed a hodgepodge.

His public relations work was just one of F.K.'s involvements for which there was no tally sheet. Had his time been well spent? How was one to know? During recent years, F.K. acknowledged, much of his time had been focused on this realm:

> [B]oth our own activities and national association ones. The AFPI Pub. Re. program has become a real factor in national thinking and I am proud of our part in it. It has also seemed important to get the cooperation of the Pulp & Paper groups. I have also tried with relatively little success to get our ideas on various subjects into action programs of the NLMA.

He then observed, sadly, that Uncle F.E. "repeatedly belittles these efforts and apparently thinks I should drop them." Rex Black had been wonderfully helpful, but Rex wasn't family. A despairing F.K. described matters thusly: Either F.E. was "crazy in his point of view or I am." But F.K. wasn't about to throw in any towels, adding that in his mind it was "of supreme importance to keep ourselves in a good light before the public and Congress."

But the public relations frustrations were just part of a much larger whole. F.K. had been trying for more than a decade to assume a greater family-leadership responsibility but with little to show for his efforts. The uncles simply weren't willing to step aside. As 1944 drew to a close, F.K. clearly viewed F.E. as the larger problem, and in his typical manner he put his thoughts on paper, hoping to clarify them and to ensure a thoughtful response. He listed the particulars of F.E.'s opposition, "sabotaging everything I have been working on for years":

> The fact is that he has expressed himself as opposing every single activity I am engaged in; the set-up of the Weyerhaeuser Sales Company, its relation to the eastern yards, its attempt to dictate to the Weyerhaeuser Timber Company, its lack of cooperation with Product Development & Fred's other activities, time spent on public relations and national lumber affairs, ABC., direction of traffic, etc.

F.K. struggled with the analysis, in the process playing the amateur psychologist, attributing F.E.'s present unhappiness to his being the youngest son of "a very dominant Father"; he "had the potential capacity to be a great leader [but] he was overshadowed by the others." F.E., now in his seventies, perhaps felt that he had failed to accomplish enough. Further, he no longer occupied a central role. On the one hand, he realized that the time had come to step down, or at least step back, but he wasn't able to do that. And he was resentful: F.K. didn't treat Fred fairly; brother Rudolph read his mail; others belittled his fundamentalist religious philosophy. Even minor complaints irritated him. F.K. noted, for example, that his uncle had recently forwarded a bank statement because "it was probably meant for me and not for him." And so it went.

Actually, F.K. himself was in a bit of a funk, feeling old and haunted by the thought that he, like his uncle, hadn't accomplished as much as he should have. Had he been "too much of an appeaser in the interests of family harmony?" What he did know, however, was that life passed all too quickly and shouldn't be wasted. And then the most basic question of all: Why weren't they, the Weyerhaeusers, happier? "What's wrong with us?" Well, for one thing, they continued to live in Grandfather Frederick's shadow and had "been looking backward too much and not forward enough." In addition, pressure was put upon young men in the family to go into business without regard to their individual interests or abilities. Work was "glorified," but at the same time the material results of business success were "hypocritically abhorred and depreciated." In that connection, there seemed to be a belief that being away from home on business was a good thing and that "vacations and relaxation" were not proper. Hobbies were also frowned upon. Even in a business sense, they had not developed enough outside interests. Finally, there was that old German tradition of seniority rule. Citing pension plans that had been introduced five years earlier, F.K. recalled the opposition of Rudolph and F.E., who had "bowed their necks and turned them down. Maybe we should have fought that one out."

It was in that almost rebellious spirit that over the holidays he planned for a January 1945 meeting with brother Phil and cousin Ed Davis, hoping that the three of them could arrive at a "course of common action." First and foremost, they must stand firmly and loyally together. Second, they must build positively, within the family and without. In this regard F.K. remembered his father's remark that the Denkmann family had called their geese swans and the Weyerhaeusers had called their swans geese, to which he added, "Maybe the D's had something at that!" Third, they should ensure their election to the positions of responsibility: Ed as president of Wood Conversion, Fritz Jewett as president of Potlatch Forests, and Phil as president of Weyerhaeuser Timber Company. And these steps should be taken soon "if the dead hand of the past will not make old men of us too." Fourth, they should either get GTS's product development on the right track or transfer it to the West Coast, F.K. admitting, "This is a hot potato and I need help."

The three met as planned and then reconvened in early March. As always, F.K. arrived fully prepared, outline in hand, complete with recommendations. Solidarity of the cousins, now including Fritz Jewett, remained a foremost requirement. F.K., having acknowledged that their family history held "some good lessons for us," recommended a practical objective: "The establishment of strong leadership by we four; maintaining of voting control of all companies, particularly WTCO.; developing, conserving and wise use of family manpower; support of competent key men; establishment of adequate financial incentives to get able men; reorganization of Boards and Officers of companies; [and the] establishment of an improved investment service in St. Paul." F.K. closed by quoting a sign that had once hung in the family office, "There is still time but it is later than you think."

By year's end F.K. had accomplished many of his objectives, but the world was a very different place. President Roosevelt had died, the war had ended, the atomic age was a fearful reality, and the uncertainties of a peacetime economy lay ahead. Within the family there had also been major changes. F.E. died on October 18, and while no formal vote took place, all understood F.K. to be his uncle's successor as leader of the clan. The family met in St. Paul at the time of F.E.'s funeral, October 22. Rudolph called the all-male gathering to order, and F.K. agreed to serve as secretary. The minutes were thus his, and so, too, were the agendas for future meetings. Several important decisions were reached.

Fred immediately raised the question of the need to continue General Timber Service, Inc. To appreciate the significance of this, one must be aware of the recent history of GTS. At its annual meeting in January 1945, F.K. had attempted to remove himself from the board, but many present, including brother Phil, would not accept that. F.K. was successful, however, in urging the election of cousin Fred as president, and Fred reluctantly assumed the position. (He had previously informed F.K. that his major interest in GTS involved product development, and that should those activities be eliminated, he preferred to depart.) Also approved was a budget of $90,000 for the "ordinary activities" of product development, "to include efforts to commercialize the panel house in Omaha but not to include the pilot plant developments which were being considered."

A few days later, Fred met with Phil, F.K., Bill Billings, and several others, at which time he proposed to increase the operating budget to $100,000 with an equal amount to be designated for pilot plant construction. Although F.K. complimented Fred for a "very fine statement," no decision was reached. The next day Fred, Phil, and F.K. met in what must have been a very stormy session.

Phil indicated that he would support the expanded budget Fred had proposed but only if "a good businessman were put on top of the whole thing to tie the loose ends together and to bring to the mills completed proposals for entering new activities." Again at the center of controversy was Neil MacKenzie. Phil agreed with F.K. that MacKenzie was an "idea factory" but was ineffective as the top manager for product development. This angered Fred, who responded, in effect, that it was none of Phil's business and that although he, Fred, did not like some of the department heads in other organizations (implying the Timber Company, of course), he felt that "each chief executive had the right to pick his own men." Phil wouldn't argue that point if Fred "would actually undertake to run the department himself and make the final contacts." There the matter ended, for the moment, Phil returning to Tacoma with the understanding that F.K. and Fred would come west in order to continue the discussion. That never happened.

In mid-March, when F.K. was in Lewiston, Idaho, attending a Sales Company Operations Committee meeting, Harry Kendall advised him that Fred wanted to know if the Sales Company would either take over product development or assume responsibility for its expenses. F.K. consulted with Phil, Ed Davis, and Fritz Jewett, after which he wired Fred as follows:

> Harry Kendall reports you want immediate decision from Sales Company reference taking over Product Development or paying expense thereof. We regret your apparent decision in GTS. If that decision final will recommend to Sales Company directors that we reestablish our former type of engineering department for sales service. Would then be glad [to] use MacKenzie in it.

F.K. and Kendall left Lewiston to spend a few days at the Bohemian Club in San Francisco, and while there Kendall received a phone call from Fred advising that MacKenzie had resigned, effective May 1, and further inquiring whether the Sales Company intended to proceed with the panel-house experiment in Omaha. When F.K. arrived back home in St. Paul, Fred indicated that since the GTS Development Department "had originally been created around the ability and person of N. T. MacKenzie," there was no purpose in continuing it now that MacKenzie had resigned. F.K. didn't agree with that assessment, contending that the department wasn't conceived with any one individual in mind; it had been created for the purpose of meeting group needs.

Given the circumstances, however, he wasn't going to insist that logic was on his side, deciding "it was better to let the matter rest," for several reasons:

1. The activity had led to so much friction and trouble over the past years, due to resultant criticism and gossip.
2. The activity was not sympathetically regarded by the operating companies.
3. The expense of the department was increasing.
4. It seemed to me that an activity carried on close to the mills would, in the long run, be more productive.
5. Any activity carried on in St. Paul is apt to become the subject of so much discussion and gossip that if it can be done somewhere else there will probably be less interference and it is more apt to succeed.

With that as background, the question posed by Fred at the family meeting of October 22 is better understood. Still, civility ruled, and in the end the family approved continuing GTS "for the purpose of rendering to the affiliated companies auditing and tax services and any other services which are needed or required." There was no mention of research or development.

The second question originated with F.K. and concerned the family meetings themselves, "which have become relatively infrequent in recent years." It was decided to meet twice a year, once in St. Paul "on the Friday before the last Saturday in January" and again in the summer at the "convenience" of family members. Those members would include all males along with Mrs. F. R. Titcomb and Mrs. W. B. Driscoll "on account of the fact that their husbands are not active in business." Further, every two years there would be "a full family meeting," attended by all, "including wives and children."

The third item for consideration was introduced by Ed Davis and involved some unfinished business, initiated by F.E., specifically the family's possible support for a history program, "involving the writing of a history of the lumber industry, a history of Frederick Weyerhaeuser, and the establishment of a centralized source of information on the history of the lumber industry." Rudolph expressed his support, and it was decided that F.K. should pursue the matter and submit a detailed report at the January 25 meeting.

Returning to the subject of GTS, Fred would continue as its president for a time, doing his best to further other activities, most importantly the auditing. But even here he was to be disappointed. As usual, it was a question of just how GTS dealt with operating companies: as an independent agency or as an associated one? Phil preferred not to make a public issue of it. Like F.K., he didn't want to make Fred's life unnecessarily complicated; he thus closed an early March 1946 letter to Fred on a conciliatory note: "My sympathy goes to you in heading up a service company which receives complaints from all sides. . . . Inasmuch as this letter seems to be critical of what you may think wise policy with reference to General Timber Service, I want to end it with the sincere expression of appreciation on my part that you are willing to direct General Timber Service in its activities."

But it was too late for sympathy to heal the wounds. Fred was finished, and he appended a lengthy explanation to his April 18, 1946, resignation announcement. After reciting his disappointment over the abandonment of the research activity, he declared the remaining activities to be insufficient, in his opinion, to warrant a continuation of GTS. If he erred in this assessment—and he allowed for the possibility—surely GTS "should have new blood as certainly under me it will fold up sooner or later." He continued:

> I believe we as a family are going to have to organize to work things out more on our own. I don't see a third generation of our associates coming along that will take the place of the second generation of associates. If this is true, G.T.S. becomes all the more meaningless as time goes on. I would favor letting one of our associates, namely John Musser, wrestle with G.T.S. from here on. I don't like to be responsible for the eventual liquidation of G.T.S., having had nothing to do with its formation and it being the only medium for group representation of the associates.

Clearly Fred was discouraged beyond repair. F.K., on the other hand, while often disappointed, seldom despaired. He was, if nothing else, the eternal optimist, especially when it came to Weyerhaeusers present and future. At the October 22, 1945, family meeting, F.K. had introduced as a subject of importance the Family Office, asking just how the family wished it to function. He, of course, had developed his own ideas, and had even circulated a memo on the subject a week prior to F.E.'s death; these would indeed lay the foundation for Family Office operations for years to come. First on this list and on those to follow was the maintenance of family unity.

FOR THE SAKE OF HISTORY

THE JAPANESE surrender was formalized September 2, 1945, in Tokyo Bay aboard the USS *Missouri*. Six terrible years, and so much had changed. The effects of war would continue to be felt, including such irritants as price controls.

There were, however, encouraging signs, some of which were very close to home, the result in no small part of Vivian Weyerhaeuser's leadership. She had relegated her wartime Red Cross uniform to the closet, but F.K. soon found that now *he* was wearing a uniform with frequency, a tuxedo. Vivian's involvement in the Women's Institute of St. Paul (sponsored by the *St. Paul Pioneer Press*) may have sounded innocuous enough, but that was deceiving. She assumed the chairmanship on April 25 at a program attended by some fifteen thousand, with pianist Oscar Levant as the featured performer. The women subsequently organized a major cleanup of their beloved city, but perhaps most important in the long term was a project called the Search for Talent, a contest for aspiring young singers in the Twin Cities area.

Many of the institute's programs in the 1945–46 season naturally featured war participants, including such well-known personalities as General Carlos P. Romulo and correspondent H. R. Knickerbocker. Violinist Mischa Elman enthralled the evening audience on October 31, preceded in the afternoon by critic and author John Mason Brown, recently discharged from the Navy. Vivian introduced them both. But the most imaginative event of the fall was a radio extravaganza celebrating the twenty-fifth anniversary of the medium, on the general theme "How Can We Keep Radio Free?" With an estimated national audience of twenty million, this was the first time that the five major networks cooperated in broadcasting from the same stage. Vivian presided, and she dutifully thanked each contributor. "The Institute has scored again," the reporter for the *Pioneer Press* wrote.

Not everything succeeded, however, and no failure was more embarrassing than one that occurred on January 30, 1946. Despite cold temperatures and heavy snows, a crowd packed the St. Paul Arena to see the Carmelita Maracci dancers. Nearly three-quarters through the performance, in the middle of the number "Por Que?" Carmelita, "in a flare of temperament," ordered a halt. Her manager later explained that "the situation was unsuited to her form of art, which demands intimate surroundings for full effectiveness." The humiliation was all the more ignominious because the troupe had performed without complaint the previous evening in Duluth. But Vivian and her colleagues weren't deterred, soon focusing on the search for the "golden voice of 1946." They prepared to welcome thirty-two contestants, two of whom would receive "grand awards."

The Carmelita flareup was the exception to the rule. Vivian's leadership culminated on the evening of February 20, when she introduced Mexican tenor Tito Guizar and his company. She took the occasion to talk briefly about St. Paul, its attractions and civic enterprise, as well as the upcoming Victory Carnival. But she herself would be absent: "When I was invited to be your chairman for the season, I was, of course pleased. But as with all wives and mothers I have definite family obligations and I knew my husband was planning his first real vacation in several years." She soon resigned. There was just too much else going on.

The same was surely true for her husband. F.K. faced some unfinished business of his own. F.E. had devoted countless hours of work to a project he called "The Record," a complete accounting of his father's business accomplishments. This would prove to be a far more daunting task than F.E. had imagined. Years passed and the typewritten pages piled up, eventually numbering more than eight hundred. Once the manuscript was completed, the obvious question was, what should be done with it? F.E. had no ready answer.

Initially, he seemed willing to permit some reasonable distribution, but he became increasingly proprietary, possibly reacting against those who recommended a wide circulation. At the same time, however, he recognized the need for greater awareness of the Weyerhaeuser-affiliated companies, and, indeed, of the entire industry. In this effort F.K. was an enthusiastic supporter.

Others agreed, chief among them representatives of the Minnesota Historical Society (MHS). Not only did they appreciate the importance of the lumber industry, but they also were considering how their state might best celebrate its centennial as Minnesota Territory, upcoming in 1949. In that frame of mind, a group called on F.E. at his home in early September 1945. Judge Kenneth G. Brill, then president of MHS, was accompanied by Theodore C. Blegen, dean of the Graduate School of the University of Minnesota and MHS vice-president; August C. Krey, chairman of the university's Department of History and a member of MHS's Executive Committee; and Lewis Beeson, MHS's acting superintendent.

The committee explained that they envisioned a commemorative centennial publication, "a comprehensive history of the state," that would include political developments as well as agricultural, industrial, social, and cultural aspects. Typically, the Historical Society (also founded in 1849) lacked funds for such a project.

In this context the notion of "mutual interest" was introduced, the visitors citing F.E.'s own work-in-progress on Frederick. "The Society could, if you chose, help to complete that work." How F.E. reacted is unclear; perhaps he thought it was already completed! In any case, the committee made its point as to the importance of lumbering and noted the absence of any historical center for the industry, contrasting it with transportation: "The late J. J. Hill established collecting centers at Yale and Michigan . . . or the special collection for the Burlington and Great Northern Railroad which Ralph Budd has established at the Newberry Library in Chicago." Organizational specifics could be decided later. All recognized that the center of lumbering activity would continue to move, "but whatever the industry shifts, its history can be best served from one systematic collection."

F.E. was by now a very sick man, suffering the final stages of leukemia, but he understood clearly what was being asked of the Weyerhaeusers, and he wasted no time in contacting other family members. In writing to Phil, he described his evening with the representatives of the Historical Society "as an unusual experience; it is not often that intellectuals come to our house to call on me." He wasn't being snide or coy. Indeed, he mentioned that he would have been "a little reticent" at sharing "my modest efforts" with the likes of Dean Blegen and Professor Krey.

Although F.E. would recall no specific dollar request, he thought that $100,000 may have been mentioned as a figure that would cover the costs of a biography of Frederick, allowing that at that point he should probably have "thrown a faint." But he remained conscious, and apparently it didn't strike him as unreasonable: "I think it is generally recognized that father was the leader of the industry for many years and perhaps the most interesting personality so far as the lumber business is concerned that could be selected." The evening ended with "a few cigars and a little charged water," the guests departing in hopes that they be allowed "to discuss the matter further with me." Again, F.E. didn't say no.

Niece Peggy Driscoll's response was predictable and representative. "The whole subject of their visit rather 'floors' me," she wrote. "I would certainly go along—myself—with anything agreed upon by you, Father, and the Cousins." F.E. assured Peggy, F.K., and other family members that their decision would have to be unanimous before any commitment was made. F.K. happily concurred, even at the $100,000 figure. (In fact, the initial request would prove to be half that amount.) But he understood that the crucial decision was his uncle's to make: "I feel very strongly that you should determine what is to be done and that if you are inclined to have the family underwrite a project for the Minnesota Historical Society I would strongly favor it being done."

In the meantime, Judge Brill smelled success. Writing to board member Homer Clark of St. Paul's West Publishing Company, he suggested that this might be "one of the greatest opportunities the Society has had." He also noted the discussion about publishing a volume on "the life of Mr. Weyerhaeuser, Senior, and history of the lumbering industry and establishing a great center for the collection of all material which can be secured on the industry."

Judge Brill acknowledged the insufficiency of the $50,000 requested, obviously unaware that F.E. had reached a similar conclusion. Still, $50,000 provided a significant start. The judge also couldn't know of a critical change in circumstances. On the very day he was writing to

Homer Clark, October 18, F.E. died. As a result, in this as in other matters, F.K. would henceforth represent the Weyerhaeusers.

F.K. soon visited the Minnesota Historical Society, located adjacent to the State Capitol, and was shown about by Judge Brill, Dean Blegen, and Professor Krey. As he would report to Phil and his cousins, he was "honestly impressed by the character of the building and the apparent high standard of the activities being conducted there." The hosts discreetly avoided much in the way of specific discussion, although a suggestion was made that were the Weyerhaeusers to lead, others would likely follow. For the moment, F.K. offered three recommendations. First, F.E.'s "Record" should be printed and distributed with the understanding that its use be limited to family members for a period of ten years. Second, family members would contribute $25,000 or $50,000, this to be considered an initial installment on a project "to develop a collection of documents, papers and historical data bearing upon the history of the lumber industry." And third, the family needed to employ "a good man to write a short history of the business . . . intended for use by employees, friends and customers." The proposal was viewed as simply an introduction for discussion of the subject at the family meeting on January 25, 1946.

The possibility of the family contributing to the Minnesota Historical Society received a good deal of attention at the January meeting, but no final decision was reached. Too many unanswered questions lingered, such as whether papers would be accepted on the condition that they remain closed for a specified period. Phil was among those in need of convincing, and he joined F.K. and Ed Davis in another visit to the Historical Society, this time meeting Arthur Larsen, its superintendent.

F.K. would report in detail, suggesting the family consider contributing $15,000 over each of the next three years. His reasoning was as follows:

(1) events are proving the need for accurate historical data on the history of the lumber industry (recent literary efforts by Sarah Jenkins Salo and Richard G. Lillard bear this out); (2) The Minnesota Historical Society is one of the best institutions of its kind in the United States, having a fine record of professional accomplishment; (3) the men behind the institution, including Judge Brill, Dean Blegen and Professor Krey are men of high standing

and fine integrity; (4) I know that Uncle F.E.W. would have favored our doing this.

At the bottom of the letter there was a space to sign if approved. No doubt for most, the inclusion of F.E.'s favor was enough in itself. (By way of explanation, Lillard had apparently shared with F.K. a draft of his article "Timber King," which would appear in the winter 1947 issue of *Pacific Spectator.* Salo's "Timber Concentration in the Pacific Northwest" was her 1945 doctoral dissertation at Columbia University.)

Final approval awaited a detailed proposal for what was to be called the Forest Products History Foundation. The three-page prospectus was largely the work of Krey and Blegen, and its key provision was paragraph 1A: "The purpose of the foundation is to establish at the Minnesota Historical Society a complete and authoritative collection of materials relating to the history of forest products in the broadest sense and to develop plans for the best possible use of this collection. No such center exists at present." The proposal also included Canada as a focus for collecting information on the industry.

A few at the Minnesota Historical Society worried that the University of Minnesota's role could become excessive, but that was a passing concern. Brill assured Larsen that he had no fear "that the University would attempt to dominate the Society." On the contrary, he appreciated the fact that university faculty and staff had been "so generously willing" to give of their time and assistance, "and we are fortunate in having their continued interest."

On June 11, 1946, Brill and Larsen met F.K. and Ed Davis for lunch. As Larsen later recalled, "The opening words were like music to us," referring to F.K.'s announcement that the family had agreed to proceed "along the lines of the outline you presented." And the next day, F.K. forwarded the first check, "a gift from the Weyerhaeuser Family for the purpose of creating a Forest Products History Foundation as an activity of your Society."

With initial financing assured, the MHS representatives immediately felt the pressure to perform. Who was to manage the project? Rodney Loehr of the university's history faculty headed the list of candidates. But would he accept, and what would the arrangements be? Larsen inquired of

Professor Krey whether one-third of Loehr's salary at the university plus another $1,200 to $1,500 might be agreeable, expressing hope that they could reach a decision "in the very near future."

Professor Loehr was indeed interested, and the arrangements with the university proved workable. But publicity about the new foundation was delayed, the principal reason being Rudolph Weyerhaeuser's illness. He died on July 12, the last of Frederick's four sons to go. Superintendent Larsen waited a week before writing to F.K. MHS's Executive Committee had since approved the plans for the Forest Products History Foundation, and now wished "to give the Foundation proper publicity, if it suits your purposes." Larsen's real question concerned any efforts by F.K. to elicit industry support. There was one other item: The Executive Committee had recommended that an advisory board be established, to assist in formulating policy and acting in a general capacity. Further, they hoped that F.K. would serve as chairman of that board.

F.K. could hardly refuse a continued involvement, although he wasn't sure about the chairmanship. In any event, he and his family were now committed to the foundation's success. Moreover, he had given a good deal of thought to which colleagues might be interested in contributing to the cause. Four of those near the top of his list—Paul V. Eames, Archie D. Walker, David J. Winton, and Edward Brooks—had strong Minnesota ties. They were contacted immediately, F.K. observing in his letter to each that there had been "so much misinformation and plain distortion of fact regarding the history of the lumber industry that there would seem to be substantial advantage in having an institution with the standing and integrity of the Minnesota Historical Society undertake a collection of this kind." They could not disagree with that.

Paul Eames, while expressing his personal enthusiasm, also suggested that they would do well to include Corydon Wagner, then president of the American Forest Products Industries. According to Eames, Wagner would be essential in their plan to garner support among Pacific Northwest operators. Cordy Wagner may have been considered crucial in regional terms, but there was little cause for such concern. The Weyerhaeuser Timber Company would lend a receptive ear, and when its leadership listened, other Pacific Northwest lumbermen did so, too. Indeed, what was more important in the involvement of men such as

Wagner was that they had no Weyerhaeuser connection, and the sooner the foundation became truly an industry endeavor—rather than strictly a Weyerhaeuser family project—the better.

In this matter of solicitation, Loehr early made his position clear, that he felt it inappropriate to accept any responsibility beyond "the technical aspects." That was understood, at least by his university colleagues and most of those in the Historical Society. Superintendent Larsen may have been an exception, but then, as he admitted, he was caught up in worries concerning the territorial centennial, which from his vantage seemed ever so close. It was "constantly on my mind," he admitted to Krey in an October 22, 1946, letter. They needed proof of accomplishment, not promises, and the Forest Products History Foundation was only one of his projects. What about the Committee for Industry and the Public Health History Project? Would it all come together in time?

At least they were ready to move ahead with membership in the advisory group, provided F.K. agreed. Larsen still assumed that F.K. would serve as chairman, assisted by Paul Eames, Dave Winton, Corydon Wagner, and Dean Henry Schmitz of the University of Minnesota School of Forestry. It seemed likely that they would increase the membership by year's end, but in the meantime this could be the "nucleus." Loehr participated in the marketing, explaining to Wagner just what they hoped to accomplish. "A calm and impartial appraisal of the history of the forest products industry might contribute to a realistic public attitude," he wrote. Cordy Wagner would likely have underlined the "might," making it clear from the beginning that he had no intention of making any substantial gift. But he accepted, and so did the others.

Wagner visited St. Paul in late February and was introduced to the other participants, Judge Brill, Dean Blegen, Dean Schmitz, Professor Krey, MHS superintendent Larsen, and Professor Loehr, who opened the discussion by describing the objectives of the foundation, as well as some of its challenges. Brill talked about how the project had come together, and Wagner added his own enthusiastic comments.

The board met again on June 24, this time with F.K. in attendance. A number of actions were taken. Stanley Horn, president of the Tennessee Historical Society and editor of the *Southern Lumberman,* was elected to membership, the first southerner to be included. They further decided that the original board members would continue "without limitation as to time of membership," but future members, to be appointed by the president of the Minnesota Historical Society, would serve terms of two years, the terms beginning July 1. A variety of other matters were discussed, most concerning prospects for support and subjects for possible study, such as the "tree farm" movement.

Although Loehr, as director of the Forest Products History Foundation, had forsworn any direct involvement in fund-raising, the realities of budget considerations soon dictated otherwise. These became all the clearer as he submitted the figures for the first year, in the process realizing that just two years remained to the Weyerhaeuser family gift. Only the Winton family had indicated a willingness to offer support "when we need it, viz. at the end of the three year trial period." Loehr visited the Pacific Northwest for the express purpose of eliciting interest, and he thought he had been reasonably successful. But he returned with no firm promises in hand. The basic problem, of course, was the absence of any established record. What confidence existed was "largely a matter of confidence in persons, rather than in institutions or publicity." To move the process along, Loehr envisioned three steps: acquainting individuals with the foundation; "building up of confidence through the continuance of personal relations and the issuance of *several* publications"; and a direct appeal for funds. They had made progress on the first; were starting on the second; and should begin the third within the year. One additional item he mentioned in passing: Earlier in the year, Blegen had suggested that they offer memberships in the foundation. Loehr now concurred with that suggestion.

Loehr faced a problem common to fledgling organizations. He had virtually nothing to show in terms of real accomplishments. The summary in his first annual report, for 1946–47 (actually covering less than a full year), clearly details the problem while also putting the best possible face on things:

The past ten months have been used in organizing a staff, getting acquainted with the industry, developing techniques, plotting a course, and laying the foundations for future work. We are virtually pioneers in attempting the history of an industry as large and old as the forest products industry. The guide-posts have been few in number, but we do have the satisfaction accorded to pioneers:

the hewing of paths which others will follow. The next year will see the quickening of our activities, and the fruition of some of the seeds which have been planted this year.

The seeds planted in those early years grew ever so slowly. Still, the Weyerhaeuser family remained constant, despite the doubts of some, notably Phil. He was briefly vexed by an article in the *Gopher Historian,* "When Lumber Was King," and he communicated his vexation loudly. He described it as "typical of the half-baked stuff which the conservationists all like to put out." Granted, the *Gopher Historian* was a publication of the Minnesota Historical Society, but it was primarily intended for schoolchildren and obviously had no direct connection with the Forest Products History Foundation. Phil worried, however, about guilt by association. He also didn't appreciate Professor Loehr's attitude, "that he could not be cooperative with the industry and still maintain his standing." In fact, Phil had had it with professors.

But not F.K. He had previously convinced Phil that the Weyerhaeuser Timber Company ought to make an annual contribution of $4,000 for a five-year period to the Forest Products History Foundation, beginning in 1950. And in the fall of 1951, F.K. requested that the family provide additional support of $5,000 annually for three years: "I am putting it up to others to get another $5000 which with $4000 from the W.T.Co. and $1000 from PFI [Potlatch Forests, Inc.] should give the Foundation sufficient opportunity to prove whether or not it can merit support from other members of the forest products industries." As for himself, he seemed already convinced. "I am much encouraged by the interest in this project and feel that plans now being made stand a good chance of creating a permanent and worthwhile institution."

He was prescient. The foundation, now the Forest History Society, has indeed endured. While never prosperous financially, it has largely realized its mission to preserve and to publish without prejudice the history of the forest-products industry.

AFTER THE WAR

WHEN WORLD WAR II ended, the general euphoria was dampened by an uncertainty about the future, at least among businessmen. There would be large changes, no doubt of that. According to Weyerhaeuser Sales Company figures, the percentage of sales cost to value in 1935 was 8.31, compared to less than 3 percent in 1945.

F.K. had big plans—brother Phil would probably have said grandiose—for the years ahead. The Sales Company would continue to strive for efficient distribution of lumber produced by Weyerhaeuser-affiliated mills, keeping sales costs as low as possible, all the while making the Sales Company "a profitable operation in and of itself." F.K. foresaw carefully planned expansion into new fields, including imported woods from the Soviet Union, Mexico, and perhaps the Philippines; hardwoods; and a variety of endeavors resulting from research applications.

The Sales Company executives met for three days in mid-July 1945 to discuss a wide range of problems. It was generally presumed that postwar lumber requirements would drop dramatically. Harry Kendall estimated that government stockpiles alone would total between two hundred and four hundred million board feet. F.K. thought that just as the Sales Company had been helpful in purchasing lumber for the war effort, it might also "assist in liquidation of government lumber surpluses," with little or no concern for making a profit in the transaction. The executives considered everything, from wholesale discounts, to lumber standards, to reinstating the sales-training program. Then there was the matter of returning veterans. That discussion emphasized the need for sensitivity in their transition back to civilian life, termed a "re-acquainting period."

While the war's end certainly precipitated numerous changes, much remained as before—too much according to some, including F.K., who was thinking especially of government regulations. (Price controls, for example, would last until November 1946, more than a year after V-J Day.) He tried to envision a new world that would recapture the best of prewar conditions. "Not a week goes by," he wrote to Phil in early 1946, "but what some of us in this office are called upon to take some action based upon our beliefs in respect to national fiscal policies and particularly with respect to those that touch upon the building industry." While F.K. felt pretty sure of his own viewpoint, he wasn't so sure about all of his associates. Were they seeing clearly? Could they anticipate the same dangers? Maybe, maybe not. Shouldn't they develop "a set of approved basic principles, both as a general guide and also to assist our representatives" serving on the various associations and agencies? Obviously, he thought so, provided they could "avoid use of such a set of policies in a manner to secure publicity for ourselves in a way that might be detrimental or unwise." Phil doubtless agreed philosophically, although he was less certain as to the application.

F.K. began a proposal entitled "Weyerhaeuser Position Relative to National Policies" as follows:

> Private Capitalism cannot exist unless it is freed from paternalistic governmental controls and political efforts to repeal the laws of supply and demand. It was possible to tolerate governmental controls and restrictions of liberty during the war but the war is now over, yet the controls and restrictions remain. They may remain forever unless business is willing to accept the risks of free enterprise and private capitalism, as well as the benefits.

He proceeded to enumerate specifics, emphasizing those factors likely to frustrate a prompt return to a "free private competitive enterprise." These included many familiar items, such as a balanced budget, low tax rates, elimination of federal subsidies, discontinuation of price controls, and no increase in appropriations for federal services, "including forest protection and research, until the federal budget is balanced and taxes are reduced."

Such an agenda, however desirable, was clearly beyond accomplishment in its entirety. In the meantime, F.K. worked diligently to bring about whatever change was possible, and heading his list was an improvement of the public relations effort of the industry itself. In 1946 that effort focused on the American Forest Products Industries, Inc. (AFPI), formerly an adjunct of the National Lumber Manufacturers Association. Soon, however, it would become an independent corporation with a single objective, "the prosecution of its Public Relations Program," a program "focused completely and solely upon the object of increasing tree growth through educational and cooperative means," or so F.K. explained to a colleague following the meetings. The president of the reorganized corporation continued to be Corydon Wagner, with Colonel Bill Greeley serving as the new chairman and Chapin Collins remaining as secretary and managing director.

Collins had prepared a draft for an opening talk by F.K. at the March 1 meeting, but F.K. wasn't interested in being in the spotlight. Attention should first be given to the AFPI program itself and then to the two most important individuals involved, Greeley and Collins. After the program was explained fully, F.K. recommended that Greeley make one of his typical statements, to the effect that, "Gentlemen, you have heard the story of what has been done and is being done, and an outline of what can be done and should be done—in the near future representatives of AFPI will get in touch with you to ascertain what part of this program you will be able to undertake." F.K. promised to be one of AFPI's representatives, contacting key individuals, soliciting their support. He did so with characteristic enthusiasm, and he included not just lumbermen. For example, he even appealed to Ralph Budd, president of the Burlington Lines, urging him and his Association of American Railroads to support the national tree-growing program. The railroads have "a great stake in the productivity of American forests," F.K. explained. Maybe so, but it turned out to be a difficult sale, one he was unable to close.

All of this was played out against a background of surprisingly strong lumber demand and accompanying price increases. High prices inevitably occasioned governmental inquiries into the cause, and such inquiries boiled down to two basic questions: Was there evidence of price fixing, or was the resource itself threatened? To many, it was an either-or proposition. For instance, the list price on Longview Douglas-fir was $60.39 per thousand, an increase of $11.33 since November 9, when price controls were lifted. F.K. noted that consideration was being given to further increases but advised the Sales Company board, "Your management is . . . of the opinion that prices on Coast woods, including our own, are getting dangerously high." He outlined the policy they hoped to follow, one "aimed at getting us on the true lumber market if possible by the end of February [1947] without resorting to extreme and fantastic pricing."

Harry Kendall concurred that the Sales Company needed to "take a very conservative price position and to slowly follow the market upward." But the market had a mind of its own and the intense inflationary pressures continued, Kendall admitting at midyear that none had foreseen the excess dollar sales, "as no one believed the market would go as high as it did." And still there was no sign "of a market reaction serious enough for us to make very broad price reductions." Still the market pressures, as well as Congressional ones, persisted. Finally, on January 15, 1948, F.K. announced an arbitrary 10-percent reduction in Sales Company lumber prices. There were dangers in this because some inferred a Weyerhaeuser influence more considerable than was the case. The intention was not to control the market—an impossibility—but rather to encourage similar responses from other sellers. As always, the market would prevail. By year's end, everyone was wondering what happened to the buyers. Phil urged that they use their "weight" to reduce the price of fir lumber further. But he wasn't interested in making another public declaration along the lines of the January 15 announcement. "Everyone is a little bit frightened of doing what we did last year as a gesture, knowing that it would do no good."

The unending frustration of trying to maintain an "industry position" was in some degree due to the personalities involved. There were some who doubted Colonel Greeley's loyalty, largely because of his Forest Service connections; he had headed that organization for eight years prior to becoming secretary-manager of the West Coast Lumbermen's Association in 1928. F.K. addressed that concern in a June 9, 1947, letter to Cordy Wagner, acknowledging "a little fear that the Colonel is too much inclined to team up with the Forest Service and that AFPI has already gotten pretty far along the road of appeasement in . . . fighting the extension of governmental control." F.K. himself wasn't among the doubters, and he contended that Greeley should remain chairman of the AFPI board.

F.K. had earlier begged off attending the mid-June AFPI meetings in New York City, explaining to Collins that he refused to leave home "unless absolutely necessary because I have to be away from home about sixty per cent of the time anyway." Surely other matters were on his mind, including family affairs and considerable discontent regarding Sales Company policy. Still, public relations occupied much of his attention, especially when he heard that his own "expert," Rex Black, was about to resign, joining the Georgia Hardwood Lumber Company (today's Georgia-Pacific).

Congressional hearings on the status of the nation's timber supply were to be held some time that summer, but the announcement of the July 11 date came as a surprise. Even the National Lumber Manufacturers Association wasn't notified of the hearing until 5:00 p.m. the preceding day—too late, of course, to prepare for any serious initial participation. George Malone, Republican of Nevada, chaired the Senate Public Lands Committee, and he assured industry representatives that they would indeed be heard. The debate centered on an all-too-familiar question: Was the country's timber supply adequate for the future? Chief Forester Lyle Watts and others predicted that need would exceed production for "one or two decades." But, under questioning by Chairman Malone, the naysayers stopped short of categorizing the United States as a "have-not nation."

Journalists well understood that fear sold copies. And so it was with *Life* magazine's November 3, 1947, issue, featuring an article entitled "The Vanishing Forest." While the message was in line with the Forest Service's propaganda, emphasizing the need for federal controls, F.K. knew it could have been much worse. Indeed, he asserted, the supposed threat of a timber failure would have been worse five or ten years ago, "before the Forest Industry through A.F.P.I. and other channels started promoting timber growing on private lands." How best to respond to attacks was a constant topic of discussion. Almost thirty years earlier, when F.K. had been a bomber pilot, he had become convinced that initiating immediate counterattacks was the most effective strategy. Now, he wasn't so sure. And neither was AFPI's Chapin Collins. He and others began to assemble materials and statistics in hopes that the editors of *Life* and other periodicals would be interested. At the time, Collins tried to put into words the AFPI's objective: "to engage in a strong, positive program of encouraging tree-growing and forest protection, in the name of the forest industries, in the belief that such a program not only will help the forest situation, but will reflect credit on the forest industries generally." That was about right, although it still didn't answer the question of how far they should go, or how loud they should be. On that score Collins continued, "I have always felt that if we engage actively in controversy, we will close a lot of doors that are now open to us." And from a public relations standpoint, "I can't imagine anything worse than a public clubbing match with the Forest Service." It was like walking a tightrope.

Another new public relations challenge involved moviemaking. Hollywood went "woodsy" in a 1947 Weyerhaeuser Timber Company-financed effort, *Green Harvest*. F.K. didn't like its story-within-a-story featuring a young honeymooning couple. Bill Billings of Potlatch agreed, complaining about the "ham." In the end, however, theirs was a minority opinion. "The 'corny' part which disturbs you and me," F.K. responded none too seriously, "seems to make a hit with the 'lower classes,' which includes my younger daughter and others who lack the civilizing effect of a life in the lumber business."

As for more important family matters, these increasingly involved the so-called Family Office and its services. F.K. felt responsible to everyone, reminding them of just what was available, from the safekeeping of securities to tax assistance and investment management. The annual family meetings no longer sufficed for business decisions, and F.K. called upon those conveniently situated—Walter S. Rosenberry, Jr., Ed Davis, and Fred—to get together in St. Paul for discussions on a variety of subjects.

In addition, there were the inevitable conflicts of interest between competing companies served by common directors. A case in point surfaced late in 1947 when Fritz Jewett, defending the honor of Potlatch Forests, Inc., let his feelings be known. It was increasingly clear that the Weyerhaeuser Timber Company was the main dog of the affiliation and felt encumbered by too many tails. Thus Phil offered to purchase PFI's stock in the Weyerhaeuser Sales Company. Fritz reluctantly agreed, but he called attention to the consequent "psychological disturbance," realizing that Potlatch would no longer be represented on the board of the

Sales Company. Phil foresaw only more bickering as Potlatch and the Timber Company competed, especially in the pulp business, and he urged F.K. to replace him on the PFI board. In addition, there was debate in the Congress over the Kefauver bill, which called into question membership on boards of competing companies. But as yet, that restriction was unclear.

In the meantime, F.K. attempted to patch things up. As he reminded cousin Fritz, "After spending the last twenty-three years trying to build up the Sales organization, which involved as a major factor securing cooperation between the various stockholders, I naturally hesitate to see anything done that will cause a rift in the relationships that have grown up over so many years." And even if PFI felt an occasional hurt, F.K. didn't believe they could "find or develop" an alternative to the Sales Company that would net as many dollars.

The logic favoring Timber Company ownership of the sales organization was becoming crystal clear. First and foremost was the fact of declining lumber production outside the Weyerhaeuser Timber Company and the increased capacity of the Timber Company plants. As a partial consequence, there was consideration of Sales Company recapitalization, a step that could be far more readily managed with single ownership. In that connection, F.K. had received an inquiry regarding "a rather vague rumor that the current scope of operations of your company has led to the consideration of employing additional capital funds." The writer, Arthur M. Anderson of J. P. Morgan & Company, had obvious interests, which F.K. immediately doused. None of the companies, he emphasized, was considering borrowing funds, and that position was unlikely to change "because the history of borrowings by forest industries has not been a happy one."

Another reason for simplifying Sales Company ownership was that the Timber Company already operated its own distribution yards. F.K. surmised that maintenance of the past ratio of stock ownership was "impractical." Indeed, "It seems to me that the only practical disadvantage which would result from having Weyerhaeuser Timber Company acquire all the stock of Weyerhaeuser Sales Company would be any resentment or disagreement on the part of Potlatch Forests, Inc." Somewhat similar difficulties also made the relationship between the Timber Company and Ed Davis's Wood Conversion Company uneasy. Again, the companies were clearly affiliated, but that did not make them partners. They were more akin to fiefdoms, loyal to single and separate lords, even if those lords happened to be cousins.

The changes sought by F.K. and Phil would be accomplished, pushed along in no small part by recommendations made by Booz, Allen and Hamilton, a firm specializing in business surveys and management counseling. The Sales Company became a wholly owned subsidiary of the Weyerhaeuser Timber Company in 1948, a year in which sales reached nearly one and one-half billion board feet. As for the Sales Company organization, Booz, Allen and Hamilton had recommended simplifying the structure in various ways. Perhaps the key change was the naming of a vice-president for sales, C. J. Mulrooney, to whom the three regional—now division—heads reported: A. N. Frederickson for the Eastern Division (Bill Peabody would henceforth be responsible solely for the Weyerhaeuser Steamship Company), A. D. Franklin for the Central, and R. S. Douglas for the Western. Of course, no perfect solution existed, but Kendall and F.K. thought they had moved in the right direction. When F.K. first outlined "the characteristics of a man who may be fitted for the job of sales personnel manager," he allowed that anyone fitting the mold would also make "an excellent candidate for President of the United States." C. J. Mulrooney should have been honored!

Despite strains and stresses among family members, there were instances of comic relief. F.K. saw to that, and so, too, did unnamed others. Evidence of such silliness was obvious on the morning of January 24, 1947, when he looked out his bedroom window and saw, to his amazement, a bison grazing on the front lawn at the end of a rope. The *St. Paul Pioneer Press* reported that "a prankster friend of the family" was responsible, and that the aim was merely to remind everyone that the St. Paul Winter Carnival was at hand and that it was time for "high jinks." Just who the "friend" was isn't clear, although all evidence points toward Walter Rosenberry, Jr., cousin Sarah-Maud's husband. This wasn't the first fraternal foolishness. A year earlier at Christmas, for example, Phil had received, anonymously, a live monkey. F.K. solved his bison problem by having the beast trucked to a nearby farm, where it was fattened and eventually provided exotic steaks and roasts for the Weyerhaeuser table. F.K. must have chuckled to himself every time he sat down to a buffalo dinner.

Uncle Rudolph, pointing at a Douglas-fir seedling, and F.K. at the Clemons Tree Farm near Montesano, Washington, 1941

Vivian Weyerhaeuser in her American Red Cross uniform in 1943, when she was vice-chairman of the organization's St. Paul chapter

Executives and directors of Weyerhaeuser Timber Company, Sales Company, and Potlatch at Glacier National Park, August 1942. Standing, left to right: Walter S. Rosenberry, Jr., Lewis W. Rick, Otto H. Leuschel, James E. Morris, S. G. Moon, Phil Weyerhaeuser, C. J. Boerner, Clarence J. Mulrooney, T. Lincoln O'Gara, C. L. Billings, Fred Weyerhaeuser, Clarence O. Graue, H. H. Irvine, James C. Gillespie, E. H. O'Neil, L. N. Riechman, W. H. Peabody, Charlie Ingram, A. J. Dickinson (of the Great Northern Railway), F.K., and Harry Kendall. Front row: D. H. Bartlett, James O'Connell, Harry E. Morgan, J. P. Boyd, Ray V. Clute, Rudolph Weyerhaeuser, John M. Musser, Ed Davis, R. R. Macartney, George H. Shafer, Don Lawrence, and Luther H. Atkinson.

On his fiftieth birthday, F.K. is joined in the St. Paul office by Uncles F.E. and Rudolph.

Vivian and Lynn Weyerhaeuser at a horse show in 1946. No doubt encouraged by their mother, the two were for a time serious equestriennes.

Gathered on the terrace of F.K.'s Summit Avenue home overlooking the Mississippi River are (clockwise from left) Rodney Loehr, Leonard Carpenter, F.K., Theodore C. Blegen, Bergman Richards, Minnesota Governor Luther W. Youngdahl, and Harold Dean Cater; 1949

Phil and F.K., who always appreciated time together, are caught by Charlie Ingram's camera on a western woods tour in 1946.

The annual Weyerhaeuser Timber Company dinner at the Winthrop Hotel in Tacoma, ca. 1949. At far left, Bill Peabody, F.K. against the wall, Joe Nolan behind the unidentified speaker, and Norton Clapp, second from right

Third-generation cousins, ca. 1955. Standing, left to right: Fritz Jewett, Carl Weyerhaeuser, Ed Davis, and Phil; seated: Fred Weyerhaeuser, F.K., and Dave Weyerhaeuser

Vivian Weyerhaeuser with Rudolph Bing, general manager of the Metropolitan Opera, in 1956, when she chaired the Met's National Council

Vivian welcoming Metropolitan Opera conductor Erich Leinsdorf to 294 Summit Avenue in 1960

George Long, Jr., and F.K. using a cross-cut saw to cut the Weyerhaeuser Company's sixtieth anniversary cake in 1960, the year F.K. announced his retirement as president and became chairman of the board

Weyerhaeuser Company directors in the old board room of the Tacoma Building, 1961. Seated clockwise from left: Carleton Blunt, John Hauberg, Jr., Thomas Taylor, John Musser, Herbert Kieckhefer, George Weyerhaeuser, Howard Morgan, president Norton Clapp, chairman F. K., Dave Weyerhaeuser, Laird Bell, Edmund Hayes, Edmond Cook, O. D. Fisher, Charlie Ingram, and George Crosby

F.K., John Musser, and New York Stock Exchange president G. Keith Funston
on Wall Street in 1963, when Weyerhaeuser stock went public

F.K. in the seat of honor at the joint Weyerhaeuser-Denkmann family reunion at the Alderbrook Inn near Seattle in 1965. The event honored the families' association dating back to the 1860 partnership of Frederick Weyerhaeuser and his brother-in-law F. C.A. Denkmann.

F.K. at the 1965
family reunion

F.K. in costume for
a party at the
1965 reunion

F.K. sips his coffee while a
youthful Howie Meadowcroft
talks to John Hauberg at the
1965 reunion

Mary Gaiser, Vivian, and F.K. being entertained at the 1965 reunion

Vivian Weyerhaeuser, honorary chairman of the Metropolitan Opera's National Council, in 1967

Two old friends, F.K. and Charlie Ingram, share a moment at the Weyerhaeuser Company's seventy-fifth anniversary dinner in 1975. F.K.'s son-in-law Stanley Day stands behind him. The event was held at the new corporate headquarters building in Federal Way, Washington.

A relaxed F.K. in 1972 at age seventy-seven

One senses that occasionally F.K. missed having a son, though he never suggested such feelings to his family. On the contrary, he included his daughters in every possible activity. Both girls attended Miss Porter's School in Farmington, Connecticut, after which they matriculated at Vassar. Their parents paid close attention to their progress, and F.K. was occasionally a bit disappointed in their performance, attributing any deficiencies to a lack of effort, for which he was overly ready to take the blame. Writing to Ward Johnson, director of Miss Porter's, he observed, "Their failure to do their best is probably caused by some neglect of mine in their up bringing." This was in the summer of 1946, prior to Lynn's start at Miss Porter's. For the headmaster's benefit, F.K. reported that daughter Vivian was taking a six-week course in mathematics, admitting, "We do not know whether she is taking this course from a desire to improve herself or because a number of her friends are also enrolled in it." She was also reading a book a week, after which she did an outline. "The rest of her time she devotes to riding, tennis, swimming, et cetera."

Within the Weyerhaeuser family, F.K. enjoyed plenty of opportunities to advise and assist the young men, especially those who entered the lumber business in some capacity. He felt a special responsibility for sister Elizabeth's boys, in part because she worried that they might not be given equal opportunities for advancement. In 1948 John Titcomb, then twenty-seven, was working in Lewiston for the timber department of Potlatch Forests, Inc. He had previously accumulated some experience in sawmilling and marketing and, as F.K. noted in a confidential letter, would have time later "to learn about the manufacture of veneers, plywood, and pulp." F.K. hoped his nephew would take advantage of his situation and "not get impatient or disturbed by extraneous matters." He reminded John that "a sound knowledge of trees furnishes the key to most of the fundamental decisions that have to be made in the operation of a forest industry," and later added with emphasis, "The forest is the important thing!" Then he delivered some serious advice to young Titcomb, in the process indicating his own feelings about work and responsibility:

> There is one thing that most of us have to learn in business, or for that matter in any other human activity, namely, that *we make our own jobs.* What you are doing can be merely a matter of rou-

tine, resulting from the past practice of somebody else, or it can become a matter of great importance depending upon how you yourself regard it and what you do about it. As soon as people around you find that you take on responsibilities and carry them out conscientiously and effectively, you get more responsibilities placed on you as fast as you can take them.

F.K. immediately apologized for his gravity, allowing that what he had written sounded much like "a sermon," though that wasn't his intention.

Heeding his own advice about the importance of the forest, F.K. headed west for the annual meeting of the Weyerhaeuser Timber Company, in those days held in mid-May. He traveled with Peavey Heffelfinger of Minneapolis, Phil's roommate at Yale, who was planning to do some fishing in Oregon. F.K. joined the party. As it turned out, they got dunked in the McKenzie River rapids and apparently were lucky that their losses were limited to their possessions. On that score, they lost nearly everything, the only items recovered being one oar and the tip of F.K.'s fishing rod. All in all, it was a little more excitement than they had expected. And that was just the beginning, for the balance of the summer—indeed, the year—was filled with activities, Vivian's focusing largely on politics. Another presidential election was at hand, and at long last hopes were high for the Republicans. She had gone to the national convention in Philadelphia as a supporter of Minnesota's own Harold Stassen. She left somewhat disappointed but firmly in the camp of nominee Thomas E. Dewey.

Next on the agenda was George H. Weyerhaeuser and Wendy Wagner's wedding on July 10. F.K. and family stayed with sister Elizabeth and Rod, and F.K. worried a bit as to where his daughters fit in the social scheme of things, "whether they are still regarded as 'babies' or mature women, the latter status being intended to signify that they are invited to the parties and the former that they are not." Young Vivian was almost eighteen and Lynn a little more than a year younger. They, of course, considered "themselves as quite advanced in years and experience," but F.K. desired his sister's "candid advice so that I can know whether to paint the lily or emphasize the educational or cultural aspect of the trip." The girls were included, and everything went according to plan.

Vivian Weyerhaeuser worked tirelessly, enthusiastically, and generally to good purpose. At the Republican state convention in Minneapolis on September 18, for example, she hosted a dinner at the Hotel Nicollet, this following a speech by Mary Donlon, the "applecheeked" chairman of the New York State workmen's compensation board. Miss Donlon predicted that Governor Dewey would win decisively and that his biggest margin would be in his home state. F.K. decided to take leave of the political scene and arranged for a pheasant hunt in South Dakota with Phil, Ed Davis, and a couple of other friends. They hunted for three days and bagged only eleven birds, leaving F.K. to wonder whether they ought to leave South Dakota alone for the next few years.

But the hunting disappointments failed to match those of election day. How could it be that once more a Democrat had been elected? There he was for all to see, a beaming Harry S Truman holding up that *Chicago Tribune* with its premature headline proclaiming a Dewey victory. Four more years. On the morning after the election, Phil summed up the situation in a letter to F.K.: "I can imagine the gloom in your household today."

POLITICS AND PUBLIC RELATIONS

THE POSTWAR economic boom did not last. Despite worry over the inflationary spiral early in 1948, by year's end conditions had changed dramatically. Phil and others complained that their prices were too high, but opinions varied from "zone to zone," in the Weyerhaeuser Sales Company lexicon. Those in the East expressed complete discouragement, while in the central region the consensus was for maintaining prices, "else we'll frighten the market down." And on the "Pacific side" there were "signs of life."

F.K. sympathized with those in the field. He knew that consumers are at heart speculators, buying not when the price of lumber is cheap "but rather when they think the price has reached a low point and then is apt to turn up." He didn't want to scare customers into delaying lumber purchases for a month or two in hopes that prices would fall still lower. "These are considerations that every sales organization has to face," he lectured, adding that he wasn't sure Phil would want to go through "all that mental turmoil." In this he was probably right. Meanwhile, he looked forward to pending sales meetings in Newark, Minneapolis, and then Tacoma. "My present efforts," he noted, "are bent very largely in the direction of re-energizing the sales organization and getting the lumber moving the way it should."

That was in some ways a curious observation, because what F.K. contributed personally to the three meetings was a carefully prepared speech that he entitled "Politics and Business." He realized that some might think he was overstepping his bounds, but he felt so strongly that he plowed ahead, explaining, "It is almost impossible to discuss the lumber business without reference to general business and without mention of economic and political trends in the country as a whole." His remarks could hardly surprise anyone. He spoke of the need for economy in government, of the dangers of deficit spending, and of the possibility of taxation levels that would discourage savings and risk-taking. Specifically, he called attention to President Truman's budget proposals, which included government entry into the public-housing field. And he mentioned the trends toward socialized medicine and various subsidies, programs requiring "taxation from you and me, spending a portion of it to maintain an organization of bureaucrats in Washington and then turning the balance back to us in the form of medical, education or other services which we may or may not need." Harry Kendall subsequently distributed copies of the talk, citing many requests, but he also included F.K.'s "admonition, that when it comes to your thinking or action on any of the problems we discussed, 'you are on your own'."

That pretty well described the problem F.K. and other managers faced time and again: how to get everyone to march in step. As for "re-energizing," it simply wasn't a necessity for many in the field. Detroit salesman B. D. Collins said as much in an early January letter. Collins had worked for the company for nearly thirty years and was now selling lumber to the grandsons of early customers. He reflected a bit after receipt of his 1948 bonus check, noting that good customers were first good friends and that "perhaps we stress SELLING too much, and the art of making friends too little." While F.K. appreciated the message, he knew that not all of the salesmen were imbued with the same spirit; and the spirit of the organization was always a basic concern of his. F.K. never forgot that it involved individual loyalties as well as enthusiasm.

Likewise, each firm was an individual within the fragmented forest-products industry. That fact seemed a secret too well kept, many assuming that somehow Weyerhaeuser was lumber's equivalent to Standard Oil or U.S. Steel. As a result, F.K. was frequently called upon to speak for the industry, a difficult assignment at best. Not only did he worry, legitimately, that the likes of brother Phil would complain, but also there were all those other operators listening critically. Previously, in mid-December, he had reluctantly accepted an invitation to appear on a seventeen-member panel of home builders, architects, politicians, and investors in what was termed the *Life* Round Table on Housing. This would result in a thirteen-page report in the January 31, 1949, issue.

As for the roundtable itself, naturally F.K. didn't get to say everything he wished, later informing a friend that he had "kept trying to get into the record as first essentials the adoption by the federal government of a financial program aimed at limiting inflation and permitting competition to function in a natural manner and also the necessity of keeping the federal government out of the housing business—but these two ideas were no more popular in the LIFE Round Table than they are nationally." Hoping to make up for his roundtable disappointment, he mailed to Russell W. Davenport of *Life* a lengthy outline of what he had prepared. In the first section, "How prices are made in the lumber industry," F.K. pointed out that there were "from 40 to 50 thousand sawmills in the United States." He also used U.S. Forest Service figures indicating that "no one company sold during the year 1946 more than 3.4% of the lumber marketed in the United States," resulting in great competition with relatively little price stability. Lumber prices, he asserted, were "one of the best examples of 'A Free Market' in our entire economy." In that regard, F.K. managed to include in his outlines many of the same points on politics and economy that he would discuss before his salesmen at their January meetings.

Perhaps the best meeting in January 1949 was that of the Weyerhaeuser family. As led by F.K., these meetings were beginning to be recognized as a welcome change from the past. Peggy Driscoll was one who noticed. "What a grand job I thought you did," she subsequently observed, appreciating the "feeling of *unity,* with complete freedom for discussion." This had to please F.K., though there were inevitably less pleasant aspects of family leadership. Recently these had involved Walter S. Rosenberry, Jr. Walter was charming, articulate, and had a first-rate sense of humor, the bison episode aside. He was the kind of associate who appealed to campaigners of any sort, including politicians. Unfortunately, he also enjoyed the partying aspect of politics. With Weyerhaeuser family approval, he had taken a leave of absence from his Rock Island Lumber Company position to work with the Stassen for President campaign, after which he never seemed quite able to return to the workaday world. F.K. and Fred got together with Walter and, in effect, read him the riot act. He had to stop drinking or else.

Some might consider their involvement meddling, but not the Weyerhaeusers. To them, personal problems were family problems. F.K. recalled that meeting later, when Walter had begun to backslide: "You said that you intended doing *everything* in your power to get yourself in shape and to satisfy the Family that you could and would carry on without any further trouble." The crucial disagreement had to do with choice of doctors and treatments, F.K. insisting on making the selection.

There would be no happy ending. Walter and Sarah-Maud divorced before the year was out, and Walter relinquished his management responsibilities. "It is with a heart full of sorrow that our family life comes to an end," Walter wrote to F.K. on July 11. He was referring to his divorce, but he might just as well have been talking about separation from the Weyerhaeuser family. John H. Hauberg, serving as president of the Rock Island Lumber Company, announced the resignation in an August 31 letter, noting Walter's significant contributions over the years. "He was responsible for the merging in 1935 of several companies into what is now known as Rock Island Lumber Company and in 1939 was the prime mover in the formation of Rilco Laminated Products, Inc." Hauberg had been an admirer, remembering that on occasion he had wondered, "What would happen if anything happened to Walter?" Now they would find out.

Even if business wasn't good, it surely had to be better than dealing with family miseries. The change from a seller's to a buyer's market was an emphatic one. For example, it was estimated that at the end of 1948 inventories of West Coast mills had doubled in one year, and there was little optimism for an early turnaround. Bob Douglas of the Sales Company opined that "1949 is going to be a year where we will have to sell lumber in a competitive market and with each species and grade having to stand on its own merits." F.K. put the best possible face on the situation: "Business is getting to be more fun with competition coming back into the picture."

Increased competition naturally meant stringencies of all sorts. One of the first involved the Sales Company's cash-discount policy. A year earlier, this had been changed from 2 to 1 percent, but now F.K. and Harry Kendall proposed to return to 2 percent, within ten days of the customer's receipt of the carload, effective May 1. F.K. noted that they were "fighting hard for business to keep the mills operating at capacity and it seems unwise to permit the continuance of a practice which, though justified by economics, has been abandoned by the rest of the industry."

Things were in such a state that Kendall began putting his nose into what would otherwise be Timber Company business. The subject of foremost concern was how the logs were sawed. Normal practice, at least for the West Coast mills, was to saw for the purpose of producing the best general average price. But these weren't normal times, and some of the mills were cutting to accommodate their orders. Kendall wished he had the authority to demand that the Timber Company follow the latter option, citing two reasons. First, they were behind in their shipments, and customers were complaining to the point of refusing to buy more until they received what had already been ordered. "Second, because the market is getting weaker every day and the longer those orders are held, the more danger we are in of getting cancellations or requests for price adjustment."

Increasingly, F.K. found himself fighting fires on several fronts. They may have been just brushfires, but he feared they might develop into something far more serious. Politics was his particular bane. Of course, he wasn't alone in his worries, but too often it seemed that others didn't recognize the gravity of a given situation. Occasionally, F.K. must have reminded cousins and colleagues of his Uncle F.E., who was at heart a Tory. In the summer of 1949, F.K. aimed at enlisting others on his team of watchdogs, including brother Phil, John Musser, now president of General Timber Service, Inc., Joe Nolan, legal counsel for the Timber Company, and C. W. Briggs, longtime attorney serving the St. Paul office. Of the group, Joe Nolan may have been the most cautious, while Charlie Briggs bordered on the reactionary.

On June 3 F.K. addressed a letter to the so-called policy committee, "In order to keep the record straight" and to provide an outline of goals. He then proceeded to list ten current objectives, many of which demanded alertness, keeping apprised of legislative efforts or possible legal actions. Perhaps the most significant objectives, at least in present terms, were items two and three: "The avoidance of federal regulation of privately-owned timber lands; [and] The defeat of any bill to create a Columbia River Valley Authority."

Phil and Joe Nolan wasted little time in sitting down and discussing F.K.'s outline, but they did so with the Timber Company's interests foremost in mind. Thus their worries were not equally shared on every item. Nolan, in his response, drew "a sharp distinction" between subjects with which the Timber Company was "particularly and perhaps peculiarly concerned" and those that were the concern of industries in general, even though some of the latter might hold special interest for Timber Company shareholders or officers as individuals. For instance, "Federal regulation of timberlands is representative of matters of the first class," whereas, "Economy in Government and even the Housing Bill is representative of matters in the second class." In short, there were priorities, and the Timber Company preferred a rifle's discriminating aim over taking a shotgun to any and all objectionable possibilities.

Lawyer Briggs saw things quite differently. "The whole is always greater than any of its parts," he asserted, adding that "an attack upon private forestry practices and utilization of timber will not be a local engagement. It will be part of a general engagement in which the issue will be nationalization, or state control, of business." He fervently believed that they must stand united, all of the "components of private business" allied to battle "the advancing forces of Collectivism." His message amounted virtually to a call to arms, and he was so exercised that he addressed his reaction to F. E. Weyerhaeuser, dead now for nearly four years. F.K. probably agreed; indeed, he indicated as much to friend Spencer Logan, "that we are in a desperate battle right now between conservative and socialistic forces which will determine the history of the country." But he immediately admitted, "Just what we can do about it here I don't know."

What he did was to follow the path suggested by Joe Nolan, directing Leo V. Bodine, Rex Black's replacement in public relations, to draft an outline of "our legislative program," with three levels—Classes A, B, and C—of importance. For example, the first listing under Class A was federal regulation of privately owned timberlands; and the first item under Class B was Socialized Medicine, with the notation "action unlikely this session." Class C, "no action recommended," began with a possible increase in the minimum wage. At the very least, that approach seemed to provide some quantification to the process.

With or without such prioritizing, the Department of Agriculture's 900-page publication *Trees* would have provoked a response. Admittedly, it contained many questionable assertions, and F.K. doubtless had good reasons for his resentment. Whether his expressed reaction was beneficial is another matter. He had received his copy thanks to Minnesota Senator Edward J. Thye, a personal friend, and it was to "Ed" that he responded with a lengthy letter. Specifics aside, F.K. observed: "Since about 1907 there has been one dominant, ever present thread piercing forest service contacts with the public . . . a gloomy prediction of forest depletion and attendant breakdown of the nation's economy. So consistent has the service been in this respect that it amounts to policy." There was no denying that. Over the years, if the Forest Service leadership had been accurate in its predictions, the trees would have long since disappeared. "The forest outlook is encouraging, not alarming," F.K. continued, "and I confess to a feeling of keen disappointment that the book TREES played down this truth—while by inference and outright petition from the chief forester it seeks to develop belief that federal regulatory laws are an inevitable necessity to survival of industry and nation."

Senator Thye did as F.K. knew he would; he immediately wrote to Forest Service Chief Lyle Watts, allowing that he was "greatly disturbed by [F.K.'s] criticisms." Laird Bell, however, wasn't convinced of the efficacy of F.K.'s approach. In Bell's words, "We are bound to lose . . . if we content ourselves with saying that the Forest Service is wrong." Simply being right couldn't compete with the government's power and particularly not when it had "effective sentimental appeal to the public." Most of the country had no forests of consequence, he reminded, and citizens in those regions thought in terms "of pretty trees and nice camping spots, and from that point of view we superficially are vulnerable." They were, indeed, and always would be.

As Laird saw the situation, they had only two courses of action. The first he termed "positive propaganda," which he thought they were doing successfully. The second required "cultivation of better relations with the Forest Service," and in this they weren't doing as well. He believed the industry had allies within the Forest Service and that therefore they should avoid attacking the whole, hitting "friend and foe alike." To conclude his piece, Laird noted that it was "surely no accident that Simpson, Crown-Zellerbach and Crossett were mentioned in *Trees* as progressive operators, without a word about Weyerhaeuser." In response, F.K. suggested that they call a meeting of those members of the affiliated companies who dealt regularly with the Forest Service "to consider whether we can evolve a plan for the improvement of our personal relationships with the members of the Forest Service."

Events soon supported Laird's position. Chief Forester Watts's answer to Senator Thye's inquiry—and F.K.'s criticisms—was downright snarling. He endeavored to respond point by point but was more political than factual. For example, replying to F.K.'s suggestion that the forest outlook was "encouraging, not alarming," Watts countered that "it may be encouraging when viewed from the position of a large timber owner," but it was "alarming to the consumer who sees lumber prices 3 times higher than they were before the war and twice as high as all other building materials, and who somehow can't shake himself loose from the old-fashioned idea that such a state of affairs stems from scarcity, not abundance." And he ended with the very idea that Laird had brought up:

> To me a serious aspect of Mr. Weyerhaeuser's letter is his closing challenge of what amounts to the sincerity and motives of the Forest Service. At another point he implies a question as to the professional competence of the many field men who participated in the Forest Service Reappraisal Project. Perhaps all I need to say in answer is that those who know the personnel of the Forest Service best generally find quite the opposite to be true.

Concurrent with these discussions was something F.K. and Phil viewed as even more alarming, which was consideration of a Columbia Valley Authority, Senate Bill 1645. The possibility of CVA, modeled on the Tennessee Valley Authority, established as part of the New Deal, clearly fell into those categories of legislation demanding immediate action. The brothers felt so strongly that they addressed identical letters to employees of the Timber Company and the Sales Company, referring to the proposed legislation, which "would set up a huge monopolistic government corporation controlled by three men whose actions would be well protected from interference by the states concerned and practically independent of Congress." They closed the letters urging that employees write their congressmen expressing views "on this important subject."

Again Laird Bell reacted, although this time it was in far less measured words. He lambasted his former junior partner and now Timber Company counsel, Joe Nolan, who later admitted, "Laird really put the whip to me." This wasn't merely a slight difference of opinion. "You just permitted the grossest error to be perpetrated," Laird admonished. "We have all kinds of shareholders and we have no right to instruct them in subjects political." Phil acknowledged, "This political business defeats me." F.K. nodded in agreement.

Maybe, just maybe, there was another way. Fairfield Osborn, author of the book *The Plundered Planet,* who had recently created an organization called the Conservation Foundation, seemed genuinely interested in recruiting industry representatives to participate, or as he put it, to inform the public of what each "is doing to protect the nation's resources heritage." Not surprisingly, he was also interested in financial contributions. Initially, Phil had been Osborn's target, but Tacoma was so far away, and Phil, typically, decided the cause could be better served from St. Paul and by F.K. Accordingly, he nominated his brother. So it was F.K. who attended a meeting of the Conservation Foundation, a black-tie affair on January 11, 1950, at the University Club of New York. He subsequently informed Phil about what he had missed. Somewhat to his surprise, F.K. found it to be a "most enjoyable evening," with Osborn a "very genial host," who "succeeded in selling himself and his services to a group of very intelligent people." The message was one with which F.K. could agree enthusiastically, "that we should save our natural resources and our personal liberties at the same time, through avoidance of big government"—or so he interpreted it.

F.K. assumed that Osborn hoped those in attendance "would leap to their feet and offer to put up funds," but it hadn't happened. All, including F.K., sat on their hands, although he felt confident "that you or I will have an opportunity to be a guest of Mr. Osborn again at which time it will be necessary to say yes or no to something." Still, F.K. came away something of a believer, reasoning that they would "come out better by joining them than by fighting them." Further, there seemed to be agreement that "we [Weyerhaeuser] had been and are doing a swell job," and he added, for Phil's benefit, "Just who sold them this bill of goods I don't know but I guess it was you."

He was right about getting the opportunity "to say yes or no to something." Osborn visited him in St. Paul the following May, at which time he shared a motion picture "depicting the need for conserving natural resources." It contained little objectionable material, "except that I get somewhat pained whenever such a picture shows trees being falled and leaves any inference of industry's guilt for the ensuing floods." But by and large, F.K. considered the position of the Conservation Foundation to be "not too far from our own." The inevitable differences regarding "facts" were not cited with any malice. The real purposes of Osborn's visit were to invite F.K. or Phil to serve as a trustee for the foundation, and second, "unrelated to the first," to get a contribution from Weyerhaeuser of between $2,500 and $5,000, which as F.K. presumed, was intended "to be an annual affair." F.K. was favorably inclined. What obviously tipped the scales was his belief that the foundation preferred to educate rather than depend on governmental action.

Phil responded promptly, enclosing a Timber Company check for $5,000 along with the expressed hope that F.K. would be the one to serve. His charge was simple enough: "To keep this Foundation, if possible, saying things which we believe to be true in reference to the forest situation." F.K. accepted, on one condition: "Namely, that if there arises a diversity of views that would make my continued participation as trustee embarrassing either to you or to me I will be free to withdraw." And so it was that he became a colleague of Fairfield Osborn and a member of the Conservation Foundation.

Somewhat related were other involvements of national importance. Through friend Henry T. McKnight, soon to be a Timber Company director, F.K. and Phil received an invitation to meet with Dwight D. Eisenhower, then president of Columbia University. At the time, Eisenhower was championing an organization called the American Assembly, and the Weyerhaeuser brothers came away impressed. Again, the focus appeared to be public education, and in his thank-you letter to Eisenhower, F.K. cited the importance of the cause: "Certainly the intelligence with which the American people meet the problems which lie ahead will determine more than anything else where we will end up." Where they would end up also depended upon the general. Already some talked about a presidential nomination, but McKnight doubted whether Eisenhower's sense of duty had as yet moved that far. In the meantime there was much to do. McKnight, for example, was also active in the Conservation Foundation and Friends of the Land, another conservation group headed by Louis Bromfield. For the Weyerhaeusers, such involvements were inescapable.

Inevitably, these commitments resulted in added responsibilities, all of which F.K. took seriously. But none of his responsibilities was more keenly felt than his leadership of the clan. Earlier in the year, the family had met on schedule. This time, he had prepared some far-reaching recommendations—he outlined them in terms of advantages and disadvantages—in what he called "A Family Proposal." This touched on several subjects, perhaps most significantly the Rock Island Lumber Company and the northern California redwood operation, the Hill-Davis Company. Included in his list of advantages was recognition of the "high degree of unity" that had been maintained as well as the fact that several family members were "currently making substantial contributions to the corporation in which we have interests." Conversely, among the disadvantages was the "danger of drifting apart and ceasing to maintain our present unity of policy and action." Then—something F.K. always noted—they might lose the interest of "our abler business men, both adult and young." Those items hardly surprised anyone, but when it came to family investment policy, he offered a new perspective. It was, he observed, "the same as it was twenty years ago even though revolutionary changes have occurred in our political and economic world."

Specifically, he recommended that the family acquire all of the Rock Island Lumber Company's ownership and give it "some of the characteristics of a partnership," using it not only to run the retail and wholesale business as before, "but also to enter other promising fields as they appear by investing earnings or borrowing." They could use The Bonners Ferry Lumber Company as a banker and would "hold our Family interest in the following as long as possible"—Weyerhaeuser Timber Company, Potlatch Forests, Inc., Boise-Payette Lumber Company, Northwest Paper Company, Rock Island Millwork Company, and Wood Conversion Company—insofar as these were "well managed properties which will appreciate in value over the years."

F.K. secured the necessary "informal O.K." and proceeded to fill in the details, implementing the proposal. Although Phil didn't agree enthusiastically with every point, he did find the matter of providing for the next generation "interesting," especially as concerned the Hill-Davis Company. There was an offer to buy, but Phil wondered if instead that might be one of those opportunities "for someone of our younger group"; that would definitely influence his own decision about whether to sell. In the end, the family would retain Hill-Davis for many years. When it was finally sold in the 1980s, the profits were substantial by any reckoning.

F.K. continued to investigate ways the children could involve themselves in business. First, the family successfully acquired all of the outside ownership in the Rock Island Lumber Company. He then, much in the manner of his father and uncles, tried to put together a "routine for college graduates which might in the shortest possible time give them a bird's eye view of our business." Upon completion, they—the male exclusiveness was understood—should be in a position to determine which area best suited them. Included in his curriculum was a bibliography of texts and technical books that they "might read with profit." The entire program would require about eighteen months, which, he admitted, "seems to be too long a time for a young man to be on the move rather than buckling down to one job." The program commenced with a one-month assignment as an assistant in a retail lumber yard, after which the apprentice would receive forestry and logging experience and work in a sawmill, in pulp and paper, and, of course, in sales.

But it wasn't all work, not even for F.K. Early in the summer, his family toured Europe, and while it was enjoyable, keeping track of three women proved a bit of a challenge. During the Christmas holidays, he invited his young St. Paul relatives, "Cousins-once-removed," to a clay pigeon party. The "shoot" would occur at the Somerset Country Club, and he advised that "Each fellow should have a clear head and a good eye." Regardless of the outcome, after the event all would convene at 294 Summit Avenue for refreshments. In this instance, "fellows" included females.

So the year ended as most years do, with a celebration of sorts. But this New Year seemed special, marking as it did the century's midpoint. For all of the many distractions, F.K. had not slighted the Sales Company, as his annual address to its personnel attested. The talk was not particularly optimistic, beginning with recognition of the likely return to a buyer's market. Many of the salesmen had little or no experience with such conditions, for over the past dozen years or so they had enjoyed the advantages of a seller's market. The change, he lectured, "emphasizes the vital importance of doing an efficient and effective selling job." As always, he had prepared carefully. "Tonight I will say a few words to you on the following subjects: 1. The nature of the lumber market; 2. What W. does to sell its sawmills' products; 3. Who sets prices on our lumber; 4. How we price our lumber; 5. Something about sales policies; 6. To whom do we sell our lumber?; 7. Lumber market prospects; [and] 8. How big is our sales organization?" When he was finished, all must have felt they knew as much about the subject as was necessary. More important, however, F.K. obviously cared; so they could do no less.

But caring didn't cure uncertainty. The big event of 1950 once again involved distant places and unknown outcomes. North Korean troops crossed the thirty-eighth parallel on June 25, and two days later President Truman committed American forces to the defense of South Korea. Military requirements would have a large effect on the nation's economy, although there would be no effort to institute controls on a level comparable to World War II. Korea was to be a "limited war," but that did not make it any the less terrible. Peace continued elusive, with the added complication of irrational fears on the home front.

F.K. THE CONSERVATIVE

ONE THING SEEMED clear in the early 1950s. Not all of America's enemies were on the Korean peninsula. Nor were they to be found only in China and the Soviet Union. They were everywhere, often in the most unexpected places— subversives, "fellow travelers," in college classrooms and on Hollywood sound stages. Although F.K. could hardly be labeled an hysteric, he did waste time, and some money, in joining the chase for a while. The most flagrant example occurred after a chance meeting with actor Adolphe Menjou at a St. Paul social event. Menjou subsequently forwarded to F.K. the names of three Yale professors "who have been associated with various Communist fronts."

F.K.'s brief involvement with Menjou was naive, doubtless stemming not so much from fear of any imminent Communist danger as from his long-standing concern about socialist tendencies. Even in his correspondence with the actor-turned-accuser, F.K. emphasized the need for responsible education, or in his terms, "sound economics." He constantly warned of what he saw as the dangers of government expansion and interference, or those trends that seemed most likely to imperil free enterprise. Indeed, in 1951 he had tried to honor an invitation from Harvard professor of economics John Kenneth Galbraith to appear before two groups, a conservation seminar followed by "our entire group in agricultural economics." But in the end, F.K.'s schedule did not permit him to attend.

His St. Paul friend Samuel H. Ordway, Jr., had suggested that Professor Galbraith invite F.K. to Harvard. And it was the Conservation Foundation that first introduced the professor to Sam. F.K. had maintained his enthusiasm for the foundation's program, although as he sought Phil's approval for another $5,000 contribution, he couched his reasoning in terms he knew would appeal to his brother: "I don't want to be soft-headed about this, but my current feeling is that these contributions tend to make them very careful about what they say." Phil's response: "I agree."

But in truth, F.K.'s interest in the Conservation Foundation was hardly as cynical as his note to Phil suggested. An example was his detailed review of Ordway's paper for the foundation, "Alaska Now." Not surprisingly, F.K.'s list of "corrections" began with an assumption that the federal government's role in the territory's future would be substantial. He did take issue with Sam's comment regarding "exploitation" of the American forest, observing that "forest wastes do not constitute real economic waste when you cannot afford to bring them out of the woods." That was an old disagreement. The question of who should own the land mattered more. F.K. knew that it was best owned by "the individual operator," explaining, "If he owns the land he has a very real stake in keeping it productive." Throughout, however, he maintained a respectful tone, closing his note to Ordway with the assurance "that our differences are more in words than in thoughts."

The subject of private ownership was not one of pure philosophy. F.K. could cite personal experiences that seemed to support his position, underscoring the importance of individual initiative as opposed to collective action. A case in point was Potlatch, Idaho, a company town that, despite positive efforts over the years, had come to look like most—drab and depressing. F.K. thought that because the families themselves didn't own the homes, they had little incentive to maintain them. W. P. "Bill" Davis was now president of Potlatch Forests, Inc., and in February 1951 F.K. encouraged him to follow up on earlier discussions about the town. Don't think about making money out of it, he advised, "but simply of getting rid of the responsibility and probably getting a better town in the long run when people own their own homes." He would later recommend more direct action, including expenditures of "$50,000 a year or more doing things to improve the communities in which [PFI] operates plants or has logging operations." He admitted that management attitudes in the past may have been "rather narrow" but reminded him that Potlatch had had no profits for a long time "and had to husband its resources."

Another evidence of change in which F.K. took enormous interest involved the forest itself. Regarding Potlatch, for example, he came away from a late-winter tour worrying about forestry practices there. He recommended that PFI hire a first-class forester and allow him to practice his profession, answering questions about regeneration, areas requiring artificial planting, and all the rest. He recalled that some years earlier a forester had criticized their practice of selective logging (i.e., cutting the large white pine, leaving behind the smaller pine and mixed woods) as ineffective, resulting "in a stagnant forest where the white pine is suppressed and very little growth ensues." F.K. didn't pretend to know the best answer, but he argued that they "ought to have a policy and that our policy ought to be developed by experts."

F.K. wasn't the only one without answers when it came to forestry matters. It is difficult to appreciate how little even the professionals understood in the early 1950s. The Timber Company's chief forester, Clyde Martin, readily admitted, "We have much to learn." He was convinced that nature "still produces better crops of higher quality timber at less cost than can be artificially grown," adding, "We hope never to have to plant more than 10% of our cutover areas." The big job, Martin contended, was "to learn how to utilize *all* of the wood our forest lands now grow." In this they had made considerable progress, harvesting 25 percent more per acre than ten years earlier.

Admittedly, F.K.'s interest was fueled partly by a significant assignment. In keeping with his self-assumed public relations responsibility, he accepted an invitation to address the Newcomen Society in 1951. Originally British, it was named for Thomas Newcomen (1663–1729), an early designer of the steam engine. The society's focus had been "the history of Material Civilization," although in more recent years its concerns centered on British-American traditions and ideals. A Newcomen invitation was viewed as an honor, and F.K. took it seriously. He delivered his speech, "Trees and Men," on the evening of May 18 at the Minnesota Club in St. Paul. His remarks were in keeping with the formality of the affair. "My story is about trees and men," he began:

It is a romantic story that appeals to the imagination. A story of men meeting the challenge of floods, snows, and droughts; of driving logs down swollen rivers, and of battling forest fires. I hope that it will bring to you a little of the aroma of Wisconsin pines, a vision of great, horse-drawn sleighs piled high with logs traveling the iced roads of northern Minnesota, the faint far cry of "timber" on the slopes of some deep canyon in the Cascades, the chug of a steam skidder, and a picture of the snowy peak of Mount St. Helens towering above heavily forested foothills against the deep blue of the western sky.

F.K. sketched the early history of his grandfather's lumbering efforts in the Lake States and then detailed the move westward and expansion in Washington, Oregon, and Idaho. He spoke of their faith in trees, of the Tree Farm movement and other educational programs, and also of their success in combatting enemies, natural and otherwise. Concerning the latter, F.K. didn't waste the opportunity to attack government interference. "The issue of federal ownership or control versus private ownership and control can be stated another way: 'Can we grow more trees by government compulsion or by voluntary private effort with the profit incentive?'" F.K. left no doubt as to the correct answer. He concluded on a positive note:

> We who have spent our lives in these enterprises have a great inheritance and we are conscious of our responsibilities. We believe a fine future of great service lies ahead for American forests and the forest industries. Certainly those who plant trees to mature *in a hundred years* give daily evidence of their faith in the future of America and in the perpetuation *of what America symbolizes!*

Coincident with F.K.'s preparations for this speech, negotiations were under way with Professor Allan Nevins and Columbia University for a history of the Weyerhaeuser Timber Company. The result, which covered far more than the company, would be *Timber and Men: The Weyerhaeuser Story* (1963). The historian initially envisioned a dramatic tale of big trees and big men. In fact, however, *Timber and Men* and F.K.'s "Trees and Men" speech suffered similarly. Lumbering could be exciting and colorful, even romantic in the abstract, but in the end, it was always business.

With considerable assistance from Laird Bell, F.K. searched long and hard for an author to write the history. Nearly as important, he had to convince brother Phil that such a history ought to be written. Early in 1951, Phil capitulated, indicating that he would "vote unqualifiedly" in favor of proceeding. "I think it's worth doing and I would like to have it accomplished before I retire and become thereby a possible subject of consideration." His earlier fears of antitrust problems would simply "have to be weighed by the historian and we will each have to get our heads down so far as the impact of personalities of ancestors as they come out of the mill." Phil needn't have worried, at least for himself. Publication wouldn't take place until seven years after his death.

The reaction to F.K.'s Newcomen address was favorable, as expected. He sent copies far and wide, forewarning some regarding the message. To Laird Bell he wrote, "As you will immediately realize it consists of a little history and a lot of propaganda." He even mailed a copy to his beloved Lake Nebagamon tutor and friend, Aimee E. Lyford. In his covering note, F.K. apologized for his long silence: "The only explanation seems to be that life gets complicated and time passes so fast with so much to cram into so little of it." He also brought her up-to-date on his own family, the two daughters now both attending Vassar. "They are fine girls," he noted, "but as father used to say, 'they need a little fixing now and then.'"

Despite F.K.'s hectic schedule, there were still occasional breaks in the action. But even vacations with family often proved demanding and occasionally frustrating. Such was the case when he was trying to plan the details of a Hawaiian visit. F.K. asked Don Watson, now manager of the Weyerhaeuser Steamship Company, about the arrangements; specifically, could they "get somewhat less expensive accommodations for the two girls at the Royal Hawaiian Hotel." But he immediately warned Watson to expect more changes. "One thing about traveling with my family is that I never quite know what is going to happen next. No doubt by the time you receive this letter there will be some other plan."

Two events demanded special attention in the summer of 1951, one quite pleasurable and the other quite the opposite. The first involved a visit, something like a triumphal tour of the United States, by Dr. Carl A. Schenck. F.K. felt privileged to host the eighty-three-year-old Schenck at a dinner in St. Paul on July 26. He was, as noted in the invitation, "one of the fathers of the American forestry movement." The second event occurred during the family's Hawaiian vacation. The Weyerhaeuser home was ransacked, but as it turned out, little of value was stolen. Perhaps the worst consequence was the publicity the break-in occasioned, publicity of a sort never welcomed.

As 1951 passed, thoughts inevitably turned to politics. The Republicans had not yet settled on a candidate for the presidency. F.K. offered "our dog Bowser or anybody else who can beat Truman, including Taft and Eisenhower, both of whom are honorable men and patriotic Americans." But there would also be politics, of a sort, closer to home within the family. F.K. had been introduced to an organization known as Spiritual Mobilization, whose purpose was to "reawaken in the hearts and minds of the American people a sense of the significance of the spiritual and moral principles which are enunciated in our Declaration of Independence, and upon which, through our Constitution, our country has prospered." At least momentarily, F.K. was sold, convinced of the organization's legitimacy. The credentials of its leaders were impressive. Its president, Dr. James W. Fifield, Jr., served as pastor of the First Congregational Church of Los Angeles, and supporters included Roger W. Babson, Dr. Norman Vincent Peale, and Leonard E. Read. F.K. personally contributed $3,000, and he did his best to convince family members to follow his example. But not all agreed, and a few thought that he had overstepped his bounds.

One of those recalcitrants was cousin C. Davis "Dave" Weyerhaeuser, younger son of F.E. One might have expected the objection that this organization was too conservative. For Dave, however, it wasn't conservative enough. And when it came to spiritual questions, he was a far more serious student than F.K. He sent a lengthy letter explaining his doubts as to the Spiritual Mobilization's credo, "first of claiming the sanction of the Christian faith, and professing that Christian teaching is the basis of the program and then of departing almost completely from what the Christian faith really teaches—that is, if the Bible is to be considered the true source of authority." Dave's disagreement began at the beginning, with the assertion that "Man is a child of God." Not so. As Dave read his Bible, "Only those who believe in Christ are children of God," and he proceeded to cite chapter and verse, beginning with John 1:12.

Dave's brother Fred also expressed doubts. Spiritual Mobilization's program focused on theological seminaries and theologians, and Fred felt this missed the mark. They ought to be concentrating on "professions such as professors, teachers, economists, doctors, etc., where a much higher degree of radical thinking exists." If they were interested in "the quality of ministry," it would surely be more effective "to actively aid and support those seminaries that are sound in their teachings."

F.K. may have been disappointed in the reluctance of others to join the cause, but he didn't give up. As Dave suggested, he checked the biblical references regarding "children of God," and came away with a different interpretation. "My own belief," F.K. answered, "is that man is potentially a child of God in that he has a soul and can be saved by the grace of God." F.K. too had given these matters considerable thought—after all, he had faithfully served as an elder of St. Paul's House of Hope Church, listened intently to sermon after sermon, sharing the messages with distant friends and daughters away at school. And thus he was sincere in saying to Dave, "I would love to sit down and talk with you at length about this because it is a subject which interests me enormously."

F.K. admitted defeat later in the year, at least in obtaining a grant for Spiritual Mobilization from the Weyerhaeuser Family Foundation. "There are too many members with other interests," he explained, "and also too many members who look at Spiritual Mobilization with a somewhat jaundiced eye." That, however, didn't deter him from contributing $3,000, "the same as last year." And he continued to preach to those who had to listen, including his daughters. In late 1953, he sent a copy of *Faith and Freedom,* Spiritual Mobilization's magazine, to Lynn, specifically calling her attention to an article, "Three Fallacies of the Left," which provided "the best answer to socialistic doctrines that I have read." He also noted the lead article, "Pinks in Our Pulpits," which pretty well described the organization's fundamental concern.

F.K. knew he couldn't count on any support from Phil for Spiritual Mobilization, even though the basis of F.K.'s position was economic, specifically his fear of collectivism and the clergy's role in encouraging what he viewed as an alien and dangerous practice. As he had tried to explain to Dave, "It is certainly not the first duty of clergymen to help protect the 'inalienable rights' of man, but also clergymen clearly have no right to help destroy these rights which many of them are doing unknowingly." While Phil was a Christian and as much a capitalist as his brother, he was no missionary. And at the moment he had far more on his mind, beginning with some broken ribs, the result of a fall. F.K. was sympathetic, as only a brother could be. "It seems to me that you are getting more awkward as you get fatter and no doubt you don't see where you are placing your feet." He concluded by citing the increasing unfairness of their athletic contests, "when you reflect on how well I have kept my figure and my agility."

Being a Weyerhaeuser could be amusing when an occasional interloper sought acceptance by subterfuge. Phil received one inquiry from a Fritz Weyerhaeuser, who claimed to be the grandson of John Weyerhaeuser, grandfather Frederick's brother. F.K. researched the claim and reported back that "Grandfather's brother Johannes was born January 15, 1838, and died on the 25th of August, 1840, at the age of two."

While F.K. enjoyed most aspects of life as a Weyerhaeuser, there were problems. Some of them had to do with providing leadership and advice in a constantly changing financial and legal environment, and others proved to be of a personally sensitive nature. Foremost was uncertainty regarding the stock of Potlatch Forests, Inc., owned by the Clearwater Timber Company, whose stock, in turn, was owned by individuals but retained by the family holding company, The Bonners Ferry Company. The problem wasn't a simple one by any means, but F.K. tried to explain it prior to the January family meetings so there could be informed discussion. "It is advantageous," he noted, for those contemplating "disposal of their interest in a corporation to have the stock of that corporation directly in their own hands rather than in the hands of a holding company which they own." The reasons were clear enough. Stock in holding companies had no real market value. Further, moving stock that had appreciated in value out of a holding company usually involved "a tax to the stockholder through the mere process of liquidating the holding company." In short, if a holding company were liquidated and the stockholder sold the stock thus received, he would probably pay two taxes. But when a stockholder sold stock held in his own hands, he would pay only one tax.

An important interim decision had been obtained from the Treasury Department, which permitted The Bonners Ferry Lumber Company to forgive accrued interest owed to it by the Clearwater Timber Company. F.K. estimated that this decision alone had saved the family about a million dollars in taxes. Clearwater still owed Bonners Ferry about

$500,000 of principal, but this could be paid by means of dividends from Potlatch Forests, Inc. (PFI) and received as return of capital without being taxed. Once that was accomplished, it would be possible to liquidate the Clearwater Timber Company, its assets going to The Bonners Ferry Lumber Company. This, however, required a decision by the family. F.K. offered three alternatives, A, B, and C, which he urged his relatives to think seriously about before discussing them at the family meeting in January 1952.

He also stated that he preferred plan C, whereby Clearwater would be liquidated with its PFI stock passing to Bonners Ferry. Then Bonners Ferry would distribute approximately $6.5 million to its stockholders without any tax ramifications. This liquidation would leave some 135,000 shares of PFI stock in the hands of Bonners Ferry, "which would represent a bare controlling interest in PFI." He concluded his presentation in the expected manner:

> The Family ought to decide this question in the light of all the facts, bearing in mind that it will have important consequences for the future. Balancing the advantages of each plan I have come to the conclusion that I favor plan C because it keeps the Family strong and united while still putting into their individual hands enough PFI stock to give them some opportunity for liquidation if advantageous in the future.

Plan C was adopted, the tax-free cash distribution subsequently being used mainly to purchase, on an individual basis, PFI stock from Clearwater at $100 per share; 30,000 shares were purchased under this option. Of all of F.K.'s many recommendations, few rivaled the Clearwater settlement in terms of increasing family financial security.

Another interesting and complicated situation caught F.K.'s attention early in the New Year. While the Weyerhaeuser Timber Company had never been active in the California redwood country, Weyerhaeuser family members were, specifically through the Hill–Davis Company. That fact wasn't initially significant in January 1952, but it would become so years later when the redwood properties of Hill–Davis were purchased by the federal government at considerable profit to the shareholders. In 1952, however, public interest in redwoods, at least in any organized sense, was in its infancy.

Fairfield Osborn's Conservation Foundation brought relative strangers together to consider the matter, but the Save-the-Redwoods League was the prime mover, along with a new organization, California Forests, Inc. F.K. studied the latter's proposed charter and immediately questioned its position, as stated in paragraph five: "All participants felt that California Forests Inc. should serve a very worthy cause and that it should be established and managed solely in the public service." In the first place, F.K. viewed redwoods as trees, admittedly large and old, but trees, nothing more, nothing less. While he agreed that "the perpetuation of our forests is vitally important to the future welfare of our people," he had little faith in a perpetual foundation. And again he stated his basic belief, that ownership of the land was "better kept in the hands of the people than to be permanently segregated in a non-profit enterprise for whatever worthy cause." The harvesting of trees ought to provide the means for more efficient utilization of other trees, and "by impounding lands in a non-profit corporation you may discourage or make impossible such investment."

To another individual, F.K. raised questions about foundations per se. They "go on and on," he asserted, becoming "creatures of their managers who wish [to] retain a living out of their jobs and tend to forget the original purpose of the foundations. It seems to me that many of the large foundations created by capitalists have become sinecures for socialists." That was F.K. at his most conservative.

Yale University presented a different sort of dilemma. The Forestry School was in the midst of a fund-raising campaign, and Colonel Bill Greeley visited F.K. to solicit support. Normally, this would not have been a problem—the Weyerhaeusers were among the earliest contributors to the Forestry School, and probably considered it a legacy. But attitudes at Yale, and lately about Yale, seemed anything but traditional from F.K.'s viewpoint. Central to the debate was the recent book by William F. Buckley, Jr., *God and Man at Yale*. Young Buckley, in what seemed to some an exposé, warned of an irreligious, socialistic point of view that threatened to rule in Eli classrooms. F.K. read the book and listened to the pros and cons. He wasn't sure just what to believe, but he feared that much of what Buckley wrote was true. To a friend he suggested that "academic freedom" was too often confused with "academic license." And while he agreed that the alumni had "no inherent right to dictate what should be taught," at the same time they had "a first class right to say whether or not they will contribute to the support or endowment of that institution."

In the course of the brouhaha, one Yale dean referred to F.K. as a "very conservative Republican." F.K. pretended confusion over that label. He admitted a religious belief and also that he supported "teaching young Americans the advantages of an economic and social system which has given the greatest degree of freedom and opportunity for individual development that any people ever enjoyed."

But Whitney Griswold was now president of Yale, and his presence was somehow reassuring; he was apparently considered a kindred spirit. Further, the Forestry School seemed largely removed from the more controversial subjects of economics and history, although one might wonder why that should have been. And, of the forestry schools the country over, only Yale and Duke were privately supported. Thus, F.K. agreed to contribute to the $2.2 million campaign, and solicited the financial help of others. There was, however, one small irritant: The Forestry School had begun to describe its curriculum as the Conservation Program. So be it. F.K. even suggested that the Weyerhaeuser Timber Company would most likely "commit itself to employ annually one graduate of the Conservation Program at Yale." The times were changing.

Nothing evidences change more starkly than the death of a friend and colleague. So it was with the loss of Harry T. Kendall, who died on May 2, 1952, while attending a meeting of the Canada-U.S. Committee of the U.S. Chamber of Commerce in Sulphur Springs, West Virginia. Kendall's Sales Company service dated back twenty years. He had been vice-president and general manager from 1933 to 1950, at which time he became chairman of the board. F.K. would miss him greatly. His announcement to employees concluded with words inadequate but sincere: "We have lost a warm friend and a fine citizen who lived a life of outstanding service to his community and to his country."

Other changes were taking place, including dissolution of General Timber Service, Inc., effectively marking the end of the "committee approach" that had been inaugurated by F.E. shortly after his father's death in 1914. GTS now consisted of the Finance Department, whose responsibility largely involved audits, the Tax Department, the Public Relations Department, and the Insurance Department. The general conclusion was that these jobs could be delegated to the Sales Company or managed as well by outside contractors. Final approval for liquidation was given by the Executive Committee on December 11, 1952. F.K. didn't mourn the passing of GTS, but some did. Ed Davis, for example, allowed that he was "sorry to see the action taken and still believe it would be of much benefit to have retained this company for the benefit of all others." The fact was, however, that the Weyerhaeuser Timber Company had simply outgrown the need for such an association. GTS was obsolete, and only those who cherished the past for its own sake shook their heads.

But the biggest change involved the Weyerhaeuser family and affiliated companies only indirectly. Another presidential election year had arrived, and once again Vivian was in the midst of the action. Again, Minnesota's Harold Stassen vied for the Republican nomination. Stassen, still a young man, had first been elected governor in 1940 and was known far and wide as the "boy governor." But he viewed state politics as a stepping stone, beginning what one historian described as "his never-ending quest for the White House" in 1948. Curiously, it was the Minnesota primary in 1952 that doomed Stassen's candidacy that year, specifically the unexpected heavy write-in vote for Dwight D. Eisenhower. Friend George Merck closed his May 15 letter to F.K. with the hope that "Vivian will switch to Ike!" She would, eventually, when left with no other choice.

F.K. also walked the political fence for a time, uncertain whether Ike's credentials were quite in keeping with his own philosophy. He, too, was surprised by Eisenhower's Minnesota primary performance, attributing it to organization and general popularity. "Personally," he acknowledged, "I like [Senator Robert] Taft better." It wasn't that F.K. thought less of the general, but he had little faith in Eisenhower's closest advisers.

As convention time neared, F.K. explained his preference for Taft to family and friends. He would cite experience as a key factor, but "the great issue of the day" came down to the basics, spending and taxes. The words were familiar. "Government solvency" was the issue:

> . . . and that immediately becomes the issue of socialism versus our historic principles of personal initiative. Spending for whatever object becomes a part of this issue. Foreign spending, that is to say the continued granting of enormous funds to foreign countries

for rehabilitation or military preparation, threatens the very foundation of our government and economy. General Eisenhower "appears to be" wedded to that program.

To underline his opposition, he expressed the fear that many Republicans supporting Ike were wolves in sheeps' clothing, New Dealers at heart, and he pointed to Senator Wayne Morse of Oregon as a prime example.

But Eisenhower would win the nomination, and with that battle over, there was no doubt about what to do next. F.K. and Vivian had previously planned a late-summer European tour, sailing aboard the *Queen Mary*. Those plans, however, fell victim to the moment. As F.K. explained to a London friend, "Vivian has become involved in politics working for the election of General Eisenhower and has decided that her patriotic duty requires that she keep at it instead of making the European jaunt." F.K. ended up going alone, flying both ways, enjoying a bit of grouse shooting in the Scottish Highlands.

Vivian spent most of the fall in New York with the Citizens for Eisenhower Committee. Her contributions were significant. She possessed managerial skills, of that there was no question. As for F.K., he took no active part in the campaign. Perhaps there seemed little need for any personal involvement since everyone he knew was committed to Eisenhower. Well, almost everyone. Laird Bell may have been the sole exception. F.K. heard via the grapevine that Laird was "working hard for Governor [Adlai E.] Stevenson" and observed in a preelection note, "I hope this is your one failure for the year." In reply, Laird admitted his preference for Stevenson, but the details would be provided "only on request."

The election wasn't even close. More than 60 percent of the eligible voters turned out, and the Eisenhower-Nixon ticket won thirty-nine states, including such Democratic strongholds as Texas, Florida, Virginia, and Tennessee. A Republican in the White House: what a curiosity. While Eisenhower may not have been F.K.'s first choice, he certainly signaled a welcome change.

PUBLIC RELATIONS AND OTHER PROBLEMS

Excitement filled the air at the Eisenhower inaugural fes-
tivities, and F.K. and Vivian were among the celebrants.
Although her efforts brought most of the recognition, he
participated fully, leaving convinced that they had witnessed
"more than just a big show." His previous doubts about Ike
seemed to have disappeared. F.K. continued to worry, however, that those around the new president had agendas of
their own, some of which carried potential threats to his
industry.

The first hint of trouble was a proposed White House
conference on natural resources. Nevertheless, it was reassuring to learn that his friend Fairfield Osborn was on the
conference-organizing committee and that Charles Eliot,
representing Resources for the Future, had been dropped
from that committee. He was a grandson of the Harvard
president Charles V. Eliot and was, in F.K.'s words, "a left-
ist do-gooder." Other than "a rehash of the old question
of what branch of government, if any, should regulate the
forests," he foresaw only more political argument at the
conference. He was troubled that many apparently did not
share his misgivings. In the meantime, he hoped that the
conference "as proposed" would never take place.

Early in 1953, he received an invitation from presidential
assistant Sherman Adams (an old friend who had once discussed possible employment with the Weyerhaeuser Timber

Company) to attend the Ninth Annual White House Conference of the Advertising Council. Secretary of Defense Charles Wilson urged F.K. to become the lumber industry's "official promoter." But F.K. declined, citing a recent bout with the flu, plans for a vacation, and the fact that "I have been soliciting money from the lumber industry for a long time, first for the tree growing program of American Forest Products Industries, Inc., and in recent years for the Forest Products History Foundation."

The now-annual late-winter stay at Hobe Sound, Florida, helped F.K. to leave some worries behind. He would miss the April 7 board meeting of the Conservation Foundation, admitting to Osborn that he "felt like a loafer and a bum to lie around the sands of Hobe Sound and fail to trek north." The prospect of a White House natural resources conference was still on his mind, and he again tried to explain his continuing fear that the extremists on both sides of the issue would dominate. At the conference he hoped the Conservation Foundation might "become the spokesman for that group of true conservationists who arrive at their conclusions and objectives by mental rather than emotional processes." That was his position throughout. He would shortly forward a Timber Company check for $5,000, trusting this would "lighten" Osborn's financial problems. His more immediate news was of nearly landing a sailfish and a tarpon.

As important as the Conservation Foundation sometimes seemed, it couldn't compete with F.K.'s commitment to the Forest Products History Foundation. He had recently received the fall 1952 issue of the *Wisconsin Magazine of History*, which featured an article by D. C. Everest, chairman of the Marathon Paper Corporation, entitled "A Reappraisal of the Lumber Barons." F.K. considered it "excellent" because "it punctures some false thinking about the part played by the lumber industry in the last century and also because it benefits the memory of some of my own forebears." And he didn't miss the opportunity to solicit Everest's support for the Forest Products History Foundation, the means by which "a truer appraisal of the industry and its accomplishments will appear in books, magazines and newspapers if there develops a better source of authoritative information on the industry." That was about as clear an explanation of his commitment as could be made.

Also of interest, and a bit puzzling, were two simultaneous campaigns focusing on research. One was an effort, under the aegis of the National Lumber Manufacturers Association, aimed at raising $200,000 in its initial year, half to finance a market survey and the rest dedicated to research. F.K. approved, noting for Phil's benefit "that it would be to our advantage to get the lumber industry into such a research program because few other lumber concerns would be in such a good position to capitalize on the results obtained as we would." He recommended that the Weyerhaeuser Timber Company contribute about half the amount sought from the West Coast group, "or a maximum of 15% of the total sum."

His position was quite the opposite concerning the Forest Products Laboratory's vigorous campaign for support in Congress. The economy-in-government efforts apparently threatened the Wisconsin-based operation, and although F.K. had been a loyal friend of the FPL, he was more devoted to government reductions than to publicly financed forest research: "Having taken the position repeatedly in favor of reducing the cost of government, it seems a little illogical for us to turn around and support increased appropriations for this particular institution, beneficial though it be to the lumber industry."

Earlier in the year he had attended to a couple of other significant matters: first, the selection of a new public relations director to replace Leo Bodine (who had accepted a position with the NLMA); and second, the final negotiations with Allan Nevins and Columbia University about writing a history of the Weyerhaeuser companies. Although both matters were primarily of importance to the Weyerhaeuser Timber Company, they were also stepchildren of the old General Timber Service, Inc., and as such had been inherited by the Sales Company. F.K. was more committed to public relations and the cause of history than Phil, who happily signed the checks if F.K. agreed to do the work.

B. L. Orell, the Washington State forester, was approached early in 1953 regarding his possible interest in the public relations position. He was thirty-eight years old and had already demonstrated leadership in reorganizing the State Forestry Department. Phil knew him by reputation, and the Timber Company's chief forester, Clyde Martin, thought well of him. Orell took his time, but in mid-May he accepted. Many years later in an interview, he would remember a conversation in which F.K. had explained his unwritten responsibilities. There would be times, F.K. advised, when Orell would have to make decisions without benefit of advice from St. Paul or Tacoma. On such occasions, he should simply do "the right thing," always mindful that the right thing had nothing to do with "bottom lines." Similarly, in 1955 D. H. Bartlett, on the occasion of his retirement from the Sales Company, recalled that whenever questions arose, if "ethics or integrity was involved, I never had to hesitate on my decision. I had the knowledge that there was only one decision that would be approved."

Not surprisingly, the public relations responsibility reflected F.K.'s foremost concerns. Before leaving for his new position with the National Lumber Manufacturers Association, Leo Bodine circulated a copy of a memorandum he had written largely for his own reference. It emphasized that public relations was essentially "the selling of a company's history, its future plans, quality of products, fairness to competition, and soundness of operational policies." It is interesting that Leo began with a reference to the "company's history." F.K. would nod in agreement, for in his view the history was merely the record of performance, and he was eager to have that record made public, confident that it was worthy of sharing.

Some months earlier, F.K. had lunched with Professor Nevins, John Krout, associate provost at Columbia University, and Professor Thomas C. Cochran of the University of Pennsylvania to start negotiations regarding the proposed history. Cochran was a newcomer to the discussions, at the moment basking in favorable reviews of his history of the Pabst Brewing Company. After lunch, Nevins demonstrated the latest audio-taping technology, and Arthur Link played some recordings. Today this seems quite primitive, but at the time it was state of the art.

F.K. forwarded a contract to Provost Krout in early January, and some of the key elements are worth noting. For example, work would begin February 1, 1953, to be completed by December 31, 1957. Cost for preparation and writing was to be $125,000, with an additional $25,000 for general university overhead. There was also mention of a contingency payment, not to exceed $25,000. Professor Nevins was assured "complete freedom in the writing of this book," although the Weyerhaeuser Timber Company would be given the opportunity "to make any corrections in fact, and to prepare suitable footnotes to be printed in the book in the event that it disagrees with statements in the book."

"As the crown of the undertaking," the contract specifically noted, "a one-volume history of the so-called associated Weyerhaeuser companies will be written by Allan Nevins." Although that was clearly the intention, things didn't work out that way. Professor Nevins would explain what happened before an informal gathering of colleagues in 1961. While discussing the importance of a historian's enthusiasm for his subject, Nevins admitted that he had lost that enthusiasm for the Weyerhaeuser project. He had pictured "a life in giant forests, the resin smell of sawed wood, the silent majesty of the lumber industry moving westward" but was soon confronted with countless volumes of business records "and rows of dull figures." In his disappointment he turned the project over to Professor Ralph Hidy.[*]

With or without Nevins, the book that was ultimately published in 1963, *Timber and Men,* would prove to be a significant contribution. The sights, sounds, and smells may have been given short shrift, but those details that discouraged Nevins are accurately recorded for all future reference. And F.K. received proper credit for his contributions in the Acknowledgments:

> . . . Frederick K. Weyerhaeuser, more than any other person, made this history possible. Not only was he among those that took the lead in initiating the project, he was unstinting in his efforts to make available the papers of his grandfather, father, and uncles as well as his own. His requests quickly opened doors from Rock Island and St. Paul to Lewiston and Tacoma. He has even extended his efforts to reading of page proof! His geniality and kindliness have lightened our labors.

Not only did F.K. contribute significantly to the *Timber and Men* project, but he also encouraged others to see that records were safely kept for future historical research through his favorite organization, the Forest Products History Foundation. Typical was a letter to Hugo Schlenk of Cloquet, in which he urged that the old records of the Northern Lumber Company be protected; such documents "worth preserving should be deposited with the Forest Products History Foundation at the Minnesota Historical Society." And to cover all bases, he sent a blind carbon copy of the letter to the foundation's new director, Elwood R. "Woody" Maunder.

---

[*]I am indebted to friend and colleague David H. Stratton, who was on the scene August 12, 1961, and subsequently transcribed notes taken by Ray Allen Billington.

If F.K., as his brother might suggest, had "too many balls in the air," Vivian nearly matched him. She had become active in the programs of the Minnesota Historical Society (MHS). In 1949, for example, she oversaw startup of MHS's Women's Organization, initially to assist in calling attention to society programs in Minnesota's territorial centennial year. Her efforts were subsequently recognized by the American Association for State and Local History, from which she received an award of merit. She was also elected vice-president of MHS.

Two years later, in 1951, Vivian served with Leonard G. Carpenter of Minneapolis as co-chairman of MHS's statewide membership drive. She participated as well in the planning of the Weyerhaeuser history room in the society's St. Paul building. This provided the institution with a much-needed auditorium, seating some two hundred people. Unusual in light of the Weyerhaeusers' general dislike of publicity was the fact that the room's name marked a public acknowledgment of the importance of grandfather Frederick. More common was F.K.'s response to a 1953 proposal regarding a memorial to Frederick: "Our family has never been enthusiastic about memorials in the form of plaques, statues, or what-not, and has been faced with many suggestions or requests of that type." But the Minnesota Historical Society would stand as the exception to the rule. (The oil portrait that hung in the room now resides in the Weyerhaeuser Reference Room of the History Center.)

For all of her interest in MHS, the Metropolitan Opera was Vivian's first love. This apparently was an outgrowth of the old "Golden Voice" talent search. Indeed, F.K. listened to his wife speaking on the "Metropolitan Opera Hour" in early March 1955, when she appeared as a recently elected member of the Metropolitan Opera Association's board of directors. She was the first Minnesotan to be so honored, and her St. Paul friends would become accustomed to seeing newspaper photos of her and Rudolph Bing smiling together. But it wasn't always Rudolph and Vivian. For example, in the coverage of the Met's opening on November 9, 1954, she was pictured with former heavyweight boxing champion Gene Tunney, whose wife was also an important sponsor. But opening nights were merely the frosting on the cake. What Vivian most enjoyed was the work that went on in support of the performance. In 1955 she was elected chairman of the National Council of the Metropolitan Opera Association. This was the council that oversaw the regional auditions, including the one in the Twin Cities, and also served as "a clearing house for information on music and technical material, new stage works and English translations of operas." Most important, in addition to managing the details of the audition process, Vivian recruited key personnel and raised necessary funds.

Other noteworthy events demanded attention. In June 1953 daughters Vivian and Lynn graduated from Vassar. F.K. combined attending that ceremony with business, including a dinner given by U.S. senators Homer Capehart and Styles Bridges. The subject under discussion there was farm subsidies, and afterward F.K. informed Capehart of his own position, lest there be any confusion. As important as the farmer was to the lumber industry—he had "always been our best customer"—subsidization didn't necessarily follow. "In principle," F.K. continued, "I don't believe in subsidies or artificial price supports for anybody, including the farmer and the lumberman because I believe they will destroy the industry which they are supposed to benefit." And he concluded, "The further we continue to tinker with economic laws, the more we will have to interfere with the freedom of the individual."

Senator Capehart subsequently invited F.K. to serve on an advisory committee, to assist in studying the operations of the Export-Import Bank and the International Bank for Reconstruction and Development. F.K. wondered whether the senator might just be "getting back at me" for the letter on farm subsidies. Nonetheless, he accepted, observing that "the subject has always interested me because of its bearing on our domestic economy."

In the wake of his acceptance, F.K. acted predictably, consulting friends and associates who were in positions of experience in such matters for their advice and counsel. All had to appreciate his sincerity even if they might disagree with his positions. One who took note of the process, Harry P. Davison of J. P. Morgan & Company, responded, "It would be very comforting to think that all members of committees of this character devoted the time and thought and care to their responsibilities as you have."

Throughout, F.K. never slighted his major responsibility, providing leadership to the Weyerhaeuser Sales Company. And selling wasn't an easy job in late 1953. To F.K., it was especially difficult, "as the seller's market in lumber transforms itself more and more into an old-fashioned buyer's market." With harder times, he became "increasingly conscious of the weaknesses and failures of our marketing techniques." It was no small task to keep 150 salesmen current "in respect to present prices and stocks at mills that will be available two weeks hence, all of which will enable said sellers to send an adequate flow of orders through 3 Divisions to 8 points of manufacture and 7 distributing yards."

F.K. knew better than to point a finger. He thought that the best way out of the dilemma was to employ consultants to study the "whole matter of sales instructions, order flow, and mill service." Thus in mid-October, the New York–based management-consulting firm of McKinsey & Company was hired. In the meantime, one of the regional sales managers proposed creation of a single stock sheet for all of the Weyerhaeuser Timber Company mills, suggesting that this alone would improve the situation. It seemed logical, but F.K. knew that there would be immediate objections:

> One big handicap to the free exchange of stocks between mills is the high degree of competition on the part of each mill management and the spirited rivalry existing between them which tends to make each management reluctant to accept other mill stocks even though such acceptance would be in the broad company interest.

There could be no better, more succinct statement of the basic organizational problem: the advantages of centralization over decentralization. F.K. knew that acceptance of a single stock sheet was most unlikely, but perhaps the inventories of Weyerhaeuser Timber Company mills (with the exception of Coos Bay, Oregon, and Willapa, Washington) might be consolidated, "setting up a system in Tacoma whereby necessary transfers resulting from such combining of stocks may be facilitated without having a civil war every Monday morning." In the end, opportunities to increase business were few. They could employ more salesmen and spend more on advertising; or they could cut prices and force unwanted items onto an unwilling market; or they could improve sawmills' efficiency in filling difficult orders. For the benefit of Charlie Ingram, he suggested that they probably had gone too far on the first two options and not far enough on the third. The letter served primarily as forewarning.

F.K. was on his way to Tacoma, where he planned to spend a week or so, "at which time we can talk about some of these possibilities."

The meetings took place, and perhaps some progress resulted. There would, however, be no single stock sheet. Not yet anyway. First, each mill manager had a responsibility "to saw his logs to the best advantage of that operation from the point of financial return." Period. It is interesting why the autonomy was deemed so crucial. For example, "The merging of stocks would theoretically permit one management to produce high value items at the expense of their marketability and thus ride upon the back of another management which keeps his product saleable." It was tentatively suggested that central authority be established within the Sales Company to order stock transfers, but in fact few were enthusiastic about such a step. First, who was the Solomon to manage the task? Besides, if ever such a job were created, it should fall within the Timber Company management.

Compromise was the key. Free exchange of stocks between mills would be encouraged. The Stock and Price Office in Tacoma would prepare "a suggested 'balanced stock' covering all the items usually purchased in a mix car order," thus furnishing something of a guide for the mills. Then there was the whole problem of selling western hemlock—against which there was a prejudice. The only answer appeared to involve greater promotional effort. It was estimated that hemlock accounted for approximately 25 percent of the annual growth. So they were talking about a great deal of timber, and lumber.

But clearly the question that mattered most, and that would be the first item on the contract with the McKinsey & Company consultants, was "Coordination of manufacturing and sales planning." F.K. would do his best to ameliorate the tensions between mills and markets:

> Theoretically a sawmill should saw its logs to items which carry the highest prices to realize the highest return. Contrarywise, to market its production at the lowest sales expense . . . [by cutting] its logs to sizes for which market demand is the greatest. In addition, from the selling point of view, stock assortments must meet the needs of customers in order to command market prices. The first procedure if carried to extreme would pro-

duce stock which could not be marketed; the second procedure if carried to extreme would probably sacrifice values inherent in the log should the log be sawed properly. The most successful procedure of manufacturing logs into lumber and marketing the product involves a continual compromise between these two theories.

Despite F.K.'s best efforts, however, and the recommendations of the management consultants, the basic problems refused to go away. The mill managers were simply too entrenched, too independent, and probably too distant from the customers. The whole question of a separate Sales Company needed to be addressed, and it shortly would be. Meanwhile, situations such as the following exemplify the organizational complexity: F.K. had recently learned that the Everett mill was manufacturing Common Boards with a width of 49/64 inch, 1/64 inch scant of the industry's American Lumber Standards. How long had this been going on, he inquired of Charlie Ingram, and how much money had the mill realized as a result? To say that F.K. disapproved is to understate. He informed Ingram, "This business of selling something that is not as represented bothers me very much." Although Charlie tried to explain the advantage of making the boards "interchangeable between water and rail shipments," he realized that the explanation was insufficient. "I concur with you that we should not misrepresent our product." And indeed, the standards would be honored, to the fraction.

Notwithstanding the obvious interdependence of the Timber Company and Sales Company, F.K. was not yet ready to merge the two. He made that point clear in a Christmas talk to the St. Paul office personnel. Predictably, he reviewed the history of the organization, beginning with its 1919 incorporation through the decision that the Sales Company should be a wholly owned subsidiary of the Weyerhaeuser Timber Company. That incorporation, however, did not mean that the Sales Company was "any less important than activities carried on in the parent organization." Not only did they operate in many states in which the Timber Company wasn't authorized to do business, but in addition to selling the products of the Timber Company, "we also operate its distributing yards and do a great deal of outside wholesale business. A separate corporation is appropriate for such an activity."

F.K. left the meetings of the Central and Eastern divisions in mid-January generally pleased with his separate corporation. "Several interesting developments" he considered worthy of sharing with such as Laird Bell. First was a dramatic drop in the average age of sales personnel, from fifty-two in 1946 to forty in 1954. Moreover, they were "practically all college graduates," the sort of chaps Laird "would be proud to meet." Second, F.K. thought he saw signs of "improved coordination between manufacturing and sales," at the same time admitting that there remained "much more to be done." Third, he sensed general satisfaction with their branded lumber. He recalled "the arguments that started about 1922 on lumber advertising between the proponents of advertising and those who said that 'you can't advertise lumber.'" Then the 4-SQUARE program commenced in 1928 and continued until 1942, when it had to be abandoned due to labor shortages. (It was resurrected, though, in the postwar era.) Trademarking had also been revived, leading F.K. to note "the high degree of preference our branded products are receiving in the market." The argument continued, however, and the ghost of George S. Long would contend that preference for branded products was simply evidence that they had done a poor job of educating buyers.

All the advertising in the world would not resolve that most basic problem of coordinating needed sales information and sawmill-production inventories. Bob Douglas of the Sales Company and Charlie Ingram of the Timber Company even struggled to agree on the scope of the McKinsey & Company consulting project. Ingram didn't care about any meddling at the manufacturing end, whereas Douglas presumed that they needed help securing "better stock assortments which would mean examination of our mill inventory systems, methods of recording stock sold against expected production and inventories, the practicality of cutting for stock in short supply, and other procedures in, or near, the areas of responsibilities of Resident Sales Managers."

At the heart of the problem was just how to get information regarding stock assortments into the hands of the salesmen. "It is in this area that we need improvement," Douglas argued, not only to satisfy customer requirements but also to provide easier shipping from the mills. He noted that his Central Division had written more than twenty thousand orders in 1953, but also had found it necessary to write nearly eight thousand special inquiries to Tacoma and the West Coast mills and an additional two thousand to the Inland Empire. In other words, nearly half of the orders had to be accompanied by inquiries, a fact that hardly bespoke efficiency in service and cost.

Regardless, together the Weyerhaeuser Timber Company and the Sales Company were doing more business than ever before and, in the case of the Timber Company, a greater proportion of earnings was being invested in plants and property. As Bernie Orell noted in his March 29, 1954, letter to Sales Company employees: "[The Timber Company] is planning ahead for a permanent supply of forest raw material. It has a long range program of research and development. It is willing to invest millions of dollars based on its faith in our country, its shareholders, and its employees." Speaking of employees, Ray Clute was retiring after nearly forty years of service in sales. He regretted it, but the rule—that retirement at age sixty-five was mandatory—left no choice in the matter. When the moment arrived, he wrote to F.K. "It has always been a real pleasure to serve your Father, Uncles, Brother Phil and yourself, and I never tired of doing all I could to further theirs and your own interest." Then he added what was doubtless most appreciated: "That I succeeded in that effort or to the extent that I did so, was due to the ideals of right, honesty and fair play which have always been your aim."

Ray may have known how much such notes meant to F.K., and the fact is that they were seldom sent. That was also true with respect to his role as family leader. F.K. tried mightily to be effective, but too few thanked him. An exception was cousin Dave Weyerhaeuser, who wrote following the January family meeting: "I am sure there is no other family in the world more united than we are, and you are making the biggest contribution to that end." He further noted his personal pleasure at seeing "the younger generation coming on, and even though they may not all work in affiliated companies, yet there is being generated a loyalty to our family interests which should never diminish." F.K. must have been pleased with such an optimistic assessment, although a year later he observed that the "younger generation seems pretty inexperienced." He quickly added, "I suppose that is the way we looked to our predecessors," writing to fellow oldtimer Ed Davis. In practice, F.K. did everything possible to encourage the youngsters. He had just celebrated his sixtieth birthday, and he knew where the future lay.

In part, that future loomed close, with daughters Vivian and Lynn. They both had plans to remain in the East for the summer, and F.K. wrote to them jointly in Washington, D.C., where they were working for the Citizens for Eisenhower to help reelect the president. F.K. would have preferred that they spend their time at home, doubting that they would have much effect on the fall congressional campaigns. He did take the time to advise them on a few financial facts, specifically that he and their mother had agreed to put $200 into each of their accounts the first of every month, and that, along with $300 monthly income "from stocks left you by your Great-aunt Elise in her will," provided $500 a month, "most of which is your own money so save all you can." And he concluded with a sermonette: "As you know, one of the most important rules of a business man or woman is to know what you have in the bank and *never* to over-draw your account."

F.K.'s advice proved to be both prescient and ineffective. Three months later he wrote again, this time in separate but identical letters. F.K. related his embarrassment at having his daughters' overdrafts mentioned at the Tuesday morning directors' meeting, on two occasions! "Normally the bank would prefer to have accounts which are continually overdrawn placed elsewhere," he observed, "but I think the bank officers hesitate to make such a request in the case of my own daughters." If they didn't mend their ways, he hoped they would move their accounts to a Washington, D.C., bank.

Another family involvement—family in its most extended sense—was a product of the times, specifically the cold war in Europe. F.K. became active—in fact, he was vice-president—of the Foundation for a Unified and Democratic Germany in a United Europe. Dr. James Pollock of Ann Arbor, Michigan, was elected president, other directors including friend D. H. "Pick" Ankeny of the Hamm Brewing Company and Joseph Uihlein, Jr., of Milwaukee and the Schlitz Brewing Company. The foundation had an agent in Germany, and its purpose was obvious. Its lack of success soon would be equally obvious.

An additional disappointment was on the horizon. F.K.'s commitment to the Conservation Foundation was lessening, although he hated to break the news to friend Fairfield Osborn. He did hint at the possibility in a spring letter, explaining reasons for missing the next meeting, adding, "I don't like to be a trustee and not do a proper job." Subsequently, he and Phil agreed that the foundation no longer served their purposes, but still F.K. hesitated to break the tie. "It's going to be quite a blow for [Osborn] to learn that we are cutting off support as well as withdrawing an able trustee." And he wondered if they might not make one last contribution of $2,500. That they would do, but it would indeed be their final gift, F.K. admitting that "the objectives of the Foundation are getting somewhat diverted into channels in which we have rather little interest." Still, when he wrote his letter of resignation, he requested, sincerely, that Osborn "express for me my regard for the members and for the activity, and merely explain that I cannot get to the meetings and that's that."

True, he was busy, but not so busy that he didn't take time now and then to play. A favorite playground was the Waterhen Lodge, an exclusive Manitoba "hunting establishment" located on the Waterhen River outlet of Lake Winnipegosis, about one hundred eighty miles northwest of Winnipeg. Getting there was a major operation, involving plane, bus, and finally boat. But the ducks, "largely Canvas Back and Red Heads," and the camaraderie apparently made the trip worthwhile. On another hunt that same fall at Diamond Bluff, across the St. Croix River in Wisconsin, F.K. accomplished little more than getting sunburned. Nonetheless, he enjoyed himself "whether the birds are plentiful or not so long as the company is good."

F.K. was promoter and organizer of the fall excursion to Waterhen, inviting friends far and near. Included in the group was fellow Waterhen member General James Doolittle, who had led the famous bombing raid on Tokyo in 1942. The Waterhen Lodge was a curiously democratic organization, regularly polling its members on possible changes in policy and procedure. As an example, the previous winter they had been asked about the need for a fire extinguisher on one of the boats and "a fire or explosion drill on the boat before we take away from the dock in the camp." F.K. was among those who favored a fire extinguisher, but he didn't think the drills "would accomplish very much. In fact, some of the members might fall in the water which would be bad."

Ducks were a high priority for many. F.K. had tried, without much enthusiasm, to solicit interest in the Second Upper Great Lakes Conference to be held at the Three Lakes Resort in Wisconsin. He had writ-

ten to thirty-seven acquaintances and had received only a single acceptance. He knew the problem: "Everyone of those birds who is able to
sit in a duck blind or hold a gun in his hand is going to be out in some
marsh shooting ducks while the Second Upper Great Lakes Conference
is in session." And in the end, F.K. was among the hunters.

But when it came to charities, he was, not surprisingly, among the
hunted. Often he didn't mind in the least. Such was the case with the
House of Hope Church and its new parish house, the Elizabeth Chapel,
named in honor of his grandmother. He happily sent a check for $20,000
to the pastor, Dr. Irving A. West, noting "with Vivian's consent" that they
had added $10,000 of their own to the $10,000 contributed by the Weyerhaeuser Family Foundation. He also continued to respond to requests
from the American University in Cairo, fulfilling a family obligation for
the favorite charity of Elise and Bancroft Hill. But when it came to his
own old favorite, Spiritual Mobilization, F.K. had almost given up trying
to convince others to enlist in the cause: "I find it increasingly difficult to
get support from the Weyerhaeuser Foundation, because of the differ-
ing points of view of its members." And he met more of the same at
church, Dr. West expressing doubts "by reason of Spiritual Moblization's
championship of Senator [Joseph] McCarthy." Still, prior to Christmas
1954, F.K. sent his personal check for $1,000 "for work during the com-
ing year." At the same time, he agreed to become a sponsor of Ducks
Unlimited, contributing $1,000, "provided the work of Ducks Unlim-
ited is conducted in an effective manner."

FAMILY MILESTONES

SOME MAY HAVE assumed that F.K. decided to limit his outside activities, particularly those requiring travel, simply because he was feeling the years. After all, he was now in his sixties. However, the basic concern was not his health but Vivian's. There is little purpose in speculating about the origin of her problems, possibly involving long-term medication prescribed to combat high blood pressure following the death of her infant son in 1929—medication that, doctors subsequently believed, may have contributed to bouts of depression. F.K. had no real understanding of her condition; she was never one to complain, and he didn't pry. But he could worry, and he did.

One fact could not be overlooked: On occasion Vivian had one martini too many. Socializing in the 1950s more often than not included alcohol, and F.K. and Vivian were required to attend a great many functions. While F.K. certainly wasn't opposed to social drinking, he did appreciate the damage wrought by excessive drinking. After all, it was he who had confronted Walter Rosenberry, Jr., regarding that very problem. But Vivian was quite another matter. First, it was hard to admit, and second, it seemed next to impossible to face directly. Finally, in the late summer of 1954, he scheduled appointments for both of them at the Mayo Clinic, explaining to his St. Paul physician, Dr. W. H. Hollinshead, Jr., "In order to get Mrs. Weyerhaeuser to take a thorough physical examination, I went down to Rochester with her and took one myself."

The results of F.K.'s examination were positive in every regard, other than familiar problems with hay fever and asthma. What Vivian may have learned is not known, nor is it known whether she was advised to be careful. Regardless, there would be no easy solution, and F.K. remained puzzled and concerned. He loved his wife without reservation; whatever problems she faced, he was always at her side. Her Metropolitan Opera commitments may have been a bit trying at times for him, but he never groused. If F.K. had been selfish he would have spent more time with friends, but he could never neglect her so callously. Vivian, for all of her public visibility, her apparent strength and independence, depended on his support and encouragement. If he was there, nodding and smiling, she was fine.

Though F.K. generally maintained a relaxed and pleasant demeanor around the house, he wasn't so easygoing at the office. There, once again, his cousin Fred had become the center of attention and exasperation. Fred was executive vice-president—in today's terminology, the CEO— of the Rock Island Millwork Company, and F.K. was a director (not that this was of great significance, as he would have been involved in any case). The Millwork Company's success or failure was important to the family. F.K. allowed as he had been a poor director, spending too little time in Rock Island and knowing too few of the management personnel. The company had "been on the very edge of my consciousness," he admitted early in 1955, "not because of lack of interest, but because of the pressure of other demands for my attention."

As had been the case when Fred was heading the research program for General Timber Service, Inc., many of F.K.'s complaints involved personnel. Further, it seemed that Fred was forever going "hot and cold on various programs." Why? Just before Christmas he had hinted at resigning, and then he suddenly proposed expanding operations by some $2 million. "I am confused by the rapid switches from pessimism to optimism and back," F.K. wrote, "and cannot help but wonder what will happen next." He thought he knew where the problem lay: "I get the impression that you have spent a great deal of time studying figures and making analyses of statements of the Millwork Company. Wouldn't it be better to let some accountant make such studies and to spend your own time at the plant or meeting customers or competition?" He offered a number of specific suggestions for ways to improve and closed with an attempt at assuring his cousin that his only wish was to be helpful, "and to see you derive pleasure and satisfaction from your part in the Mill Company's activities."

Fred wasn't buying any sugarcoated criticism. He answered F.K.'s suggestions item by item, but that sort of response was beside the point. Little more needed to be said than the following: "I have therefore reluctantly come to the conclusion that I should step aside so as to enable the Directors to obtain management they will have confidence in and to carry out the programs they feel should be adopted." Following a discussion with the directors living in St. Paul, F.K. regretfully accepted Fred's resignation in early May.

With the onset of serious winter, F.K. and Vivian naturally tried to take advantage of their Hobe Sound home. They did so in early February 1955, but Florida temperatures weren't very warm either. Still, F.K. could play golf, describing his game as "not good—but spectacular!" Their break didn't last long enough from his perspective, cut short by the necessity for Vivian to attend the Met's regional auditions in St. Paul. F.K. meanwhile headed to the Pacific Northwest for a series of meetings. The hectic schedule continued into the spring. In mid-May, Vivian was back in New York City, in F.K.'s words, "on some Metropolitan Opera business, and our communications have all broken down."

Partly because he knew that Vivian could hardly limit her involvements, F.K. tried to limit his own. There may have been another factor— Phil's health. Some years earlier, he had been diagnosed with chronic leukemia and had started treatment at the Sloan-Kettering Clinic in New York City. Everything seemed to be going well, but of course the future was uncertain. Gradually, almost imperceptibly, F.K. had begun paying increased attention to matters that fell more properly within the province of the Weyerhaeuser Timber Company. Although Phil might disagree with F.K.'s position on this or that, he offered no general complaint about prerogatives. Indeed, he admitted, to himself at least, that the Timber Company needed encouragement to move in new directions, and he had already been casting about for someone who might provide leadership assistance. In this search, Phil's eye had settled on John Aram of Boise Payette; Aram would eventually come to Tacoma for just that purpose.

So F.K. had important reasons to save himself from peripheral responsibilities, even including service on the board of trustees of the House of Hope Church. In a letter to its chairman, A. J. Dickinson, F.K. allowed that he had been honored to serve on the board for the past several years but suggested that there would be benefits to some rotation in membership. Thus he asked that his name not be submitted for reelection. More easily managed was his refusal to serve as a trustee for the Foundation for American Resources Management. As he explained, "My trouble is that I cannot adequately take care of my present responsibilities, and I am finding it necessary to eliminate a number of things which I would like to have continued." He did agree to keep serving on the National Council of the United Negro College Fund, but forewarned John D. Rockefeller, Jr., that any increased support was unlikely.

Forestry, Sales Company operations, and Timber Company expansion—these were his highest professional priorities. As to the first, *Life* magazine featured a story in its November 8, 1954, issue concerning a citizens' committee that was working to save a "primeval" oak forest in New Jersey. With that purpose in mind, a Rutgers University professor solicited F.K.'s support, citing William and Elise Hill's long interest in Rutgers (although he made the mistake of referring to Elise as Elsie). Instead of support, the professor got a lecture: "It is difficult for a lumberman to become enthusiastic about preserving a tract of old over-ripe dying trees," F.K. began. "Our modern conception of forest land is to keep it productive, but an old, old forest is not productive because old age, wind and disease will at least offset any growth that remains. I would much rather spend money growing young trees than preserving old ones." That doubtless represented a novel point of view to those in New Brunswick.

Another recent campaign—and in this F.K. didn't enjoy the unconditional support of Phil—was to move Timber Company operations into new areas of manufacture. The Huss Lumber Company of Chicago and the production of corrugated boxes, for example, seemed a worthy prospect for merger, and F.K. encouraged Phil to come east and meet with Alvin J. Huss to discuss the matter.

The Huss Lumber Company merger would never happen, primarily because Alvin Huss had second thoughts about surrendering his independence. But this didn't deter F.K.'s general interest in such expansion. "Mergers seem to be in the air," he wrote to Phil in midsummer. When he looked at the Weyerhaeuser Timber Company, he saw an organization that was certainly provincial geographically and probably in production terms as well: "I think I would favor merging activities leading to acquisition of marketing facilities in pulp and paper fields or acquisition of desirable timber property in the South." Phil, however, held to the old view, simply that they should avoid manufacturing products that competed with those of customers; and paper, of course, fell within the restriction.

F.K. argued otherwise. The policy might have been "right to start with, but with the passage of time gets more and more questionable." What were they to do with their profits? Return every dollar to the shareholders? Hardly. That would fly in the face of tradition. If they continued investing "the dollars that are coming out of our operations in constructive enterprises, we are driven into fields that compete with more and more of our pulp and paper customers—at least I think so."

But neither brother felt equal to the task of investigating merger opportunities. Moreover, they knew of no one sufficiently qualified, which encouraged F.K. to make a significant recommendation:

> I believe the Weyerhaeuser Timber Company should employ a
> first-class business man whose sole job would be to investigate and
> recommend with reference to the acquisition of properties;
> whether primarily for the investment of company funds or to
> complement our manufacturing or distribution facilities. Such an
> individual should report directly to you and should work along-
> side your Research Director. It seems to me that we are badly
> handicapped in this era of mergers by lack of someone to initi-
> ate deals in which we are interested. As you know, it is often eas-
> ier to buy a company than to start a new one.

Although they may have differed on details, F.K. and Phil agreed entirely that they should be planning seriously for future expansion. Phil's interest in John Aram spoke to his concerns, specifically the need for some fresh thinking on the tenth floor of the Tacoma Building. Nonetheless, business was booming in 1955. "It is fun to see the wheels go around so fast," F.K. confided to a friend. Fortunately, when either F.K. or Phil was tempted to worry too much, the other could be counted on to restore a healthy perspective. For example, when Phil was updating his résumé, he included mention that he continued to serve as captain of the *Wanigan*. The *Wanigan* was an inboard launch, one of Phil's few indulgences, built in Florida and transported west thanks to the Weyerhaeuser Steamship Company, and now occasionally plying the waters of Puget Sound. F.K. took proper note: "I am glad that the WANIGAN is not yet sunk," he wrote. "I am somewhat surprised to learn that you are Curator of the Washington State Historical Society—it sounds pretty impressive."

F.K., too, was required to bring his own résumé up-to-date, in part because he had reluctantly accepted an invitation to be the banquet speaker at the American Forestry Association's October 5, 1955, meeting in Jacksonville, Florida. (F.K.'s résumé concluded with the assertion that he was "an ardent hunter, fisherman and golfer.") He felt obligated to participate because the Weyerhaeuser Timber Company was to receive the 1955 Conservation Award in the Field of Business and Industry, and besides F.K. never minded preaching his gospel, even if the congregation was made up of believers. He also received numerous suggestions from the director for suitable subjects, followed by a partial apology: "But knowing of your modesty with respect to the accomplishments of your own Company, I did want to indicate that it would be entirely appropriate and acceptable for you to use the Weyerhaeuser Company as the example of the unity between practical forestry and practical forest industry."

The Jacksonville visit encouraged the first serious consideration, in any specific terms, of Weyerhaeuser entry into the South. F.K. talked with several southern operators, most importantly with Floyd McGowin of the W. T. Smith Lumber Company, which owned some two hundred fifteen thousand acres in southern Alabama. F.K. later shared some of the details with Phil. "The Alger-Sullivan Lumber Company, with headquarters at Century, Florida; and the M. W. Smith Lumber Company, Inc., of Jackson, Alabama, own substantial blocks of timber which are not far distant from Chapman, Alabama, headquarters for W. T. Smith. I understand from Floyd that these three concerns own or control approximately 700,000 acres of the best timber in southern Alabama." Thus southern timberlands, so long ignored by the Weyerhaeusers, were introduced as a subject worthy of discussion. Soon Dave Weyerhaeuser, accompanied by Timber Company forester Ed Heacox, was tramping through those woods, taking pictures and making notes, beginning to understand the facts of southern forests and forestry as well as some of the characters holding forth.

While the pines weren't as impressive as Douglas-fir and its neighbors in the Pacific Northwest, they grew fast and straight. Further, the big trees west of the Cascades were fast disappearing. An old friend of the Weyerhaeusers commented on that point in a letter to F.K., recalling a 1914 conversation with F.K.'s Uncle Rudolph. Prescott Buffum remembered asking Rudolph what the Weyerhaeusers were doing about reforestation. Rudolph's answer was typically terse: "Buffum, it takes fifty years to grow a twelve inch tree and you can't get anything out of a twelve inch tree. We haven't got time to wait and we are doing nothing." But, as Buffum noted in reading a later Timber Company publication, what demanded greatest interest was reforestation. "It beats all how things change," he observed in closing.

By far the biggest event of the fall was the announcement of daughter Lynn's engagement to Stanley Ray Day, a youthful Detroit businessman. The news appeared in papers the country over on November 2. During the holidays, F.K. found himself in what he described as "the hush before the storm." The wedding was scheduled for January 6, but as was now the custom, he also had to prepare for the week of family meetings, beginning on January 23. He prefaced his agenda to family members with the admission that it was "difficult to focus our minds on events following the wedding," but he hoped that he and Vivian would get away for some rest after the nuptials and before commencement of the meetings.

The wedding went off without a hitch. F.K. proudly escorted Lynn down the long aisle of St. Luke's Church in St. Paul. Sister Vivian served as maid of honor, and Stanley's father, Ray Emmet Day, was best man. Archbishop John Gregory Murray of the Archdiocese of St. Paul performed the rites, after which there was a gala reception at the Minnesota Club. But it seems likely that all gave one large collective sigh when Lynn and Stan left for a brief West Indies honeymoon. F.K. and Vivian could be forgiven if they recalled their own wedding, with its attendant stresses. Whatever details may have gone awry in daughter Lynn's nuptials had to seem trivial by comparison.

As for the family meetings, F.K. seemed pleased, especially regarding the attendance. Peggy Driscoll was among the few absentees—she was traveling in Europe at the time—but F.K. told her of the important events. Included was a move that would turn out to be noteworthy, although none could realize it at the time, unless it was F.K. himself. As he informed Peggy, they had voted to replace her as a director of The Bonners Ferry Lumber Company with her son John, and John was also added to the board of the Rock Island Company. To explain, at least partly, the significance of these moves, Bonners Ferry was, and Rock Island would become, the focus of family financial activity. As well, John would eventually replace F.K. as head of the family.

Returning to work had not been easy, although even while he and Vivian were traveling to and from Florida, neither had been able to put their responsibilities entirely behind them. F.K., for example, solicited support from his new southern lumber friends for the Forest History Foundation. (*Products* was no longer part of its name.) The foundation had fallen short of its $50,000 goal, but F.K. figured funds were sufficient for current operations.

Upon his return to the office, F.K. found the usual assortment of mail and memos, including, of course, political solicitations. Most of these he tossed, but he gave special notice to two. The first was from the American Heritage Foundation. John C. Cornelius, new president of that organization, assured F.K. that his acceptance of board nomination "would add importantly to the prestige and effectiveness of the Foundation." F.K. may have wondered about that, noting that besides such illustrious members as General Walter Bedell Smith, Charles Wilson, and Henry Ford II, the board also included Walter P. Reuther. Bernie Orell didn't see any problem with that. He agreed that there were "a number of people on the Board who are considerably left of center," but their presence was "necessary in order to cover the field of all walks of our economic and social structure." Moreover, the foundation traditionally avoided controversial issues, "confining their support to such programs as the Freedom Train, the Get Out the Vote campaign, etc." After brief consideration, F.K. agreed to serve, with the provision, "I don't know how many meetings I can attend, but will do my best."

Considerably further to the right was the Campaign for the 48 States, whose purpose was clearly delineated in its letterhead: "To limit and restrict the centralized powers of the Federal Government; to strengthen the sovereignty of the individual States, and to protect the solvency of the Nation itself." F.K. promptly enlisted, citing his commitment to the cause while acknowledging that accomplishing those goals might be impossible. Still, he felt that the only possible road to success was "by getting grass roots support." The funding effort involved a variation of the popular pyramid club, with every new recruit endeavoring to enlist two more, and so forth.

Nonetheless, his unswerving conservatism occasionally showed itself in silly, almost quixotic ways. As an example, in March 1956 he received Harry Truman's *Memoirs* from the Book-of-the-Month Club. Normally, he would simply have returned an unwanted book, but not this time. He felt compelled to include an accompanying note. "I don't know whether you sent me these because they are good literature, because they contain great political wisdom, or merely because they were written by a former President of the United States. Whatever the reason, I would rather spend my time reading something else."

It is true that he never lacked for things to read, and when he did find an occasional spare moment he could always review old files. One evening, while doing just that, he came across a poem that had seemed important in his youth, thanks to grandfather Frederick. And now he sent a copy to both daughters, assuring them that it would make "more sense" as they got older. The poem was "The Water Mill," its refrain, "The mill will never grind with the water that is past."

One thing that he had been reading, actually studying, for several weeks was the McKinsey Report, which included a recommendation that the Timber Company embark on a new national advertising campaign. But F.K. had numerous other items in mind, notably acquisition of timberlands and possibly manufacturing plants in the South, Canada, and overseas. In addition, he again argued in favor of expanding production into end-product lines. For example, in the pulp-and-paper operation, their only customers were other industries. "The public hardly knows we make paper and pulp." Indeed, lumber was the only product with which Weyerhaeuser was identified, "and even that is usually bought by a contractor." He closed his lengthy memo with unusual vigor. "I strongly advise *against* avoiding the manufacture of consumer products too long for fear of how it will affect our present customers. A continuation of that policy may put us in a straight jacket [*sic*] that we cannot get out of until it is too late."

At first glance, it may appear that F.K. was exceeding his authority in Timber Company affairs, but he had succeeded Laird Bell as chairman of the board in 1955; and as earlier noted, Phil was genuinely seeking assistance. So, no toes were being stepped upon. One of the frustrations plaguing F.K. was his first experience presiding as chairman. The inefficiencies were obvious. Everyone had an opinion to express, and not all of them were relevant, much less informed. The biggest offender was O. D. Fisher. He was now serving as a senior counselor, without a right to vote but permitted to enter the discussion. A fellow member suggested, only half facetiously, that they had got it wrong: Let him vote but not speak!

Frustrations with O.D. aside, maybe they should consider reorganizing the board, forming committees to deal with single subjects. Laird Bell could see some advantage to that approach, but, with the exception of the executive and compensation committees, F.K. wasn't convinced, primarily because the directors were so scattered and so busy with other matters. They couldn't devote the time required to serve better. And as he evaluated the most recent meeting, he blamed himself for much of the problem:

> Our Board meetings should provide to all directors a chance to express their views and have them discussed to a conclusion. Our recent meeting (due to my ineptness) was largely a monologue by one director—some of it interesting, but most of it off the agenda. I think that future meetings of the Board should be presented with a detailed agenda which gives the Chairman a better chance to hold the meeting to subjects you want discussed.

Plainly, they were experiencing growing pains, and they had reached the point where important decisions were demanded. F.K. countenanced what had become a litany. He favored diversification "into other regions and into other related fields. I believe we should make a move toward vertical integration, perhaps by acquiring the Kieckhefer operation." He closed his memo to Phil citing the company's "biggest problem," which was "to select and train successors to Charles [Ingram] and yourself."

Phil certainly agreed with the final observation. Earlier, when discussing the question of organization with Laird Bell, he had noted, "I won't last very long, and what we are talking about is organizing for a long time." As for expansion of operations, he seemed on the verge of moving. "We are now in a stout financial condition and generating funds pretty fast, so that we can do whatever we like about acquisitions." In this situation, Laird was of little help. It is curious that he could be so liberal and progressive when it came to politics and so conservative when it came to business, but that position was one the Laird-Nortons had consistently maintained through the years. Now, in the spring of 1956, Laird dreaded the "thought of just in general looking for investment opportunities," adding, "I am even nervous about spreading into our own field in the South, but I probably should not make a point of that."

In the meantime, F.K. genuinely enjoyed one unusual break in the routine, a nine-day Joint Civilian Orientation Conference put on by the Pentagon, which included visits to Quantico, Englin Air Force Base, and the aircraft carrier *Coral Sea*. To a World War I pilot, the new technology was all pretty impressive. The group was of course given VIP treatment. He later expressed personal thanks to those responsible, in turn receiving a note from Air Force Chief of Staff Nathan F. Twining. The latter wasn't entirely unexpected, General Twining being a fellow frequenter of the Waterhen Lodge.

Undoubtedly, one aspect of the Orientation Conference F.K. most appreciated was the absence of duties required in exchange. The group was entertained and educated simply because they might be useful somewhere down the road. Few involvements were so undemanding. More typical was an invitation from Whitney Griswold, president of Yale, requesting that F.K. become a member of the University Council and chairman of the Forestry School Committee. F.K. replied that such service "would be both interesting and stimulating," but he also noted the many demands that would likely get in the way. Nonetheless, he promised to give it serious thought, even though for the balance of 1956 he seemed overly committed; 1957, however, looked more promising. "So if you feel that a committee that will do a real job in 1956 is essential to carrying out the program of the Council (and you probably do), I am compelled to say in all honesty that I cannot accept." But President Griswold thought otherwise, and in the end F.K. accepted, although his prediction of greater availability in 1957 couldn't have been less accurate.

In the meantime, he continued his investigation of merger opportunities, one of his principal targets being Walter Paepcke, president of the Container Corporation of America. He detailed his discussions with

Paepcke for Phil's benefit, prefacing with the reminder, "You know that I have been anxious to see us get into the container business for a long time because it provides such a large market for pulp and paper & hence for waste wood." It also seemed profitable, and F.K. feared that unless they moved quickly, any reasonable opportunities would be lost forever. But perhaps more interesting than the reasons for merger were the "wide differences" between Paepcke's thinking and their own. For example, Paepcke considered it foolish to own one's own timber: The return was too small and the risks too great; and most compelling, there seemed to be sufficient pulpwood and chips available on the open market. Conversely, in F.K.'s words, "We would not feel safe investing millions in paper mills without land & tbr. ownership." Other opposing points were cited, but the final one probably headed F.K.'s list: Paepcke considered "his sales operation as of first importance," whereas, "We consider sales of least importance (and always have)."

F.K. had no ready answers for such questions, beginning with the profitability of owning timberland. "What sort of profit are we making in that one activity?" he inquired. "In other words, what return can we expect to get just growing trees?" The negotiations with Paepcke continued through the summer and finally reached the point where Phil agreed to come east for face-to-face talks. But fate intervened. Phil took a nasty fall on his boat, and as F.K. informed Paepcke in late August, "The doctor insists on observing the recovery of his shoulder injured in his recent accident."

In the end, nothing came of the discussions with the Container Corporation, but the exercise was beneficial. F.K. received, for example, an estimate from W. P. Gullander, the Timber Company's financial vice-president. The figures assumed "a typical acre of Company [Douglas-fir] forest land," which would "produce 53 M Bd. Ft. after 80 years with artificial reforestation or after 90 years with natural reforestation." The conclusion indicated an annual yield of 4.5 percent to 6.25 percent from growing trees. It assumed no appreciation of stumpage values "in relation to other goods" or "the inflation hedge represented by the growing forests."

While those figures may not seem impressive, one must remember that they referred only to the trees themselves, not to forest products. Beyond that was the presumed security of owning the forest lands, at least in the Weyerhaeuser mindset. F.K. was not discouraged, and he advanced the cause at every opportunity. In writing to young Ed Titcomb, now in Cleveland with the Rock Island Lumber Company, F.K. argued against further investment in retail lumber yards, suggesting that they should "be thinking about an opportunity in a different industry like the paper container field."

Besides all the other concerns, 1956 was a presidential-election year. Both Vivians, mother and daughter, went back to work on behalf of Eisenhower, and F.K. continued to solicit support from friends and colleagues. He enjoyed an occasional success, among many rejections. One of his more difficult sells involved the Campaign for the 48 States. Even friend Peavey Heffelfinger turned him down. Peavey cited several objections, including the Campaign's support of the so-called Bricker amendment. The attacks on the United Nations contained in the amendment were particularly controversial. And he closed expressing his unhappiness with Harold Stassen: "You can have him!!" Perhaps the most discouraging thing wasn't the expressed opposition but the fact that Peavey's reply was the only one F.K. received among ten solicitations.

Despite all of the political and business excitement, F.K. and Vivian finally decided it was time for a vacation. The Iberian Peninsula was their objective, and they flew to Lisbon via Pan American, soon settling into a "lovely ocean resort." Writing home, F.K. sounded like the happiest of tourists. "We are completely carefree and don't care whether the price of lumber goes up or down." In fact, the price of lumber was going down, but that would prove the least of their worries. It is well they took the time off. Future vacations would be few and far between.

President Eisenhower was reelected in another landslide. But elsewhere the news was sad. "I am sorry to tell you that Phil is seriously ill in Tacoma General Hospital," F.K. advised the Timber Company directors on November 27, 1956. "He has been under the doctor's care for some time for treatment of chronic leukemia and has been optimistic that the disease could be succesfully controlled for a long time to come. During the past week it has flared up in very serious form."

Phil died on December 8. F.K. was there and had been for several days. Cousin Fritz Jewett had died November 23 in Spokane, so there was much mourning throughout the family. Everyone tried to help, especially with Timber Company matters. Norton Clapp would offer recommendations; Edmund Hayes made himself available, and, of course, the Tacoma office staff tried to pull together. But as F.K. must have realized, only he could replace his brother. Work went on, F.K. noting that Howard Morgan of the Timber Company was visiting the Kieckhefer Paper Company's Austin, Minnesota, plant. He also stayed "busy answering a mountain of correspondence," then partook of a brief respite with Vivian at Hobe Sound, after which he would head for Tacoma on January 7. "We will plan a meeting of the Executive Committee to suit the convenience of all members during that period."

TACOMA

Probably F.K.'s last personal letter to his brother was written from Madrid on October 16, 1956. He touched on a variety of topics, including the future of Phil's younger son, George. John Aram would soon be leaving Boise Payette to come to Weyerhaeuser's Tacoma office as the president's handpicked assistant, thus creating an opportunity in Boise. What about George? Should he be considered? F.K. wasn't sure. "In a way," he noted, "it might be a great experience for him. And he would always be on tap for the bigger job," meaning, of course, to replace his father at some future time. Well, they had best let George make up his own mind.

In that same letter, F.K. responded to a draft agenda for the next Timber Company board meeting. He favored agendas for any meeting, and this one seemed particularly useful, largely because "any agenda will help hold O.D. [Fisher] in check." F.K. also suggested that Phil solicit comments and recommendations from the other directors. "Such a request could prove embarrassing but it would clear the decks of any unexpressed ideas or criticisms (if there are any)." One item caught F.K.'s attention, long-range planning. This raised all manner of questions—"Which way should research be headed? Should we enter chemical & plastics industries & how? Should we make foreign investments? etc." Another question occasioned a very definite answer from F.K.: "Sure we should be listing our stock."

At the end of October, F.K. and Vivian had returned from their European tour to the discouraging news about Phil. A month later, F.K. was in Tacoma, literally at his brother's bedside. He canceled a scheduled appearance at a meeting of the Forest History Foundation in Victoria, British Columbia, sending his regrets along with a brief statement:

> The ownership by forest industries of the large areas of land necessary for the growing of timber crops places them somewhat in the position of trustees who must now and then render an account to the public of their stewardship. It is important to those industries that the people of Canada and the United States understand the history, current program and aims of these industries if they are to be left in a position to carry on as free enterprises. It is also important to the peoples of our two countries that their business activities remain free from government ownership and control if they are to remain free peoples.

On December 11, three days after Phil's death, F.K. was elected president at a special meeting of the Weyerhaeuser Timber Company's board of directors, Charlie Ingram was appointed executive vice-president, and St. Paul board member John Musser became a member of the Executive Committee. F.K.'s succession seemed automatic. There plainly was no other choice. But just how would it work? Would he simply hold down the fort? Or would he take charge?

Two years later, a western Washington colleague recalled doubts widely shared. William Reed of the Simpson Timber Company remembered being "nervous" at the time, observing that Weyerhaeuser "didn't seem to have a second line of defense. We feared the idea of running a big company like that by committee. We were afraid they'd get cumbersome or slow or else do something so foolish that the whole industry would suffer."

F.K. would prove equal to the task, but he must have had his own doubts. One can't imagine a good time for such a transition, but this was awful. Phil was only fifty-seven when he died. While talk of his successor had been frequent, it usually ended with a general shrugging of shoulders. Charlie Ingram was himself on the verge of retirement, and John Aram was still an unknown quantity. Now, however, there could be no deferring. F.K. was sixty-two, and though he may not have been contemplating retirement, neither was he thinking about taking on any major new responsibility. Then there was Vivian to consider. The prospect of spending more time away from Summit Avenue was unappealing in the extreme, and a move to Tacoma seemed out of the question.

Norton Clapp, who would replace F.K. as chairman of the board, was sensitive to many of the uncertainties, and in a lengthy pre–Christmas letter he shared some of them. F.K. had returned to St. Paul, intent on getting his personal affairs in order. Norton told of sitting across the table from Chuck Young, the Timber Company's economist, Young inquiring as to how F.K. might be dividing his time between Tacoma and St. Paul. "I mention this," Norton continued, "merely as it may be symptomatic of a certain uneasiness that comes when the whole program is not too clearly defined."

Included among those uncertainties was how best to use John Aram. Likely complicating that question, Charlie Ingram announced plans to bring young George Weyerhaeuser to Tacoma from Springfield as an "administrative assistant." Then what about expansion into the South? "No one has worked out a policy as to how much land we should or should not buy down in that country," Norton noted. In short, plenty of problems awaited resolution. Phil hadn't left a clean desk.

F.K. had already begun consideration of John Aram's assignment. They met before F.K. departed for St. Paul, and on the same day that Norton was writing to F.K., F.K. was writing to Aram. He informed John that they had already determined where Aram's office would be, between Charlie Ingram's and Phil's old office. As for the job description, it was "to assist me in various of my responsibilities as President, and to take on some special assignments [involving] legal, financial, resource relations, public information, research, and economic services," F.K. directing that Aram pay particular attention "to the last four of these subjects." Then he added a timeless topic, "the whole matter of organization of the Weyerhaeuser Timber Company. I would like to have you study other organizations and consider whether we should make some drastic changes in our own picture."

Thus from the outset it was apparent that F.K. had more in mind than being an interim leader. But he couldn't foresee all that would be involved. For example, initially he planned to be on the West Coast only part of the time, explaining, "I do not anticipate moving my residence out there permanently."

By far the single most important item on F.K.'s agenda in late 1956 had been long in the making, a proposed merger of the Timber Company with the Eddy Paper Corporation and the Kieckhefer Container Company. The Kieckhefer and Eddy companies primarily manufactured corrugated shipping containers, milk cartons, and folding cartons, with thirty plants nationwide. In addition, the North Carolina Pulp Company was a subsidiary, with a large Kraft pulp and paperboard mill at Plymouth, North Carolina, and some four hundred thousand acres of timberland. The merger fit Weyerhaeuser's stated policy of efficient forest-crop utilization exactly. Shareholders approved the merger at a special meeting in April. While this made great sense, putting such pieces together inevitably was a challenge. Initially, Kieckhefer-Eddy would operate as a division, or a branch, of the Timber Company, retaining its former name. In time, it would become wholly integrated, but the "in time" was a long time coming and required a good deal of effort and patience.

Perhaps it was partly in response to facilitating the Kieckhefer-Eddy merger that F.K. decided to undertake a basic review of Timber Company objectives and organization. It seemed only logical to begin at the beginning, with agreement as to objectives. The working paper stated the fundamental objective, "to produce over the long term the maximum possible profit by wise use of the assets entrusted to it by its shareholders," and followed with nine "inherent" supporting objectives, beginning with "Complete integrity in dealing with customers, employees, and shareholders." It is interesting to note that the existing objectives as stated in the Policy Manual began not with a statement on integrity, but with "Operation of the timberlands on a scientific sustained yield basis to insure a perpetual supply of raw material."

As anyone familiar with such reviews understands, they are seldom easily managed, leaving many wondering whether the results are worth the effort. But F.K. was convinced that they needed specifics on paper lest they continue to drift. If he was an "interim" manager, he wanted to provide for the future as best he could. One question he asked in his own working notes put the matter clearly: "Can the long-range future of the company be improved by adoption of a carefully worked out plan based on past experience and charted trends?" He wasn't going to wait for the obvious answer.

F.K. called a meeting of top management on May 24, 1957, to review company objectives. He opened by sharing his own thoughts, allowing that Phil's death had put them all into "a period of transition." Looking ahead, Charlie Ingram's retirement was "imminent, as well as that of Mr. F. K. Weyerhaeuser." F.K. gave the marching orders. They were "to set up by sometime in August an impersonal plan for the company organization to be attained by the year 1960," the year he would turn sixty-five.

As noted, F.K.'s plans to be a part-time Tacoman were naive. Given the content of his character, it was impossible for him to let things drift. He knew where he belonged—at his desk in the Tacoma Building. So, reluctantly, he and Vivian moved, putting together two apartments atop the new Vista del Rey, at the corner of North Fourth and Tacoma Avenue. It was certainly adequate, but in their eyes, no St. Paul. F.K. even had to skip the family meeting on June 3 in St. Paul, sending along his regrets to Ed Davis. F.K. explained that on June 3, 4, and 5, the top managers of the Timber Company and Sales Company were assembling to discuss "manufacturing, sales, product, and promotional problems." And on June 6 there was to be a meeting of the Research and Development Committee and the Timber Company's Executive Committee. For the moment, the family would have to get along without him.

Ed Davis not only missed F.K. at the family meeting but also missed having him around the St. Paul office. "You have the kind of job to which you can devote ten hours a day or five hours every other day," he observed. And he added, "Have the impression there is not a great deal that can be accomplished during the interim period." F.K. doubtless smiled at that, before heading off to another meeting. He had made one arbitrary decision, officially designating John Aram as vice-president. Aram would supervise the company's economist, the director of public information, the manager of special products, and director of research.

Throughout, F.K. tried to read as much as possible about other managers' activities in similar circumstances. A continuing concern was that of advancing good people from within; with that in mind, he was briefly curious about a recent study, "A Humanistic Re-Education for the Corporation Executive," developed under the Fund for Adult Education. Soon, however, he lost interest, concluding, "The rewards for the company seem to me to be too vague." He also observed, for the benefit of the program's chief proponent: "Incidentally, Mr. Fletcher, it seems to me that one of the characteristics of this age is that each of us is trying desperately to 'educate' everybody else. I guess it is a good thing but sometimes wonder."

At the late-summer family meeting in St. Paul several matters were discussed. There was a consensus that it would be in "the long range interest of the individual members of our family (particularly those who might be called controlling persons)" if the stock of both the Weyerhaeuser Timber Company and Potlatch Forests, Inc., were publicly registered and listed. This had been debated for years, but finally, at F.K.'s urging, a decision was reached. "Controlling persons" was a phrase suggesting the possibility of antitrust violations. Although the legalities weren't entirely clear, the assumption was that a handful of people with collective ownership influence in competing corporations could—had the power to—take actions in restraint of trade and beneficial to themselves. Quite naturally, in this regard family holding companies were suspect.

This family decision was of particular importance in the case of Potlatch, but the eventual listing of both Potlatch and the Timber Company went forward simultaneously. The Timber Company had tested the waters back in 1950, undertaking a "dry run registration" to learn what needed to be done in order to ensure that it was in compliance. While no major roadblocks appeared, at the time no further action was taken. F.K. was impatient to proceed with the listing, moved primarily by two considerations. One was simply the lack of fiscal flexibility for the shareholders. If family members were in need of funds, what price would their shares bring? Without public trading, there was no definite answer. Weyerhaeuser Timber Company stock was marketable, but the same wasn't the case with PFI. The second consideration involved the aforementioned legal concern. They had spent, F.K. reminded, "a lot of time worrying about controlling persons and the problem of arranging private sales," and wouldn't they "save a lot of valuable time and effort" by simply registering the stocks, selling them through normal markets?

To illustrate just how unusual it was for the Weyerhaeuser Timber Company to have remained private as long as it did, one need only note some comparative figures. For example, in 1957, the *Fortune* directory of the largest 500 companies included only twelve that were unlisted, of which Weyerhaeuser ranked first. The top three, based on net income, were Weyerhaeuser (thirty-seventh overall), Eli Lilly and Company (seventy-eighth), and Time, Inc. (one hundred twentieth).

Although they may have moved at a snail's pace, the objective of public listing for both Potlatch and Weyerhaeuser was finally achieved in 1963. In behalf of the Timber Company, F.K., by then chairman of the board, appeared on the floor of the New York Stock Exchange to mark the occasion. Finally, anyone was free to bid for and buy "WY" stock, and many did.

F.K.'s campaign to update the objectives of the Weyerhaeuser Timber Company went forward nearly on schedule. The "improvements" seem almost superficial, but a closer reading suggests that they involved important changes. For example, the listing opened with a new general statement speaking to "the long range interests of shareholders, employees and the public." The founders in 1900 would most likely have been confused by the thought of including the public. Additionally, the first of eleven substatements was in accord with F.K.'s earlier draft: "To deal fairly with its customers, employees, shareholders and others, and to maintain in all its affairs the highest ethical standards."

With agreement as to objectives, they could now proceed to review the organization itself. F.K. began by creating a President's Advisory Committee, its function strictly to advise, "not to exercise authority." Members included vice-president and general counsel; financial vice-president; director of personnel; vice-president of the Pulp Division and president of the Kieckhefer-Eddy Division; manager of the Wood Products Division; manager of the Sawmill Division; vice-president and assistant to the president; and manager of Forestry, Lands, and Timber. The Advisory Committee was to get together every Monday morning at 9:30, with meetings limited to one hour "except in case of emergency." Subjects for discussion were up to the members themselves, and no official minutes would be kept. It was just the sort of thing that Phil would have avoided at all costs. He would have begun twirling his watch chain; but not F.K. Ideas didn't have to be in any final form to merit consideration. The surest progress was achieved by moving together, however slowly.

Comparative openness was one of the first qualities colleagues noted in F.K. Although both brothers were unassuming, F.K., unlike Phil, relished group participation and debate. F.K. also was far more willing to make public appearances than Phil had been, and speaking opportunities were unlimited. One with special appeal was an invitation to address a November 8 banquet celebrating the fiftieth anniversary of the University of Washington's College of Forestry. In responding to Henry Schmitz, president of the university, F.K. observed that he was "much flattered" to be asked, and then added, "You probably think I am a much better speaker than I am. However, such an invitation from you, in particular, is compelling, and I will attend and do my best."

F.K.'s speeches, which he often wrote and always edited, followed a predictable pattern. Invariably, they began with some historical reference or sketch, putting the present in context. And invariably they noted progress that had been made in forestry practices with the accompanying assurance that as a nation we ran absolutely no risk of running out of timber. Finally, they mentioned the dangers from governmental regulations and restrictions, as well as the great benefits deriving from freedom and free enterprise. That was the basic message he offered at the College of Forestry's banquet. When he spoke in-house, the message varied somewhat. For one thing, in front of what was often an all-male audience, he could occasionally employ an earthy story, at least slightly ribald, the sort that today would seem adolescent.

At the "first annual office party" on November 20, 1957, he opened with a story about two conventions in the same hotel, of lumber salesmen and of ministers. Spiked melons had been ordered for the salesmen but were delivered by mistake to the ministers. Answering the question, "Did the ministers like it?" the waiter allowed that he didn't know, but they were taking seeds home in their pockets. There were guffaws galore. Nevertheless, the purpose of the gathering was serious, at least in F.K.'s mind. He served as emcee and indicated that the program was "not a speech by a physicist, nor sleight of hand performance, nor impersonation, but: A family party." Then he introduced Norton Clapp, chairman of the board; Ed Hayes, chairman of the Executive Committee; and Herbert Kieckhefer, representing, of course, the recently merged Kieckhefer-Eddy operations. Each made a brief statement. But the key element of the program was F.K.'s outline of changes in store for the organization.

Charlie Ingram was scheduled to retire on January 1, 1958. With Ingram's departure, the position of executive vice-president would be eliminated. There would subsequently be five senior staff positions: Financial, headed by W. P. Gullander; Law, Joe Nolan; Forestry, Land, and

Timber, Dave Weyerhaeuser; Personnel, headed by newly hired Lowry Wyatt; and John Aram, assisting the president generally, with his particular responsibilities for public relations and research and development. In addition, there would be three line, or operating, groups: pulp and paper, under Howard Morgan; special products, under Bob Pauley; and wood products, headed by George Weyerhaeuser, with the added note, "The services of the Weyerhaeuser Sales Company will, of course, be at the call of the head of Wood Products."

Perhaps F.K.'s "of course" most bothered the oldtimers in the Sales Company, notably Bob Douglas, now nominally serving as general manager. F.K. tried to explain the changes in a Christmas Eve letter. Setting prices was the key element: "While the Sales Company will continue in a broad way to exercise its price judgment as in the past, it seems to me the head of the Wood Products group should have the ultimate price authority." On New Year's Eve he tried again. "I thought you had understood the plan from our previous conversations," he began, but apparently that was not the case:

> The administration of the Sales Company will remain subject to its Board of Directors and officers, as in the past. George will normally depend upon the Sales Company for the pricing of his products, but must have the final veto power over price if he is truly to be in charge of the Wood Products Group. He should also be completely informed on pricing policies and practices. My feeling is that this will tie sales and production closer together and perhaps lead to a better understanding all the way around.

Bob Douglas wasn't the only one with questions about the reorganization, although he may have been the most worried. Ed Davis, for instance, counted a total of ten people reporting to F.K., "so in effect you are president, executive vice president and general manager." He further observed, "Guess this means you can't stray far away until you thicken up underneath you with somebody who might be called 'executive vice president,'" adding that it seemed strange for the company's lawyer to be a vice-president when the manager of Wood Products was not. "Hope George W. will be elected a VP at the next annual meeting." Others also thought George should be a vice-president, and he would be so elected at the March annual meeting.

F.K.'s changes were, to him, preparations for the future, a future belonging to the next generation. While he may not have been an interim president, he surely saw himself as a transitional figure. Most others did, too. Moreover, it wasn't just the Weyerhaeuser Timber Company that was important; there was also the Weyerhaeuser family to consider. The January family meetings took place as scheduled in St. Paul, marking a milestone, "the first meeting of the male members of the younger generation." As Ed Davis commented, "It shocks me to realize that you [F.K.], F.W., Dave W and I are the only ones still actively interested in our generation."

Significant, at least in retrospect, was F.K.'s recommendation that young John Driscoll be elected a director of the Northwest Paper Company. John had already caught F.K.'s eye as a possible successor in terms of family leadership. But that was not imminent. Indeed, Ed Davis expressed the hope that F.K. would soon be able to return to St. Paul and would "remain president of the family companies here until you reach 70." As a matter of fact, F.K. had no intention of relinquishing family leadership before age seventy, a day that wasn't very far away.

Much work remained in Tacoma, beginning with something that had become known during Phil's tenure as Hell Week. This actually involved more than a week in time, but for many the "hell" part was accurate. Board members and senior management moved from operating site to operating site, listening as each branch manager reported in detail on that branch's performance for the year. One major difference in 1958 was that the new Kieckhefer-Eddy Division and the North Carolina Pulp Company branches made their reports in Chicago on February 3 and 4. In the course of the tour, F.K. explained further the reorganization along product lines, emphasizing his desire "to clarify job descriptions and delegate powers in such a manner that responsibility and authority go together." He also expressed hope that the wood products and special products groups would make "a strong effort to integrate our manufacturing and sales functions," the old, all-too-familiar problem. It was becoming ever clearer that the days of the old Sales Company were numbered.

Hell Week ended in Tacoma, on the eve of the annual meeting. But this, too, would change. First, F.K. doubted the legitimacy of Hell Week itself, and he also wondered about its label. Additionally, the date of the annual meeting was poor on at least two counts, the weather and the

short time between January 1 and the first week in March. His initial recommendation was to change the date to the second Monday preceding
the last Thursday in May. In 1958 F.K. kept his remarks very brief, deferring to the newly elected vice-president of the Wood Products Group,
George H. Weyerhaeuser, so that he might "tell you some of the interesting facts of its organization, its operations and its problems."

In early June, F.K. sat down with George and John Aram to consider problems associated with wood products and the special products
groups "in the field of sales." Both George and John left little doubt as
to their preferences. George observed the obvious, that the very "separation of sales from manufacturing creates a problem," and he went so far
as to wonder if they might not change the name Weyerhaeuser Sales
Company to something like "Sales Department." John agreed: "We must
find ways of making our advertising activities in Saint Paul and in Tacoma collaborate effectively and eliminate friction and misunderstanding."
Tucked away in the notes of the meeting was mention of acquiring Roddis Plywood of Wisconsin. This would happen, eventually.

Although he had already delegated Sales Company authority to
George Weyerhaeuser in the matter of setting prices on lumber and plywood, at the heart of F.K.'s concern was the Sales Company's relationship to Special Products. He expected great things of new items in the
marketplace and, as he tried to explain to Bob Douglas, while they had
been successful "over a long period of years" in selling lumber, "we have
not yet proven that we can manufacture and sell hardboard, Ply-Veneer,
particle board, et cetera, and get a new dollar back for an old one."

The importance of Special Products was soon underscored when
John Aram asked to be relieved of other responsibilities so as to concentrate on "the principal task at hand." He would henceforth "devote his
entire time to reorganization and management of the Special Products
Group, the Research and Development activities," and related efforts.
At the same time, Bernie Orell was elected a vice-president of the Timber Company, "to be in charge of the Department of Public Affairs and
of Resource Relations."

More details of change were announced at the second pre–Thanksgiving banquet for western Weyerhaeuser management and staff. Some
two hundred fifty attended what F.K. described as "an annual tradition."
He began referring to the history-in-progress of the Timber Company

and "its *antecedents*." Six years had passed since the beginning of the project, and "drafts are now coming out and a number of us are busily engaged in criticism and correction." This was an exaggeration, but he hoped that some day they would have "a good history." And he continued, in typical fashion:

> To me, the most impressive part of this story of a century in business is the *character* of the people who associated themselves together back in the 60's and 70's on the Mississippi and on the Chippewa; of the people they gathered around them, and of their successors in Minnesota and the West, right down to the present day. We have had a succession of wonderful people in this business, great men with vision and courage. They created a great American tradition which we share as associates in the Weyerhaeuser Timber Company, and we can be proud to follow in their footsteps.

F.K. then explained recent organizational changes. For example, the three operating functions, formerly called businesses, were now to be known as groups; and the third had a new name, Silvatek and New Products Group. It was further determined that this group would have its own sales organization. F.K. also announced the retirement of C. Davis Weyerhaeuser as vice-president in charge of forestry, changing the name from Forestry, Lands and Timber Department to simply Timberland Department, a division of the Wood Products Group. And in conclusion, almost in passing, F.K. noted that the board had recently authorized employment of a New York firm, Lippincott and Margulies, Inc., "to study our trade names, trade-marks and advertising; in fact all of the words and pictures we use in describing our products and ourselves to the public." That announcement probably didn't seem very important at the time.

The significance of the Silvatek and New Products Group was made even clearer at the board meeting of November 19. John Aram presented a five-year plan, which, as F.K. summarized, was "aimed at developing a successful and profitable Group activity in fields not covered by the traditional activities of lumber plywood, pulp, paperboard and containers, and assumes the existence of a forward-looking research and development program." The effort was surely sincere, but success would be uneven at best.

The biggest event at year's end, however, had little to do with the Silvatek and New Products Group. Daughter Vivian was engaged to Frank Piasecki, an aviation engineer, actually a pioneer in vertical flight and the founder of Piasecki Helicopter Corporation. (The name was changed to Vertol in 1956 and today is Boeing Helicopters.) Vivian and Frank were married on December 20 at Hobe Sound, another cause for celebration. Once again F.K. and mother Vivian felt proud and blessed.

TREE IN A TRIANGLE

Concluding his remarks at the November 1958 dinner, which had become an annual tradition, F.K. couldn't resist adding some political commentary. He had just welcomed Gordon Lippincott, noting the recently signed contract with the New York design firm Lippincott and Margulies. The object was to improve the corporate image, even if that should require "abbreviating the name Weyerhaeuser." Years earlier, anglicization had actually been suggested as a possibility!

Then came the commentary, including the warning that taxes were "destroying the initiative of people to work or risk their savings in productive and job-producing enterprises." He also spoke of the dangers of socialism, and the irony that while the Russians were "adopting capitalistic incentives to increase products and improve performance . . . America is adopting socialistic measures which discourage production, thrift, and savings." Finally, he encouraged one and all "to make politics in the party of our choice our business, too!" "In the party of our choice" had been penciled in, no doubt reluctantly. And, of course, political concerns carried over into the New Year, 1959. It was the national deficit that was most worrisome, specifically a predicted $12.5 billion for the fiscal year. Although from the vantage of the 1990s that seems paltry, it wasn't so then. As F.K. wrote to Minnesota Senator Eugene J.

McCarthy and others, "Without minimizing the external threat of Soviet Russian aggression, the internal threat of deficit spending to the fiscal, economic and moral integrity of this country is a far greater long term risk."

If the nation's economy needed a new direction, that certainly wasn't the case with Weyerhaeuser. Market conditions had improved considerably since the disappointments of 1957, and F.K. urged his assistants to keep their eyes open for new investment opportunities. In the meantime, he concentrated on recommendations from Lippincott and Margulies. He and Norton Clapp went to New York for an early conference, primarily regarding a new logo. While it may seem curious that such seemingly trivial decisions should prove so difficult and frustrating, that is probably to be expected when tampering with tradition. At this March 19 meeting, two "candidates" were presented, one of which featured triangles. No choice was made; rather, it was agreed that both would be offered to the final Management Presentation in Tacoma on April 24. Obviously, F.K. had realized the futility of seeking unanimity.

Not only did discussion of a new logo cause friction, but there was also a new name to consider. All of this became public knowledge at the annual meeting, the first to be held in May. F.K. opened with very welcome news of the company's first-quarter performance, announcing earnings of more than $18.5 million, an increase of 28 percent over the first four months of 1958. He next reviewed recent efforts, which had resulted in the amended company objectives and the reorganization. Then he turned, almost tentatively, to the subject of corporate identity. F.K. reminded all shareholders that it had been two years since the merger of Kieckhefer-Eddy and the Weyerhaeuser Timber Company, and he spoke of progress made in that integration. But one aspect remained troublesome, "namely the confusion of names, trademarks, and slogans which no longer seem entirely appropriate," and he offered as an example: "The buyer of milk cartons and folding boxes is surprised to be solicited by a 'Timber Company.'"

Then came the bombshell, a recommendation from Lippincott and Margulies that *Timber* should be dropped, and henceforth the corporation would be known as the Weyerhaeuser Company. The board agreed to this change, and F.K. spoke briefly in support of the proposal:

I personally feel that the matter should be decided not on a sentimental basis but purely on practical and business grounds. The following argument for the change appeals to me. Our two biggest problems are: first, to sell our products up to the capacity of our plants and forest lands. Second, to represent ourselves in a favorable light to the public and to government. The word timber emphasizes to the customer our raw material—while we are more interested in emphasizing the products we sell. To the public and to government it [timber] emphasizes "Bigness," an unpopular concept, it may suggest locking up a natural asset for value appreciation, likewise unpopular and it certainly reminds them that the Company has lots of a scarce commodity which others would like to get a part of.

The new name was officially approved. As usual, the majority didn't bother to vote and were thus recorded as being in favor. Quite a number, however, made an effort to voice their objections. At the annual meeting, several stood up and spoke in opposition, and many more wrote afterward. Some simply didn't want to change what had become so familiar over the years, but there were other reasons. One complained that they were "trading the meaningful word 'Timber' which denotes strength, beauty and an earthy well-rooted quality . . . leaving only the meaningless word 'Company.'"

Weyerhaeuser secretary George S. Long, Jr., himself a strong opponent, informed chairman Clapp that "employee shareholders are voting pretty nearly 100% against the proposed change in name." And he added, "For whatever it is worth, we have received no comments either by letters or written on proxies expressing approval." Although Long exaggerated slightly, even F.K. admitted to ambivalence. "Most of us who have been with the Weyerhaeuser Timber Company hesitate to see the name changed, but feel it is probably the wise thing to do in view of the wide variety of products which the company is now manufacturing." The old name didn't die easily. As late as the 1983 annual meeting, when Edmund Hayes formally nominated candidates for the board, he inadvertently referred to the Weyerhaeuser Timber Company. Many in the audience smiled and nodded nostalgically.

But in 1959 it was full speed ahead, F.K. announcing implementation of the new program in late June:

> We will now be moving into the application phase, during which time the new corporate signature, the new Weyerhaeuser mark, and the system recommended by Lippincott & Margulies will be applied to everything that identifies us visually to the Company's customers, its employees, and the general public.
>
> It is my belief this corporate visual program is today an indispensable part of corporate public affairs and that it will make a substantial contribution to our marketing success in the years ahead. If the maximum benefit is to be obtained, however, effective implementation of the system and use of the mark through all management functions is absolutely essential.

F.K. was right, and four decades later, Weyerhaeuser's tree in a triangle looks as fresh and agreeable as it did in 1959.

The advertising campaign received an unsolicited boost in the summer of 1959, thanks to an article about Weyerhaeuser in *Fortune*. It wasn't the first time the company had been featured in that magazine; a lengthy story had appeared in April 1934, and a comparison of the two suggests just how much the worlds of journalism and Weyerhaeuser had changed. F.K. was generally approving of the 1959 piece. He had naturally been fearful, but in the end he really couldn't complain. "I want to tell you that we think the article is very flattering," he wrote to the editor. "We appreciate tremendously the cooperative attitude of the staff."

William G. "Bill" Reed, president of the Simpson Timber Company, felt a bit chagrined at his characterization in the text and wrote Norton Clapp a letter of apology, particularly concerning a reference to young George Weyerhaeuser as the "crown prince." That phrase, Bill explained, must have been the "reporter's license. Certainly I am aware of the impropriety of my saying what I think you will or should do." What had amused Reed in the course of his interview was the *Fortune* reporter's statement that he "had been unable to find anything bad about the Weyerhaeuser Company or its management." Reed allowed that he had been of no help in disclosing an underside.

A few items remained on F.K.'s own agenda. Chief among them was updating the five-year projections of capital expenditures for the three operating groups; these would be presented to the board the first week of August. In his directive, he noted a significant underlying assumption, specifically, "Because of the legal and other problems involved in acquiring any more going concerns in our own lines of business, we should plan in terms of building new facilities and developing our own place in the market, even though this is a slower and more difficult route."

In addition, there was the Sales Company. On July 30 F.K. distributed a memorandum, "Moving Weyerhaeuser Sales Company General Office from St. Paul to Tacoma." He opened with a brief history, recalling that the general office had been in the west, in Spokane, from 1919 to 1931, and then listing reasons it had been moved to St. Paul. He did not, of course, note F.E.'s preference to live in St. Paul, and certainly not his own. But what had been regarded as a reason for relocation in 1931—independence from the mill managers—was anything but that in 1959. Indeed, experience had shown that the opposite was true. As F.K. described the situation, "One problem has always been the corporate barrier." And he admitted, "Sales Company personnel looks at the Timber Company as a foreign enterprise, and Timber Company personnel looks at the Sales Company as a foreign activity somewhat hostile to its own interests."

To no one's surprise, it wasn't simply a move of headquarters that was under consideration; it was the elimination of that "corporate barrier" entirely. Maintaining a separate sales company, however appropriate in the past, was now impossible to justify. "Under today's conditions," F.K. continued, "the closest kind of coordination between manufacturing, sales, product improvement and development . . . is becoming vitally necessary." And the logical question followed: "Should the Weyerhaeuser Sales Company corporation be continued?" The answer was obvious, even to F.K. "Sales and manufacturing are two principal arms of the Wood Products group and should be under the same direction."

Little time was wasted in bringing about the dissolution of the Sales Company. Final action was taken on August 25. It must have seemed anticlimactic to F.K. and many others present, as so much history, so much effort, and so many frustrations were all dismissed rather summarily. The key resolution began, "[T]he holders of all the shares of this corporation [the Weyerhaeuser Timber Company as represented by F.K. and George S. Long, Jr.] believe that the dissolution and winding up of this corporation is in the best interests of this corporation and its shareholders." A memorandum was sent immediately to Sales Company customers, noting first the change in name effective September 1, from Weyerhaeuser Timber Company to simply Weyerhaeuser Company, and that on October 1 the Sales Company would cease to exist as a separate corporation.

The board had already acted upon recommendations growing out of the five-year plans. On August 5 and 6, F.K. opened the sessions enumerating "our past mistakes." Leading the list were overbuilding in terms of market pulp and a tardy entry into the field of paper packages and products. Similarly, they had entered the plywood field too late and now found themselves with too much lumber and too little plywood in the marketplace. Third, they had missed excellent opportunities to buy timber and cutover lands in the South as well as in Oregon and northern California. Now, even if belatedly, they proposed that the Company invest some $500 million "in land, timber and plants over the next five years." Specific recommendations were included in individual presentations from the three groups or divisions, as they were coming to be called. One resolution would have unexpected consequences: "That this Board hereby express itself as favorable to investments in foreign countries where the risk of failure through instability of government or other causes be not out of proportion to the benefits anticipated."

F.K. again addressed the board on November 18. He began by observing how attitudes had changed since the founding of the company in 1900, particularly regarding their present belief in a "sustained yield timber crop." But the core of his message centered on investment policy and the five-year plans. One of the principal motivators involved possession of $100 million in surplus funds, which, if simply held, earned 2 percent, clearly not competitive with funds invested in a business earning 10 percent after taxes. The solution was clear, "that we should follow a vigorous policy of construction and acquisitions if we are to maintain satisfactory earnings and achieve a good rate of growth." And as if to underline the extent of his convictions, F.K. surprisingly recommended that they should not "fear incurring reasonable amounts of debt if good investment opportunities appear." This constituted a 180-degree change in attitude, and, it should be emphasized, F.K. himself continued to have a few doubts; after all, it was new territory.

He was not proposing any leaps into the dark. On the contrary, he preached caution. While they did employ Arthur D. Little, Inc., and Stanley Morgan to recommend likely fields of investment, throughout he kept in mind the old proverb, "A shoemaker should stick to his last." Nonetheless, F.K.'s most important legacy to the Weyerhaeuser Company, at least in the short term, may have been an increased receptiveness to expansion.

Consistent with this thinking, and as one of his final acts as president, F.K. circulated an article from *Mechanical Engineering,* "Management's Changing Responsibilities." The article emphasized how rapid technological advances were occurring, advances that could "leave us far behind unless we use all of our resources in the field of research and development and in the acquisition of new techniques through a program of acquisition and innovation." Following his own advice, he immediately appointed John Aram, Howard Morgan, and George Weyerhaeuser as the President's Central Research and Development Advisory Committee. That president would not be F.K. He would be sixty-five on January 16 and would become chairman of the board, in effect trading places with Norton Clapp. But everyone could plainly see that Norton was taking over direction of a different organization from the one F.K. had joined just three years earlier. F.K. had left his mark, and it amounted to more than a tree in a triangle.

TWENTY-FOUR

ST. PAUL AT SUNSET

F. K. Weyerhaeuser officially retired as president of Weyerhaeuser Company on February 1, 1960. Although he continued to serve as chairman of the board for another five years, his responsibilities lessened, many of them becoming procedural, almost ceremonial. He would certainly miss much of the day-to-day activity, but he also appreciated the increased leisure hours. In a handwritten note to Ed Hayes from Hobe Sound, he admitted that he couldn't help wondering about deliberations in the Executive Committee meetings, "but believe it's wise to keep out of Norton's way for a while—besides being lazy myself." It was just as well. Norton had already called in "the experts" to dismantle F.K.'s office.

Surely F.K. and Vivian had earned rest and relaxation. Still, F.K. paid attention to matters he found of special interest, such as retirement policies for Weyerhaeuser managers and members of the board. Not surprisingly, the first was decided more easily; managers retired at sixty-five. It would eventually be decided that board members could serve until the age of seventy; but in deference to two who had already exceeded that age, O. D. Fisher and Laird Bell, a special "emeritus" category was instituted. Actually, it was Laird who suggested the compromise, allowing ex-officio service for two years beyond age seventy; senior counselors, they came to be called, who participated without voting. F.K.

also pushed for recruiting "outsider" members to the board, but it was too early for that change to be accepted.

In the interim, F.K. found more than enough to do, especially in his role as family leader. In addition, there was the job of being a grandfather; Vivian Weyerhaeuser Day was born in 1957, the first of eleven grandchildren.

The grandparents naturally took great delight in their growing families, but F.K. felt a particular responsibility to pass along words of wisdom, much in the manner of his own grandfather Frederick. On one occasion, he purchased a wallhanging for the Days and Piaseckis that featured a "poem" by one Dorothy Law Nolte, "Children Learn What They Live." It started:

> If a child lives with criticism,
>   He learns to condemn.
> If a child lives with hostility
>   He learns to fight.

And it ended:

> If a child lives with approval,
>   He learns to like himself.
> If a child lives with acceptance and friendship,
>   He learns to find love in the world.

Later, he shared an anonymous poem, "The Guy in the Glass"—the glass being the mirror—whose concluding stanza summarizes the whole:

> You can fool the whole world down the pathway of years,
> And get pats on the back as you pass,
> But your final reward will be heartache and tears,
> If you've cheated the guy in the glass.

In truth, daughters Vivian and Lynn had little need for poems and proverbs; they had learned the lessons of family in a better way, by example. If family life wasn't always perfect, it was surely happy and caring in the long term, and for that F.K. and Vivian deserved credit.

Grandmother Vivian stayed busy, both with family matters and her other interests. While in Tacoma, she encouraged the Pacific Northwest Metropolitan auditions, leaving behind a stronger organization. Nonetheless, she was relieved when they finally moved back home to 294 Summit Avenue in 1960. As president of the National Council of the Metropolitan Opera, she returned to Seattle for the auditions. Not all would go well, as the 1961 auditions demonstrated. The winner was one Heather Thomson, a twenty-year-old soprano from Vancouver, British Columbia. The extent of Miss Thomson's talent isn't known, but apparently she already had a diva's personality. Refusing to accept advice regarding her program, she was eliminated in the semifinals in New York. Although Heather would charge prejudice, a Met executive, John Gutman, countered that she was "just a little girl who is too big to learn." Controversy was inevitable, of course, all the more so as the years passed and the auditions assumed ever-greater importance.

During the summer of 1961, Vivian was wounded in action, breaking her foot when stepping back off a raised platform in the course of a talk. Her recovery required a period of inactivity, and with F.K. serving as principal nurse, she had lots of time to reflect, including, of course, about her beloved Met. The famous audition program had all begun with Vivian in St. Paul. Later, in an interview with a *Minneapolis Tribune* staff writer, she recalled its genesis. The article, published Sunday, January 5, 1964, described the course of events:

> Mrs. August Belmont of New York, founder and first president of the National Council of the Metropolitan, conceived of a national talent search. Her vice president was Vivian, and Mrs. Belmont simply passed the conception along, suggesting a pilot project in St. Paul. Vivian accepted the challenge, confident that "we really DO care about music here in the Upper Midwest." The first audition was held at Northrop Auditorium of the University of Minnesota on February 12, 1954, and more than a hundred singers participated. The rest, as they say, is history.

By 1965 auditions were being held in sixty cities, with sixteen regional finals. Many contestants went on to even bigger things, fifteen eventually singing with the Metropolitan Opera. Although the Met was obviously her first love, Vivian also contributed to the Women's Association of the Minneapolis Symphony Orchestra, and, as noted previously, the Minnesota Historical Society.

As for F.K., he became increasingly involved in history of various sorts, placing recent accomplishments in historical context. Such was the case with resolution of the Potlatch Forests, Inc., stockholders' dilemma. It had been a complicated and arduous journey, F.K. likening it to "the travels of Ulysses back from Troy." Finally, with the help of favorable rulings by the Internal Revenue Service, there was a distribution of PFI stock held by The Bonners Ferry Company to individual shareholders. In his letter to the family, F.K. recalled that in 1900 grandfather Frederick, along with F. C. A. Denkmann and John A. Humbird, had purchased lands on the north fork of the Clearwater River, forming the Clearwater Timber Company, predecessor of Potlatch Forests, Inc. "Now in 1964," he continued, "we merge Clearwater and Bonners Ferry with PFI and get the PFI stock into our own hands."

This represented a notable shift in family affairs. No longer would a large holding company such as The Bonners Ferry Company manage shares on behalf of the family. Henceforth, the holding company would be insignificant, and the Family Office would instead concentrate on financial planning, taxes, trust preparation, and estate planning and settlement.

An ongoing historical saga, perhaps also analogous to Ulysses' travels, was the Columbia University history "of the joint business undertakings" of Frederick Weyerhaeuser, his associates, and successors. Although the initial agreement promised completion by 1957, F.K. didn't receive a draft of the first chapter until the spring of 1958, along with an accompanying promise that the remaining chapters would be finished by July 1. That also proved overly optimistic. But F.K. enthusiastically accepted his responsibility, enlisting the help of others in the task of reviewing. He referred to those who eventually agreed to help—some fifteen in all—as "The Critics." The review process seemed endless.

By mid-November, F.K. had received original drafts of thirty-one chapters, which did not include Chapter Seven or the concluding chapter, still being written by Ralph Hidy, the Isidor Straus Professor of Business History at the Harvard Business School. To his team of critics, F.K. explained the holdup: The book that was to have been completed a year earlier had been "delayed by the fact that Professor Nevins took on too many jobs in the intervening five years." Nevins had since retired from Columbia and undertaken a new "career" at the famous Huntington Library in San Marino, California.

Nearly a year later, F.K. still wasn't finished. He tried his best to be patient, at the same time encouraging Hidy to appreciate the crucial points, the essence of the story. As written, thus far they had failed "to adequately interpret or sum up the significance of the past thirty years," and F.K. listed four subjects demanding further emphasis, beginning with "making industrial forestry a reality." Then he noted efforts at improving forest utilization by broadening manufacture into pulp, linerboard, plywood, "and products from logging and mill leftovers." Third, he cited the many efforts to improve marketing; and finally, "the attempt to explain ourselves and our ideas to the public, government, and industry through movies, advertising, financial reports and public statements." Implicit in his summation was an appreciation of the continuum:

1. Over the years timber has been a good investment.
2. A guiding principle of the associates has opposed borrowing.
3. There has always been a high sense of obligation to keep contracts and to make good on promises either written or verbal.
4. The associates have believed in decentralization of management. They have never believed in the concept of tight or military management.
5. Generally speaking, over the years the associates have preferred to have executives from stockholding families rather than go outside.
6. Doubt whether even today they would agree to the theory that professional management is the answer of the future rather than stockholder management.

He closed with words of encouragement to Hidy and his colleagues, that they had a fine book "in the making," even though much work would be required "to make it a real credit to the authors and a worthwhile investment to us."

Professor Hidy wasn't deterred. In January 1960, he sought F.K.'s support for the Business History Foundation and its plans to sponsor "the first comprehensive history of business in the United States." In response, F.K. allowed that he had "been promoting the importance of business history so long around these parts that I don't have the nerve to suggest another investment in that field at this time." He was referring to his record of soliciting on behalf of the Forest History Foundation. Besides, there was *Timber and Men,* still three years from publication. "Let's wait until we get our own history done," F.K. admonished.

If the history of grandfather Frederick, his associates, and his successors had become something of a cross to bear, such was not true of F.K.'s gradual relinquishing of business responsibility. He enjoyed his role as chairman of the Weyerhaeuser Company board, watching many of the developments he had envisioned take place, among them the maturation of nephew George H. Weyerhaeuser. In F.K.'s opinion, George was the hope for the years ahead. In the meantime, much was happening. Weyerhaeuser entered the hardwood lumber business in 1960 through a merger with the Roddis Plywood Corporation of Wisconsin. This was soon followed by acquisition of the Hamilton Paper Company and then another paper producer, the Crocker Burbank Company. An event little noted, but significant in terms of future operations, was the logging of 135 acres in the St. Helens Tree Farm. The significance was due to one simple fact: This was the initial logging of second-growth timber. What was a first in 1961 would soon be the norm: It would all be second-growth.

Although F.K. understood that he should generally stay out of Norton Clapp's way, some issues troubled him to such an extent that he couldn't keep quiet. A major concern was the manner in which the old Sales Company was dissolved, especially the treatment of its personnel, many of whom were on the verge of retirement. Other areas to which F.K. called attention involved the continuing difficulty of effecting the merger of Weyerhaeuser and Kieckhefer-Eddy. From a later perspective, this seems to have been completed with relative ease, but that wasn't apparent in the early 1960s, the problem exacerbated by losses suffered in the milk-carton and folding-box divisions. Then there was the large matter of increasing overhead expenditures. Finally, F.K. wondered whether expansions were wise. As he wrote to Norton, "You and I have repeatedly heard the comment that we ought to get present activities operating efficiently before we undertake to create or acquire new ones."

These concerns persisted. Three years later, in the fall of 1965, F.K. reflected upon one of them, the question of borrowing. "We have a tradition of not borrowing money at all," he reminded friend Ed Hayes, who needed no such reminding, and one of the principal reasons was that their timber reserves amounted to "money in the bank." That wasn't quite true, of course; timber was hardly a liquid asset. F.K. could not ignore the evidence that borrowing often made good business sense. But would what worked for others work as well for Weyerhaeuser? He wasn't sure. As he explained, "My basic reason for avoiding debt at this time is to insure that Weyerhaeuser management prove its ability to pick out the really good opportunities for investment." So, in the end it wasn't the principle he questioned. At heart, it was a personnel matter.

But these were times of expansion, and the Weyerhaeuser organization seemed determined to keep apace. Many developments involved the opening of overseas offices, in Tokyo in 1963, and subsequently around the world, including a joint venture with the Kamloops Pulp and Paper Company, Ltd., which would evolve into Weyerhaeuser Canada, Ltd. Much was happening in the Tacoma headquarters. But F.K. didn't allow his directors to concentrate solely on the moment; he often reminded them of past times, equally exciting and more enjoyable, at least in retrospect. He recalled a meeting in 1936, before the Snoqualmie Falls Lumber Company was merged with Weyerhaeuser Timber Company. An "Oath" was circulated among the directors, the purpose of which was gently to embarrass O. D. Fisher. In part, the oath read that the undersigned would "faithfully comply with, support and observe all of the constitutions, laws, rules and regulations of all Labor Unions in the State of Washington, and elsewhere within the jurisdiction of the United States of America; that he will vote the Democratic ticket; that he will cause all earnings of the corporation to be distributed to its employees; and be personally liable for all obligations of the said corporation: So Help Me God." Phil signed, in F.K.'s words, as "Pied Piper," and the rest dutifully followed, beginning with O.D.

The torch was passed again at the Weyerhaeuser annual meeting in April 1966. F.K. announced his retirement as chairman of the board, to be replaced by Norton Clapp. Thirty-nine-year-old George Weyerhaeuser was elected president and chief executive officer. With the exception of Helen, George's mother, and wife Wendy, no one could have been prouder than F.K. Although the timing was not perfect, it had been understood by most that George was to be Norton's successor. F.K. had certainly encouraged his nephew at every opportunity, and George did not disappoint him.

Perhaps with the Tacoma pieces in place, F.K. felt he could relax and enjoy family, friends, and old St. Paul. One of the activities that he and Vivian most enjoyed was entertaining at their Summit Avenue home. Some evenings had a serious purpose, such as fund-raising for various Twin Cities causes, often involving Vivian's musical interests. But many gatherings were simply for the fun of it, although even these were characterized by a certain ritual. F.K. would usually say a few words to the assembled group on an appropriate subject. For example, when hosting a wedding party for close friends in the summer of 1971, he made his habitual preparation, writing down thoughts that he wanted to be sure to share. Sincerely extending hospitality "to you, our good friends," he nevertheless launched into one of his hopelessly corny stories. This concerned a man who took his old hound dog to the veterinarian, requesting that the vet cut off the dog's tail "as far back as he could." The dog was wagging that tail, and the vet demanded an explanation. And so the man explained: "Because some relatives are coming for a visit and I don't want any sign of hospitality around our house." Everyone laughed of course, F.K. most heartily.

This particular party was held on the eve of a grand tour to the Far East. F.K. and Vivian hadn't traveled there since 1929, following the loss of their second child. The tour included stops at several new Weyerhaeuser Company operations. Starting in Tokyo, they went on to the Philippines, Malaysia, Australia, and New Zealand. F.K. noted all manner of strange and exotic details, such as one species of Philippine mahogany they were logging, "a beautiful wood and floats in the water whereas several other species do not." He also wondered about the precautions he saw, the presence of soldiers toting machine guns. The atmosphere was foreboding, suggesting just the sort of political instability they had feared in such overseas operations.

That trip constituted F.K.'s last major Weyerhaeuser Company involvement. His attention increasingly focused on more personal subjects, starting with the family duties and including his old World War I comrades-in-arms, the so-called Sesta Squad. To Doug Farquhar he described his current situation: "Vivian is still on the Board of the Metropolitan, while I have no urgent responsibilities except family matters which never seem to end." Actually, family matters were fairly well resolved in the early 1970s. John Driscoll had assumed leadership, and Joseph S. Micallef replaced Donald

Hanson as executive vice-president of WF [Weyerhaeuser Family] Associates, Inc., the Family Office in St. Paul. (Shortly, WF Associates, Inc., would become Fiduciary Counselling, Inc., today's organization.) John addressed family members in a November 24, 1971, letter, noting the changes: "I am your representative most closely associated with the day-to-day operations of the company." And so he was, although F.K. remained the titular head, the patriarch, in the eyes of the family.

As had become customary, F.K. addressed the family formally whenever they convened for a meeting. In Sun Valley, Idaho, in June 1970, for example, he spoke at length—his last major speech—beginning with statistics, proceeding with a detailed history, and concluding with his hopes for the future. In 1970 the Weyerhaeuser family numbered more than one hundred fifty, over one hundred of whom attended the Sun Valley reunion. "I can imagine how surprised Grandfather and Grandmother and their 7 sons and daughters would be to see this great gathering of their descendants," he said. "They would be very proud—not only at the numbers of family members who thought it worthwhile to come to this meeting, but also at the diversity of personalities, abilities and attitudes that exist among us." Looking ahead, he expressed hope that the family would continue as in the past, that they would "stick together," reminding all that "sticking together takes work and conscious effort."

Two years later, at Alisal Ranch in southern California, he offered much the same message. "I suppose that I am the luckiest person in this family," he began. "I have a lovely wife Vivian whom I love dearly; she has put up with me for nearly 50 years. We have two fine daughters and 2 fine sons [sic]; also 11 grandchildren—the 3 girls are beautiful and the 8 boys are smart (I hope)." And again, history:

> There are few families as large as the Weyerhaeuser Family that have succeeded in sticking together for 112 years. Large numbers of people tend to drift apart through disagreement or lack of a common purpose. Grandfather told us the story of the Man who picked up many branches in a forest and tied them together. When he tried to break the bundle in two he could not; but when he untied the bundle he found he could break each branch separately. That was his way of teaching us the importance of sticking together as a family.

I hope and believe that we are building our association together on a sound foundation and that our family relationships will
be lubricated with the spirit of mutual love and understanding.

F.K. would not be disappointed. In 1974, meeting in St. Paul, the
group that had been dubbed "young people" at Alisal discussed the future
of the family. Rod Titcomb, Jr., now thirty-two years old, chaired the
gathering and subsequently shared his thoughts. Included was a "unanimous opinion" that there was indeed "a purpose and necessity in keeping the Family together. But, in the same vein, it should not be a blind
historical devotion. We feel that there is an affinity amongst ourselves and
a discerning sense of responsibility to our Family, our fellow man, and
each other." And so the heritage was clearly recognized, although maintaining it would require, as F.K. had earlier observed, "work and conscious effort."

Sadly, F.K. may not have understood all that was then happening.
Beginning in 1973, he was hit by a series of small strokes, eventually losing the power of speech. His last five years were extremely difficult. For
a time, he continued to go to the office, more out of habit than anything else; to the casual observer he may have looked about the same.
He wasn't. Ironically, he became the subject of headlines in the fall of
1975 when his name appeared on the assassination list of the so-called
International People's Court of Retribution, the self-avowed followers
of Charles Manson. An FBI agent was quoted as saying that the threat "was
not directly against [Frederick K.] Weyerhaeuser, but against the company." Vivian, trying her best to protect her husband, could only say that
he was "the finest man that has ever lived. We've had a magnificent 50
years of married life and I can't imagine anything happening to him."

There was one particular curiosity in his last days. He began escorting Vivian to her Catholic church; her company was more important than
his own preference for the services at the House of Hope. Perhaps she
took this as an indication of a change in heart. More likely, she only wanted to believe that they would end up together, in the same heaven. In any
case, when F.K. weakened physically, she arranged to have a monk—an
acquaintance of her brother, Lincoln—come to his bedside and accept
what was interpreted as a conversion. To some, including the archbishop
and F.K.'s daughters, that simply wasn't playing fair. At the same time,

however, how could it possibly have hurt? Vivian was happy, and when Vivian was happy so was F.K.

F.K. died on September 16, 1978. Vivian followed him five years later. The Weyerhaeuser Company continued to prosper, much in the manner he had foreseen. The Weyerhaeuser family was together, just as he had wished. And assuming the triumph of faith, so, too, were he and Vivian.

BIBLIOGRAPHIC ESSAY

LUCKILY FOR ME, most of my historical research over the years has involved studying primary sources. All discoveries are exciting, but nothing quite equals learning through original letters and papers, with only time separating the student and the subject. Many have experienced similar good fortune, but my situation is a bit unusual insofar as each of my last three major projects was based largely on a single collection.

In the case of *Phil Weyerhaeuser: Lumberman* (Seattle: University of Washington Press, 1985) that collection was the papers of John Philip Weyerhaeuser, Jr., housed at the Weyerhaeuser Company Archives in Federal Way, Washington, home of the company's corporate headquarters. In *George S. Long: Timber Statesman* (Seattle: University of Washington Press, 1994) it was, of course, the George S. Long papers, also at the Weyerhaeuser Company Archives. For the present project, the Weyerhaeuser Family and Business Papers at the Minnesota Historical Society (MHS) in St. Paul served as the principal source, supplemented by the F.K. Weyerhaeuser papers in the company archives.

The private papers of Edmund Hayes (some of which have recently been deposited at the Weyerhaeuser Company Archives) have also provided special insights. Ed, a cousin of longtime Weyerhaeuser Timber Company general manager Charlie Ingram, was himself an important board mem-

311

ber for many years and chaired the Executive Committee during F.K.'s tenure as president.

Though the decision to forego footnotes was made with some misgivings, annotated copies of the manuscript are available at MHS and at the Weyerhaeuser Company Archives.

By the way, the Weyerhaeuser Family and Business Papers were intended for inclusion in the Forest Products History Foundation collection. That foundation—today's Forest History Society—was originally associated with the Minnesota Historical Society, but when Forest History left St. Paul for New Haven, Connecticut, the Weyerhaeuser papers stayed put, in the possession of MHS. At that time F.K. apparently had some second thoughts about a couple of files, specifically numbers 36 and 51, the first labeled "Personal Material from Family Correspondence Files, 1940–1956" and the second, "Misc., 1938–1948." Evidence suggests that these were removed and that perhaps some of the material was destroyed. But the greater part, happily, ended up in an old filing cabinet in daughter Lynn's attic. Tucked away there are other items of interest, including miscellaneous notes and letters and F.K.'s "Recollections," which he put together in 1968 at age seventy-three.

Of course secondary sources contributed significantly to the study, beginning with Ralph W. Hidy et al., *Timber and Men: The Weyerhaeuser Story* (New York: Macmillan Company, 1963.) For F.K., *Timber and Men* was both window and mirror. His own life's work makes for a portion of the story, but far more important to the final product were his contributions as consultant and editor. For personal and family background, two books I wrote for the Weyerhaeuser family need to be mentioned: *A Bundle of Sticks: The Story of a Family* (St. Paul: Rock Island Company, 1987) and *The Tie That Binds: A History of the Weyerhaeuser Family Office* (St. Paul: Rock Island Company, 1993). These are not widely circulated, but copies are available at the State Historical Society of Wisconsin library in Madison and at the Minnesota Historical Society Research Center. I might add that *Phil Weyerhaeuser* and, to a lesser extent, *The Tie That Binds* constitute parallel studies contemporaneous with F.K.'s career.

In the summer of 1916, brothers Phil and F.K. had their first serious woods experience, working under the legendary Weyerhaeuser Timber Company cruiser John M. Markham. An account of this expedition is found in Markham's book, *Seventy Years in the Northwest Forests* (Chehalis, Wash.: Loggers World Publications, 1977).

F.K.'s World War I record begins at Yale; for a general accounting of that time and place, see Morris Hadley, *Arthur Twining Hadley* (New Haven: Yale University Press, 1948). On the personal side, there exist also some "recollections," compiled by F.K. on July 9, 1941, at the request of his uncle F.E. F.K.'s best friend in 1917 was his classmate and fellow aviation enthusiast, Louis Bennett. Bennett's impressive combat record is recounted in James J. Hudson's *In Clouds of Glory: American Airmen Who Flew with the British during the Great War* (Fayetteville, Ark.: University of Arkansas Press, 1919). See also George H. Williams, "Louis Bennett, Jr.: No 40 Squadron, RFC/RAF," *Cross and Cockade Journal* (winter 1980); and Norman L. R. Franks and Frank W. Bailey, *Over the Front: A Complete Record of the Fighter Aces and Units of the United States and French Air Services, 1914–1918* (London: Grub Street, 1992). For a detailed account of training, see James J. Hudson's "Frederick K. Weyerhaeuser's Air War in Italy, 1918," *Cross and Cockade Journal* (winter 1982).

One of F.K.'s early business responsibilities involved an assignment with the Potlatch Lumber Company in the Inland Empire. Contributing to an understanding of that experience is an outstanding work by Keith C. Peterson, *Company Town: Potlatch, Idaho, and the Potlatch Lumber Company* (Pullman: Washington State University Press, 1987). For an excellent overview of Minnesota history, the obvious choice is William E. Lass's *Minnesota: A History* (New York: W. W. Norton, 1977).

I have made extensive use of periodicals and newspapers; when appropriate, I have noted these in the text. Special mention should be made of two articles in *Fortune* magazine: "The Name Weyerhaeuser" in the April 1934 issue and "Weyerhaeuser Timber: Out of the Woods" in the July 1959 issue. Chicago newspapers supplied details regarding Vivian's upbringing and social involvements. In addition, Minneapolis and St. Paul newspapers, particularly the *St. Paul Pioneer Press,* often featured articles on the F.K. Weyerhaeusers.

While I continue to recognize the inherent limitations of individual memory, interviews have added essential understandings. In the course of my research on Phil Weyerhaeuser, those interviewed inevitably saw fit to comment on F.K. also, sometimes for the purpose of contrasting the brothers' skills and styles but more often simply to complete the picture, describing the other member of the team in double-harness. Sharpening the focus on F.K., daughters Vivian and Lynn, along with Lynn's husband, Stanley Day, were most helpful. Nephew George H. Weyerhaeuser also contributed significantly, along with cousins John Driscoll, Edith Greenleaf Weyerhaeuser, and, most important, Walter S. Rosenberry III. In addition, key members of the Family Office staff—Donald Hanson, Gordon Hed, and Joseph S. Micallef—were enthusiastic participants. At times I think I enjoy the interviewing part of research too much, and so it has been in this instance. I thank these individuals one and all.

INDEX

Photograph Credits

The photographs on the jacket and in the two photo sections of this book appear through the cooperation of several repositories and individuals. The source (and photographer, if known) of each photograph is as follows:

Jacket, front, Weyerhaeuser Company Archives, Tacoma; back, St. Paul Pioneer Press (John D. Pappas).

Photographs in section I, following page 118
Pages 1, 2, Fiduciary Counselling, Inc., St. Paul.
Page 3, top, Weyerhaeuser Company Archives; bottom, Fiduciary Counselling, Inc.
Pages 4, 5, 6, Weyerhaeuser Company Archives.
Page 7, Lynn W. Day.
Pages 8, 9, Vivian W. Piasecki.
Page 10, Minnesota Historical Society Collections (Paul Stone-Raymor, St. Paul Daily News).
Page 11, Fiduciary Counselling, Inc. (Kenneth M. Wright Studios).
Page 12, top, Fiduciary Counselling, Inc.; bottom, Weyerhaeuser Company Archives.

Photographs in section II, following page 214
Page 1, top, Fiduciary Counselling, Inc.; bottom, St. Paul Pioneer Press.
Page 2, Weyerhaeuser Company Archives.
Page 3, top, Weyerhaeuser Company Archives; bottom, St. Paul Pioneer Press (George Miles Ryan).
Page 4, top, Time-Life Syndication, New York (*Life* photo by Hank Walker); bottom, Weyerhaeuser Company Archives.
Page 5, Weyerhaeuser Company Archives.
Page 6, St. Paul Pioneer Press.
Page 7, Weyerhaeuser Company Archives (bottom, Richards Studio).
Page 8, Weyerhaeuser Company Archives (Agner International Photos).
Pages 9, 10, Weyerhaeuser Company Archives (Richards Studio).
Page 11, top, Weyerhaeuser Company Archives (Richards Studio); bottom, St. Paul Pioneer Press (Friedman-Abeles Photographers).
Page 12, top, Weyerhaeuser Company Archives; bottom, Lynn W. Day.